The

Gift of Sex

CLIFFORD & JOYCE PENNER

The

Gift of Sex

A Guide to

Sexual Fulfillment

THOMAS NELSON
Since 1798

NASHVILLE DALLAS MEXICO CITY RIO DE JANEIRO

Published in Nashville, Tennessee by Thomas Nelson. Thomas Nelson is a trademark of Thomas Nelson, Inc.

Thomas Nelson, Inc. titles may be purchased in bulk for educational, business, fund-raising, or sales promotional use. For information, please e-mail SpecialMarkets@ThomasNelson.com.

Unless otherwise indicated, all Scripture quotations are from the HOLY BIBLE: NEW INTERNATIONAL VERSION®. Copyright © 1973, 1978, 1984 by International Bible Society. Used by permission of Zondervan Publishing House. All rights reserved.

Scripture quotations noted NASB are from the NEW AMERICAN STANDARD BIBLE®. © Copyright The Lockman Foundation 1960, 1962, 1963, 1968, 1971, 1972, 1973, 1975, 1977, and 1995. Used by permission.

Scripture quotations noted TLB are from *The Living Bible,* copyright © 1971. Used by permission of Tyndale House Publishers, Inc., Wheaton, Illinois 60189. All rights reserved.

Scripture quotations noted *The Message* are from *The Message: The New Testament in Contemporary English.* Copyright © 1993 by Eugene H. Peterson.

Scripture quotations noted KJV are from THE KING JAMES VERSION of the Bible.

The Scripture quotation noted NKJV is from THE NEW KING JAMES VERSION. Copyright © 1979, 1980, 1982, Thomas Nelson, Inc., Publishers.

Library of Congress Cataloging-in-Publication Data

Penner, Clifford.
  The gift of sex / by Clifford and Joyce Penner.
    p. cm.
  ISBN 13: 978-0-8499-4415-4 (pbk.)
    1. Sex instruction. 2. Sex in marriage. 3. Sex—Religious aspects. 4. Intimacy (Psychology)
I. Penner, Joyce. II. Title.
HQ31.P44659 2003
613.9'6—dc21   2003009657

Printed in the United States of America
14 15 16 17 RRD 25 24 23 22 21 20

CONTENTS

129755

ENHANCING THE SEXUAL EXPERIENCE

PREFACE

We would like to share with you some information about our pilgrimage from a mutual rural Mennonite heritage to where we are today.

Even though we were raised two thousand miles apart, we could have grown up in the same community. The German Mennonite tradition had a strong impact on us in the unique foods we ate, the yearly church festivals, the speaking of the Low German dialect, similar dating patterns, and common values. Those values included a hard work ethic and an expectation of setting and attaining goals, yet a strong pacifistic approach to life, and not just in regard to war. While on the one hand we were taught to push and scramble to get what we could out of life, on the other we were taught to pursue fulfillment of the capacities within us without trampling underfoot those around us. One example of this philosophy occurred when a lawsuit seemed the best business decision but was not pursued because, "As Christians we don't sue."

This mind-set about life has affected our sexual lives together. We came to marriage with the expectation that marital and sexual happiness was a goal we could strive for and attain. Yet neither of us would pursue that happiness at the expense of the other. The pacifistic,

Christian-love style mellowed out the aggressive "go-after-your-goals" approach to life.

Another integral dimension of our Mennonite church and home emphasis was that a personal relationship with God through Jesus Christ was the necessary beginning of a Christian life. Even though there was a legalistic approach to Christian growth, one did not automatically become a Christian by being born into a Christian home or religiously following the legalisms of the church. As a result of this spirit and the strong biblical teaching we received from childhood on, we both made clear decisions at an early age to commit ourselves to Christ and his teachings. The meaning of that commitment has continued to develop in line with our understanding and experience. The going has not always been smooth. There have been and are struggles, doubts, and our own subtle (pacifistic, probably) kinds of rebellion.

What was probably most beneficial to our Christian and emotional development was that our childhood homes were warm, safe, family- and church-centered environments. Growth and achievement were encouraged intellectually, educationally, musically, athletically, socially, biblically, and spiritually; yet, as was typical in that era, sexual awareness and understanding received very limited, if any, encouragement. Our families were not unique in their limited sexual communication and expression; rather, their attitude was typical of the day. So our parents were not remiss in following the standards they had been taught or that were common to their culture.

Given this setting, sexual feelings or sexual behaviors were not discussed openly or freely. There was, however, direct positive instruction about growing up to be a man or a woman. Good feelings were communicated about breast development; buying the first bra was a special event; menstruation was well-prepared for and was experienced as a positive sign of becoming a woman. Shaving, muscular development, and voice change were all welcome signs of emerging manhood.

The conflict was that specific instruction about sexual interaction between men and women was either absent or limited. Instruction regarding sexual involvement within marriage was lacking; at the same time the church, with the messages that surrounded us, clearly warned about "keeping oneself pure." Rigid rules were defined for acceptable dating habits. Dating was permissible only with "one of our own kind"—Mennonite—promoting a narrow view of the biblical concept of being "unequally yoked together." Holding hands with a member of the opposite sex was perceived as serious business.

Caressing and making out were obviously unacceptable, and kissing was to occur only with the person you were sure you would marry. In fact, the feeling often came across that if you did weaken and kiss your partner on a date, such action destined your marriage to that person.

The absence of positive sexual teaching, combined with the rigid rules about sexual expression, seemed designed to lead us to believe that sex between a man and a woman was questionable or nonexistent. But neither of us felt that way.

We are not exactly sure why we did not assume this negative stance. Probably the natural peer input that occurred in our rural, extended-family type of communities allowed us to be very free-spirited as young children. At large family gatherings, with cousins of about the same age and of the opposite sex, we had freedom to roam and explore. We played fun games like jumping in the hay in the nude or playing nudist colony in the cornfields. Thus we came to adolescence rather naive but with good feelings about ourselves sexually. But then the struggles of adolescence—the awkward sexual feelings along with the rigid controls on behavior—caused some doubt about ourselves sexually; we experienced a reduction of freedom during the growing-up years.

A beneficial factor was that we went through our broadening or stretching experiences simultaneously. We met during our first year at a mainly Mennonite college. From our similar backgrounds, we came together and learned as we moved away from the rigidity of our history. Together we went through a variety of church and Christian growth experiences that brought us to where we are today.

Probably our most enriching emotional input and education

about sex occurred while we were attending, respectively, a Baptist school of nursing and a Baptist liberal arts college. Through taking a class on preparation for marriage and talking with professors, we received accurate sexual data, along with warm, positive feelings about the lovemaking experience we were anticipating in marriage. It became clear to us, with the help of people we valued as sound Christian believers and mentors, that the sex drives we felt so strongly were God-given, normal, and natural. While behavioral decisions had to be made about how those urges could be handled before marriage, our sexual feelings were positively affirmed with much anticipation of their full enjoyment in marriage.

> Is it a good thing to have sexual relations? Certainly—but only within a certain context. It's good for a man to have a wife, and for a woman to have a husband. Sexual drives are strong, but marriage is strong enough to contain them and provide for a balanced and fulfilling sexual life in a world of sexual disorder. (1 Cor. 7:1–2 MSG)

Why the sexual part of our marriage started out so positively, we are not certain. Maybe the determination that sex in marriage could be positive was our way of rebelling against our past. Whatever the case, the sexual dimension of our marriage has, for the most part, continued to be very satisfying. This is true even though the level of our knowledge has changed with time and experience. When we look back, we wonder how our initial experiences could have seemed as satisfying as they did, but at the time they were all we knew, and they contributed to our growing intimacy and deepening passion. That is not to say we have been without the times of sexual difficulties typical of any couple wanting enhancement—times of varying interests, a difficult adjustment after a new baby, focusing on performance rather than on enjoyment, or adjusting to interim birth-control measures. But underlying all this, we have enjoyed our sexual relationship and have experienced it as being right for us.

As a result of our positive sexual experience and the questions this raised for us, during our first year of marriage we used our Bible study time to look at what the Bible had to say about sex. We came out convinced that the Bible is a very pro-sex book. We had heard our church's message about the "don'ts" of sexual behavior outside marriage and, lacking a balancing positive input about sex in marriage, had generalized to the point that we thought the church's message was entirely negative. Our conclusions from this study were probably the beginning of our current emphasis on bringing a positive sexual teaching to the Christian community.

After the issue was settled for us personally, we did little with it until long after we completed our formal education. Joyce received her bachelor of science and master's degrees and then taught nursing at the college level. Cliff finished his seminary and doctoral degrees and then began private practice as a clinical psychologist. Our professional energies were focused on areas such as training lay counselors and dealing with grief, death, and dying.

One day we were asked to teach a class for seminary wives on sexual adjustment in a Christian marriage. In an initial survey of the class members, we discovered much the same confusion about sexual feelings and Christian beliefs that we had experienced. For many, this confusion had led to unfulfilled sexual lives. We took this teaching assignment with no expectation that education would produce change in actual sexual behavior and satisfaction. Assuming that such change would have to come through therapy and counseling on a much more intimate level, we saw the class as a way to help the women define their needs (if there were needs present) and find the desired professional assistance. Much to our surprise, some of the women reported dramatic sexual changes in their marriages. Others were able to enrich already good relationships. These reports demonstrated the ability of such education and communication to produce behavioral change in and of themselves.

The timing was right. Word of what we had to offer spread, and the churches were ready. As a result, we have continued to share our findings and offer enhancement opportunities for couples throughout the United States and in other countries. Some couples receive help for specific problems, others revive the spark that has been lost, and still others identify the need for further treatment. Those who identify the need for additional help may come to our offices, work with one of our associates via telephone or the Internet, or obtain a referral to a counselor or counseling team more convenient to their location.

Early in the history of our sexual adjustment seminars, we realized the need to prepare ourselves further, so we pursued training from the Masters and Johnson Institute and from other experts. This specialized preparation, our personal experience and professional backgrounds, and the fact that we have led as a team are the assets we believe we bring to the individuals, couples, families, and professionals we teach, counsel, and mentor. Our modeling as a husband-wife team and the representation of both the medical and social science fields are essential benefits to those who attend our seminars or visit our office.

Working with individuals in discovering a wholesome sexuality and with couples in finding new and more positive ways of relating sexually has been a most rewarding calling. Whether couples come as a last-ditch effort and find relief after years and years of pain or a newly married couple comes for just a few sessions to work out a minor adjustment issue that will prevent years of pain, the reward is incredible! *Sexual retraining* is short-term therapy that changes lives and relationships far beyond just functioning in bed.

What have we learned about men and women and sex in marriage after almost thirty years as sexual therapists? Not long ago, our friend and colleague, Dr. Neil Clark Warren, sat us down and asked us, "After all these years as sexual therapists, what have you learned that makes for a great sex life in marriage?" We rambled for a couple of hours, and out of that rambling came some basic premises that you will find throughout this revised *The Gift of Sex* that were either not present or not as well developed in the original *The Gift of Sex*.

What we shared with Neil surprised him, surprised us, and will probably surprise you, because our findings go against conventional assumptions about men, women, and sex.

Our most convincing finding is that *men* make the difference when it comes to sex in marriage. Because of the natural differences between men and women, we are convinced that the most vital factor in building intimacy and keeping passion alive in marriage revolves around the role of the man. This is true whether he has a problem, she has a problem, or there is no problem. Men may be saying, "But that doesn't sound fair." It isn't fair, but it is true!

Let's back up. What has become clear in our studies and listening to thousands of couples' sexual stories is that men are simpler than women.

Men are more like a stick-shift Chevy pickup truck. They are reliable and predictable but often not too exciting. Women are more like a Maserati. They are exhilarating when they're running, but they spend a lot of time in the shop for fine-tuning. That is because women function on two tracks: the emotional and the physical. Those two tracks have to be in sync in order for the woman to be interested sexually. Men function on one track: when physically aroused they tend to be ready emotionally.

Men and women are different. Women desire sex and open up sexually when they feel loved by and connected with their husbands; men connect and feel loved through sex. And that is precisely why it usually works best if the man starts the process of sexual change by connecting with his wife. It is the way a man loves his wife like Christ loved the church (Eph. 5).

It goes like this:

> The husband loves, adores, and connects with his wife;
> His adoration allows her to open up sexually;
> His affirmation ignites her passion;
> She invites him sexually;
> He feels validated, so
> They both end up happy.
> It's a win, win!

For this formula to work, however, the *woman* needs to be able to take and to lead sexually. That is her part of the deal. To be able to take in sexual pleasure and receive her husband's affirmation, a woman has to believe that she is worthy and that she has a right to be sexual. She has to know that her body was designed not only for reproduction, but also for her sexual pleasure and satisfaction.

When the woman leads with her sexuality, it works. It works because a turned-on woman is usually a turnon to a man; whereas, a turned-on man can be a demand or pressure to a woman. Women can easily feel used; men are more likely to say, "Use me!"

Once the woman accepts her God-given sexuality, she leads, not by control or demand, but by *listening to her body's desire,* by *taking in the good feelings of being touched,* and then by *inviting him to enjoy her body as she enjoys his.*

When this system of the husband loving, adoring, and connecting with his wife and the wife taking in and leading sexually is put into practice, it is the woman who keeps sex interesting! We believe it is the combination of male constancy and ever-changing, complex femininity that keeps sex alive in marriage over a lifetime.

Since the man is never truly satisfied unless the woman is, he has to go her way. When he accepts, understands, respects, and goes with her complexity, he has to shift his natural drives to compete with, conquer, achieve, and score to her process orientation. Ultimately, her way will work best for both of them. Sex will be more interesting, less results-oriented, less pressure-filled, more focused on the total person, and more deeply satisfying long-term.

In addition to what we have learned about men and women in relation to sex in marriage, we have affirmed that *passion in marriage will only last if pleasure is the goal.* It is not arousal, not intercourse, and not orgasm that are central to a life of intimate, passionate sex in marriage. Those are likely to be the result when pleasure is the focus, but the success of a sexual experience is not measured by goal-oriented responses and actions.

For pleasure to be the "goal," the couple has to accept that *slow is better than fast.* They need to learn to take time to bring their worlds together and to enjoy each others' bodies, while giving themselves to each other.

We have become deeply convinced that for sex in marriage to

bring the joy and fulfillment that God intended, *healing from past hurts is a must.* For the woman to be able to take and lead, for the man to connect with and affirm his wife, and for both to delight in the pleasure of each other's bodies, healing is a prerequisite. The time, space, and the work of healing from past trauma, such as having been raised in an alcoholic home or having been in a destructive relationship, is a necessity.

And finally, we have learned during these almost thirty years as sex therapists and forty years of marriage that *sex is a lot more fun when you work at it!*

Our culture promotes spontaneity. Spontaneity works before marriage, early in marriage, outside of marriage, on vacation for some, in the movies, and on the soaps. But intentionality works best in marriage.

For most couples, the anticipation of planned times builds quality; the allotment of those times increases quantity. True passion and great sex don't just happen, but we can make great sex happen in our marriages by being deliberate about what we know works.

∽

So what we've learned as sexual therapists is

- Men make the difference by accepting and getting with the woman's ever-changing complex sexuality;
- Women keep sex interesting by learning to take in sexual pleasure and to set the sexual pace for sex in marriage;
- Both keep passion alive in marriage by focusing on pleasure, enjoying a slow pace, healing from past hurts, and being deliberate about their sexual relationship.

So with our roots still deeply planted in our Mennonite heritage, we have branched out through our broadening church experiences: first within the Baptist community; then in a large Presbyterian church; and now as leaders and pastor in a growing multiethnic, urban, evangelical setting (Lake Avenue Church in Pasadena, CA). Our personal life experiences and our years as therapists, speakers, authors, and involved parents and friends have also added extensively to our present views.

We trust that where we are and what we have to offer will reach you at your point of interest and need.

For further information, please contact:

Dr. Clifford and Joyce Penner
200 East Del Mar Blvd., Suite 126
Pasadena, California 91105
Phone: 626-449-2525
Fax: 626-564-1250
E-mail: penners@attglobal.net
www.passionatecommitment.com

1　IS THIS BOOK FOR ME?

With our busy lifestyle there is little time for intimacy between my husband and me. When we do get together, we seem to lack the passion we both enjoyed before our children came along. Sex seems to have become rather perfunctory and infrequent. What can we do—what steps can we take—to get some spark back?

As you open this book to read about sex as a gift from God to be affirmed and enjoyed in marriage, you may be asking, "Is this book for me?" If you are a couple interested in learning all you can about the God-given gift of sexuality in order to enhance your sexual experience, this book is for you!

THIS BOOK IS FOR YOU . . .

If You Desire Knowledge and Enrichment

When a young man and a young woman are experiencing the full flush of their love during those months just before marriage, they usually don't talk much about their sexual knowledge or experience. Rather, they hope and expect that the excitement, the joy, the delight they now experience with each other will carry over into their sexual relationship after marriage. Yet, without knowledge and deliberate preparation like what we offer in our book *Getting Your Sex Life Off to a Great Start* (Word, 1994), many couples find they have difficulty transferring their premarital passion to their marriage. They have many questions about sex—questions that leave them perplexed. There is no easy, natural place to find the needed information. *The Gift of Sex* offers answers to your questions and provides information that is practical and will enrich your ongoing sex life as a couple. You will find your sex life will take on new delight as you read this book out loud together.

Our knowledge about sex and about each other is always in the process of discovery. Sex is not learned by observing others. We have not observed anyone else involved in this behavior. We have learned by reading, by talking, and by teaching each other as a couple. We are confident this book will help you in your search for knowledge and enrichment of your sexual life, resulting in the freedom to make your own discoveries in the process of learning.

If You Experience Uncertainty or Stress and Want to Avoid Sexual Difficulties

You may be unsure of yourself in the sexual act or experience stress about your sexual relationship. Stress or uncertainty does not diminish on its own. In fact, it is likely to increase if you are concerned about how you are functioning. So you may be looking for help to gain more confidence or to reduce stress and help to avoid difficulties.

One young woman was raised in the Midwest in a family that was very hesitant about anything sexual. She was convinced that all sexual feelings and responses were sinful, and so she shut down her own as a way to control her sexual actions until she married and was ready for a full sexual experience. She discovered, along with so many others, that the anxiety and tension about the sexual experience did not go away, and her feelings and responses did not automatically click on at the marriage altar. As she and her new husband began their married life together, she was anxious about how to function sexually, concerned about the various sexual activities, and preoccupied with her own lack of responsiveness. As she and her husband read *The Gift of Sex* together, talked about her hesitancies to be sexual, and applied what they were learning to their sexual experience, she began a process of affirming and releasing her feelings and responses.

If you experience tension or uncertainty about your sexual experience, this book can help you find ways to discover all the potential God intends for you in your married sex life.

If You Brought Sexual Blocks into Your Marriage

You may have specific sexual blocks or habits that hinder your sexual satisfaction. These blocks may impede your sexual activities or interest to the point that your life together is jeopardized. A young seminary student found he was seldom interested in sex even though he was clearly devoted to his wife. Deeply in love with her, he enjoyed every part of their life together but had little interest in any kind of sexual activity. He sought help because he believed that eventually his lack of sexual interest was going to damage the marriage, a concern that was certainly justified. Much in his past led him to this position.

Reading *The Gift of Sex* helped him gain a better understanding of what he had brought to marriage and gave him the tools he needed to seek help.

Couples raised in the church and living as committed Christians have heard and read many things describing the sanctity of marriage, as well as the beauty of the sexual experience and the concern that it not be misused. Some of these couples may have questions about the appropriateness of enjoying pleasure—enjoying their own bodies—from a biblical and Christian viewpoint. For a couple with this concern, we will point to the Bible's clear message validating sexual pleasure in marriage (see Chapter 4).

If You Are Looking for Newness and Enhancement

Couples whose sexual lives are happy and fulfilled are continually looking for ways to add new joy and delight to their sexual experience. We might compare them to people who are wonderful cooks. They have enough recipes and cooking concepts to keep them happy for years to come. Yet they are continually looking for new ways to put meals together, new ways to make sauces or desserts, new ways to enjoy creating delicious flavors. In the same way, couples who are satisfied in their married life, whether they have been married ten years or forty, are often looking for additional input, knowledge, insight, or awareness to add to their already full experience.

If You Want to Spark a "Ho-Hum" Relationship

Many couples do not experience much excitement in their sexual relationship. Even though everything is working well from a technical standpoint, their experiences are boring.

For the couple suffering from a "ho-hum" relationship, reading this book together will add a new spark. It provides suggestions for building an experimental, creative sexual lifestyle in your marriage.

If You Are Looking for Help with Problems

It is possible to have a stable foundation in a relationship and yet face sexual problems. There are many such difficulties: The man may ejaculate too quickly, not be interested, or have difficulty getting or keeping erections. The woman may experience pain, lack of interest, difficulties with arousal, or have problems letting go orgasmically. All such dilemmas get in the way of the sexual experience and usually cause people to pull away from each other as time goes on.

For some readers with technical difficulties, this book provides information that will help you work out problems yourselves; for others, it will help you define the problem so you can seek outside help.

If You Are Making a Last-Ditch Effort

You may be reading this book as a last-ditch effort to find the hope you are so desperately seeking. One couple told us they had purchased *The Gift of Sex* in an attempt to work things out sexually but failed to read the book. Finally, years later and at their point of despair, they started a process of reading together, talking about what they were reading, and experimenting with some of the suggestions. After twelve years of a good marriage, but a tension-filled sex life, they were able to talk about issues related to the shutdown of the wife's sexuality due to childhood abuse. Learning new information and talking about sexual conflicts helped them discover what was required to find the fulfillment they so deeply desired.

∽

This book can provide needed information. It will also guide you through steps that intend to open communication and sharing so a process of mutual discovery and openness may be initiated in your relationship. We are writing for all those who seek to explore and discover together.

The following are three distinctive approaches to a healthy sexual experience that will be found throughout this book:

1. Responsibility with Freedom

We want to promote an attitude or mind-set of individual responsibility. As we see it, one of the biggest difficulties couples experience is that each partner feels responsible for the spouse's sexual satisfaction and fulfillment. This concern has grown somewhat naturally out of the correct emphasis on love, care, concern, and submission to one another. And yet, we have discovered that for many people a major barrier blocking their enjoyment of sex is the pressure or sense of obligation to provide the other with sexual satisfaction. If there are problems, many feel it is their responsibility to "fix" those problems—that it is their fault if the other person is having difficulty. For example, if the man is not able to respond with an erection as he would like, the wife may feel it is her responsibility to produce this response. If the woman is not satisfied, the man may feel it is his fault she is not experiencing release. So the emphasis throughout our writing and teaching is on each spouse's taking responsibility to identify, communicate, and ensure the best conditions for their sexual experiences rather than expecting one's partner to assume that responsibility. Each spouse obviously does his/her best to pleasure and stimulate in a way that is most pleasing. But we cannot be responsible for each other's emotional barriers, nor can we read each other's minds.

2. Integrated Biblical, Psychological, and Physical Knowledge

Our intention is to combine and integrate what we understand about traditional theology, generally accepted psychology, and physiological discoveries. We are confident that theological and biblical truths are not in conflict with psychological understanding; rather, the latter functions as an endorsement, confirmation, and amplification of the scriptural teaching. It is true that many new and contradictory theories emerge in current theology and popular psychology. But when we go back to the basics of the Bible and to the broadly accepted truths about human behavior and feelings, these do not contradict each other. We examine and describe the physical side of sex because it is important for us to accept and enjoy the full potential God has given us.

3. Embracing Individual Differences Brings Fulfillment

Although there *are* general principles that can be applied to enhance our sexual functioning as couples, there are also many ways in which each couple is unique. Each person is different—each woman is different from all other women, and each man is different from all other men. A person's feelings are different from day-to-day and even from moment-to-moment. What is satisfying and pleasurable at this moment may not be satisfying and pleasurable at another time. "Easy steps to success" is an approach that creates a sense of failure because couples do not achieve the sexual satisfaction and delights promised.

The search for deeper intimacy and sexual fulfillment must be multifaceted and incorporate the whole person. To focus only on the physical will not help a couple perform more skillfully or experience a more fulfilling response. To function in a physically accurate manner is important. But knowing all about the physical aspects of sex is not the total answer to a satisfying relationship any more than attending to the relational and spiritual without the physical will make the difference. Any time we focus on one dimension of the sexual relationship to the exclusion of the others, we lose something. For communication purposes, we deal with one dimension at a time; but when we bring our biblical understanding, psychological awareness, and physical skill into one total relationship experience, we discover the full joy and satisfaction that can be ours.

2 WHY ALL THE CONFUSION?

The sexual part of us is simple, yet complex. It is predictable, yet changeable, diverse, unknowable, mysterious, and forever beyond our full understanding. If this sounds confusing and contradictory—it is. We have all come to our present understanding about our sexuality by different routes and through different experiences. We have received messages from many sources: family, school, church, society, friends, college, spouse, experience, and our reading. We gather bits and pieces of information as we go along, often unsure how they fit with what we already know. Sex is a topic that frequently leaves us confused or uncomfortable. Messages often are not spoken directly but rather are implied or inferred. This is not to say that society is quiet on the subject. On the contrary—we are bombarded with sexual innuendos in advertising, sexual assistance in family and women's magazines, sex education in the classroom, sexual guidance in the latest marriage book, and jokes about sex in everyday interactions.

Why, then, the confusion? There seem to be several reasons. Organized, systematic opportunities to learn about sex are limited in any setting—family, church, or school. Every other body of scholastic knowledge is communicated in age-appropriate ways, beginning when we are very young. When we teach a child to read we begin with the ABC's, move to short one-syllable words, and then to brief phrases with only one sentence on a page. We gradually add to this until the educated person can read and understand long words in complicated sentences that express elaborate ideas. In contrast, sexual information is often gained mainly by osmosis and disseminated unsystematically.

To get the most out of sex, we recommend you sort through the sexual information and attitudes you have accumulated over the years. Determine the accuracy of the information and the appropriateness of your attitudes, and define your sexual goals.

WHAT YOU BRING WITH YOU FROM YOUR HOME AND FAMILY

You may come from a home in which absolutely no reference was made to anything overtly sexual at any time. As far back as you can remember, even words with a sexual connotation were avoided, disregarded, frowned at, or punished. You may have developed a natural curiosity because the subject was avoided so carefully. Any time you ran across a sexual word or a sexual reference, it held special interest for you. Or whenever you saw a magazine article, an ad on the Internet, or overheard a conversation dealing with sex, it tended to be titillating. At the same time, you may have felt guilty about this response.

On the other hand, the total absence of any reference to sexual material may have had the effect of overprotecting you emotionally, making the sexual part of your life or anyone else's seem unnatural and uncomfortable to you. The restraints on sexual information hindered the normal, natural learning process that would have occurred for you if this had been an open subject. As you grew up, each new step of discovery may have caused a great deal of anxiety, perhaps even avoidance, because of the conditioning you experienced in your home. Eventually you may have learned to accept the "sexual you" as a natural, God-created gift in your *mind,* but even at this point, you may still have emotional barriers to that reality. It may still be hard for you to *feel* or *be* sexual.

In contrast to the absence of instruction, you may have come from a home where there was some very positive teaching about the sexual part of you. Yet at the same time you may have found it confusing. That confusion could have arisen from several areas.

You may have been confused because what you heard did not coincide with what you saw. Your mother and/or father provided a confusing model. They told you that sex was a delightful part of adult married life, and yet also communicated a message that said, "This really isn't all that natural and comfortable for us."

It may be that you received a positive message concerning your own body and your own sexuality—but it became confused with the expressions of legitimate concern about saving that sexuality for your marriage partner. The preoccupation with keeping yourself pure may have made all sex seem impure.

You may have come from a situation where parents or others gave you good, clear teaching, but the message was clouded by additional input from older brothers and sisters, cousins, or peers. The double message left you in a confused state.

Perhaps your environment was totally negative. You were raised in a home where the sexual messages were very loud and clear, nothing was hidden—but they were all negative. If you are a woman, you may have been taught that sexual experience is for the man, not for the woman; that it is something to be avoided if at all possible, even in marriage; that there is no enjoyment in it; that the naturally occurring sexual feelings in your body are disgusting, and the best thing to do with this part of your life is to avoid it as much as possible.

A woman raised in a small rural town reported that she had received no instruction regarding male-female sexual interaction until two weeks before she was to be married. At that point her mother took her aside and lovingly and caringly communicated three basic warnings: First, the honeymoon would be awful; second, she should expect to feel very tired; and third, "Don't let him use you."

If you are a man who was raised in an atmosphere hostile toward sexuality, you may have received messages critical of men who were sexual. Sexual activity was spoken of with disgust and distaste, communicating the idea that you certainly wouldn't want to behave in this way—and that you should not do so as you grew up. You received the message that sexual behavior is abusive toward women and to be avoided.

Or you may have had the good fortune to be raised with good teaching and positive modeling. If that is so, you are probably reading this book for further understanding and enhancement, rather than seeking to undo the effects of your upbringing.

MOTHER AS A MODEL

Modern research has confirmed what has been preached for generations: What we do speaks more loudly than what we say. The mother in the home is clearly a model to both her sons and her daughters. The attitudes she communicates about her body, bodily pleasure, or affectionate gestures from her husband will reveal to her children how she feels about herself as a sexual being. How she answers questions about sex will also shape the child's view. If there is embarrassed silence, sputtering attempts to answer, and finally obtuse responses, again the message is clear: "We don't talk about this. It is uncomfortable for us to have you ask us. You shouldn't be interested anyway."

On the other hand, if children are answered simply, openly, without judgment or guilt, they learn the naturalness of this part of their lives. This is one of the easiest times to teach them the moral standards surrounding all sexual activity. At this time we can begin to plant the seeds of moral responsibility that go hand in hand with the enjoyment of sexual pleasure.

Another important part of the mother's modeling has to do with what she communicates about women and sexuality. Her daughter will learn whether sex is fun and satisfying or a burden to be endured. Is it a male conspiracy to be avoided, a duty to be accepted with grace, an area where the woman has to watch out for herself since the man will automatically want to use her? Or is it a source of great fulfillment of her sexual appetite as it expresses the love she feels for her husband? Usually these attitudes are transferred without any direct communication.

A son also learns a great deal about women and sexuality by what he observes in his mother. If he senses in her the same excitement and pleasure he sees in his father, he will not grow up viewing sex as a battleground. Rather, he will learn that sexual interaction is a source of pleasure for both parties.

On the other hand, if mother pulls away even from a kiss on the neck, the son learns that the woman always objects, but the man goes after what he wants anyway.

Every one of us has had a mother or some adult woman as a model. Think about the female model in your life for a moment: What did she communicate to you directly or subtly about women and sexuality? These were the attitudes instilled in you early in life, so it is not surprising that you may still be living in accordance with them even if you no longer totally accept them on an intellectual level.

FATHER AS A MODEL

Most of what we learn from our father about the sexual aspect of life is based on how we see him interact with our mother. If the only time Dad touches Mom is when they're going into the bedroom and closing the door, we learn that habit pattern. We don't understand it at the time, but we have learned that men are interested only in overt, genital sex. On the other hand, if Dad communicates ongoing warmth and interest in Mom, we learn that a man values the personhood of his wife rather than seeing her only as a source of sexual satisfaction.

Father's openness in the expression of his feelings, especially his softer feelings of warmth, care, tenderness, sadness, and hurt, will probably be the example we use in our own understanding of "how men are." As he is able to share the full range of his emotions, he is also able to respond to his wife with the total intensity that makes for a fulfilling sexual life. In homes where the father has difficulty with the expression of his emotions, the children often grow up to experience difficulty expressing themselves sexually.

A son, particularly, will model himself after his father. How much did your father feel free to touch and stroke you or other family members? How free was he to express his feelings? How willing was he to admit his mistakes? What kind of care and respect did he show for your mother? Was he tentative and unsure in relation to her, or confident and caring? Were you able to sense that he loved her totally, not just as an object of his sexual release? All these issues are the threads from which your sexual attitudes are woven.

One other area where fathers make a major impact is the influence they have on how their daughters feel about themselves as women. This influence begins at birth but reaches a particularly critical point during the early teen years when the girl is going through puberty. It is during this time that she is becoming a sexual person. If the father can be honestly supportive and affirming through this process, without being seductive or sending put-down messages, he will help his daughter build good feelings about herself as a woman and a sexual being.

Whether we are male or female, there are obviously many ways our father affects how we view ourselves and our partners. In trying to understand what has influenced you, review your father's role in your sexual self-concept.

SOCIETY'S INPUT

You may have come from a community where all the families were very similar. Thus you and your peers received the same kind of sexual message. If you explored or discovered together, you were doing so outside the limitations of your homes. If your family was less open than the rest of your community, you probably gained a lot of your knowledge about sex from the other children in your world. If your family was more open than most, it would not be surprising if you felt a kind of superiority, and at the same time a kind of isolation, as a result of being different.

Other variables may have contributed to your present attitudes and understanding. If there was a big controversy in your community about sex education, this will have left its mark on you. If someone close to your family, either friend or relative, became pregnant out of wedlock and you heard discussions on the situation, you will have picked up some attitudes about sex. If any sensational sexual events happened in your family or community, such as kidnapping, molestation, or rape, these will have affected your view of the whole sexual world. This will be especially true if there was a great deal of excitement or hush-hush conversation about these events.

As you moved into your adolescent years, your dating experiences, reading habits, discussions, and the social customs in your community added more to the already large database of information and misinformation.

If you became involved in activities that were outside the acceptable standard set by your church or society, or a biblical norm, the consequent emotions interfered with your natural development.

THE CHURCH AS AN INFLUENCE

If you were raised in a church setting, the church had its effect on your sexual attitudes. For some the message was at least hesitant if not negative. As one pastor mentioned, "The church has often dealt with sex by having the pastor make his annual visit to the youth group with the challenge to 'keep thyself pure.'" This is an important message for the youth to hear, but by itself it is incomplete.

Until recently, the church has often failed to address issues regarding sexuality. Also, since sex involves intense emotional feelings, many of us experience discomfort around the subject because of our natural modesty. Sex is a private dimension of our lives. The indirect message associated with this sense of privacy has often been that there is something wrong with having a sexual nature.

Much of this negativism has grown from scriptural limits set on sexual behavior. There is no doubt that the Bible has much to say about the misuse of our bodies in unacceptable sexual behavior with partners other than one's spouse. But the church's emphasis has not been balanced by the Bible's loud pro-sex message. So we have heard plenty about the sexual rules but little that builds positive attitudes about our God-designed sexuality or sex in marriage.

The church is becoming more and more open about sexuality as it recognizes the severe problems that plague its members. Everyone is exposed to the effects of a rising divorce rate and the unrelenting sexual exposure in the media. Findings by researchers and professionals have helped the church (both pastors and people) face the sexual realities.

Whether you were raised in a church setting where sexual issues were dealt with in a rigid, austere manner, or in one with a more contemporary, understanding approach, the church has influenced who you are today. Some of the messages you have heard may not fit with your own experience or knowledge, and hence they have added to the confusion already present.

EARLY SEXUAL EXPERIENCES

Our adult sexual understanding is greatly shaped not only by our home and social environment, but also by our early sexual experiences. For example, if you had any frightening experience as a child, such as molestation or kidnapping, early introduction into sexual activity, or sexually arousing play, that experience will shape who you are today and will influence not only your sexual knowledge but also your sexual response. If you came from a home where moral values were clearly taught, early sexual involvement probably produced a significant amount of guilt, and that guilt will affect your adult sexual experiences. We find that a person who, during the formative years, engages in sexual activity while feeling guilt will tend to, as an adult, associate the positive feeling of sexual pleasure with conflicting negative guilt feelings.

You may be a person who has learned to feel guilty even though there is nothing specific to feel guilty about. This is sometimes referred to as "inauthentic guilt." You have learned a pattern of responding with guilty feelings whenever you experience sexual feelings or arousal. As you read this book, you might look for ways to accept the God-given naturalness of your sexual feelings, feelings of pleasure, and bodily responses.

EARLY MARITAL EXPERIENCE

Your early marital experience also affects your sexual attitudes today. As you became involved with your spouse, habit patterns grew out of the accumulation of the experiences you had together. If these were positive, rewarding experiences, your current sexual self-image will probably be a wholesome one. If, on the other hand, these experiences turned out to be negative because of an unfulfilling process and an unsatisfying conclusion, then you may feel somewhat inadequate, incompetent, or unfulfilled.

The honeymoon is supposed to be that delightful time when two blissful, innocent young lovers discover all the joys and delights of sexual life together. Unfortunately, it does not always turn out that way. We see many couples in sexual therapy who have never recovered from the jarring disappointments of that first experience together. Because so much hope and anticipation went into that long-awaited event, a major letdown occurred when the first sexual experiences were not as satisfying as expected.

If your early marital experiences were disappointing, you may still be suffering their effects. This book can help you sort through those memories and begin to overcome the negative ways they have influenced you.

THE EFFECT OF CHILDREN IN THE HOME

Radical changes take place when children come into your life. Your sexual experience is not exempt from those changes. You must give much attention to the new child or children; you have added fatigue and heavier financial responsibilities. It all takes its toll.

It is not uncommon for women to experience sex differently after going through childbirth for the first time. Not only is the vagina altered by the birth experience, it also has a new function (birth), which can bring attitude changes.

Some couples find they never quite recover from the effects of adding children to their family until the last child leaves home. If this is your situation, the chapters ahead offer encouragement and hope.

Remember, where you are today is a result of the accumulation of all the input you have received and all the experiences you have had up to this point. Some of those experiences have impacted you more than others. You may be very aware of your past and how it is affecting you now, or you may tend to disconnect past family or outside influences from your present situation. If you are in the latter category, we encourage you to work actively at reviewing your past. Bring to mind the feelings you had in various situations. You might do so by talking about this with your spouse or writing a sexual autobiography. As you continue to grow, it is our hope that this book will help to further unravel any confusion hindering the embracing of your sexuality.

A

BIBLICAL

PERSPECTIVE

3 SEXUALITY IS A GIFT FROM GOD!

The worlds of theology and sexuality are commonly viewed as being miles apart. People tend to think of themselves as being divided into two parts, body and soul, with the soul being the good part and the body the evil or bad part. We do not agree with this view and hope to present what we see as a more holistic, biblical model.

Although the Bible is not an instruction book for sexual functioning, it gives a clear picture of

- God's value of our individual sexuality and
- His high regard for the sexual relationship in marriage.

Scripture's high view of the human sexual dimension elevates sex as something to be cherished, like a family jewel or heirloom. It is a precious gift to be stored carefully and not allowed to tarnish until it is shared with a special person. However, in society today, sexuality is often treated more like a piece of junk jewelry, something given to a child at age fourteen to be worn to school and later thrown into the bottom of the bike bag.

The Bible speaks about sexuality as a prized gift. It designates sex for marriage because it is within this commitment that the qualities of a highly held view of sexuality can be fulfilled. The Bible portrays sex as a symbol of the relationship between God and his people. It puts sex in the context of the deepest commitment one human can make to another: a lifelong commitment to honor, cherish, and be faithful until death. When we accept sex and sexuality as a precious gift from the Creator, it clearly sets us apart from those who misuse it as junk.

In the book of Genesis, the Bible tells how Adam and Eve were "naked and unashamed," experiencing a free, open relationship that had no barriers. Their relationship was not based on power, intimidation, social myths, or cultural control. Later, Scripture refers to Christ as the "last," or new, Adam and teaches that believers bear Christ's image (1 Cor. 15:45–50). This makes sex without shame a viable potential for the Christian. Unfortunately, the church has let social culture dictate many distorting images of sexuality. When we can rid ourselves of these limitations and live lives of freedom and openness in marriage, then we can be sexually free and fulfilled.

We hope this biblically based view will become central to your attitude in enjoying your sexual relationship with your spouse. We can affirm our body, including our sexuality, as a God-given gift to be enjoyed as it is used responsibly. Our sexuality is part of our total being—not merely a physical, fleshly, or "evil" part of us. It reflects the image of God in us.

Many of the biblical assumptions found in this book come from Genesis, particularly the creation account.

GOD'S PLAN

Sexual by Creation

Sexuality is part of God's plan of creation. Our maleness and femaleness, our sexuality, is not something added on or part of our sinful natures; it is part of the original perfect creation of mankind. It's in our bones. By implication, then, our sexuality is nothing to be ashamed of, but rather something to enjoy.

In God's Image

As we see in Genesis 1:27, not only were we made male and female, but that maleness and femaleness are representative of God's image. We don't know exactly how, but in some way our sexuality reflects the image of God.

Genesis 1:26–27 tells us: "Then God said, 'Let *us* make man in *our* image, in our likeness, and let them rule over the fish of the sea and the birds of the air, over the livestock, over all the earth, and over all the creatures that move along the ground.' So God created man in his own image, in the image of God he created him; male and female he created them" (emphasis added).

It is clear from this passage that mankind was created by God in accordance with a particular model or design. That design is described as the "image of God." We should point out that it is not the male alone whom God made in his own image, rather, "male and female he created them." Man and woman, male and female, are created in God's image.

What else can we learn about the meaning of our creation in the image of God? We see that the man and woman, created after the animals, were the only part of creation identified as being in God's image. God's image is something we have and animals don't. So God's image cannot be anything we have in common with the animal world. We have physical bodies, and so do animals, so the body can't be a distinguishing factor. The meaning of God's image is that we are created to be in relationship. That means we have the capacity to be in relationship with God, which the animals do not have, as well as the capacity to have relationships with one another.

Our image, as it reflects God and as it relates to sexuality, includes two dimensions: our sexual functioning and our functioning in relationship as a couple. The first command given to mankind was to "become one." This is a sexual function. The second command involved dominion and choice. These are relationship functions. As we move farther into this passage, the freedom of choice includes the choice of obeying or disobeying God's commands. Therefore, being in the image of God includes higher levels of function than just animalistic sexuality.

Physical, Emotional, Spiritual

To understand the high view of our sexuality, we must understand the Hebrew view of the human person as an integrated whole. The Hebrews never divided people into body and soul, as did the Greek dualists, or into body, soul, and spirit, as some of us tend to do today. Rather, the Hebrews thought of a person as a unity of the physical, emotional, and spiritual. These various dimensions of a person were closely related and were often used synonymously or interchangeably.

Lovemaking cannot be just physical. That does not mean there is never a time when only physical release is needed, and you provide that for each other. But if there is to be a fulfilled relationship, there must be more to it than meeting physical needs. The total person—intellect, emotions, body, spirit, and will—becomes involved in the process of giving ourselves to each other.

God-Given Sexuality Includes Sexual Intercourse

In the beginning, the perfect, sinless state of man and woman included sexual union, and this, too, was a perfect and beautiful part of God's creation plan—part of our being reflections of him, here on earth.

The two of us grew up with the implicit view that sexual union occurred after man's fall into sin. Yet Genesis 2:24 occurs in the account before any report of sin. It says, "For this reason a man will leave his father and mother and be united to his wife, and they will become one flesh." The phrase "become one flesh" refers to sexual intercourse. But this means far more than a mere physical meeting of bodies. The Scripture is talking about that mystical union between husband and wife that unites two people as *total persons*. This becoming one also reflects our being created in his perfect image. Furthermore, "The man and his wife were both naked, and they felt no shame" (v. 25). Apparently there was a completely open relationship between male and female, and there was a completely open relationship between God and man. This honest fellowship continued until Adam and Eve disobeyed God; then sin interrupted both relationships.

Sexual Oneness Symbolizes the God-Man Relationship

The husband-wife sexual relationship is used throughout Scripture to symbolize the God-man relationship. This imagery begins in Genesis.

Read Genesis 3:7–22. When sin interrupted the communication between man and God, interestingly enough, it also interrupted the communication between man and woman. Notice verse 7 of chapter 3: "Then the eyes of both of them were opened, and they realized they were naked." Apparently they became ashamed. "They sewed fig leaves together and made coverings for themselves." One result of the Fall was that mankind lost some of the image of God that had been given them. Adam and Eve no longer had that unashamed, open, perfect relationship with each other as husband and wife. And then an even more interesting thing happened: Adam and Eve hid from God. They no longer experienced openness with God. They felt the same kind of embarrassment with God that they had demonstrated toward each other.

Now God enters the scene. He comes to deal with Adam and Eve in their disobedience. The first action he takes is to make permanent coverings for their genitals. Have you ever thought about what a strange sequence of events this is? Why, after these two people disobeyed God, would God enter the scene and make loincloths to cover their genitals? Why would those two events be connected? We believe that somehow human sexual organs and their potential are symbolic of the human potential to have a relationship to God.

It would seem that the *total* way in which two people get involved with each other in a sexual experience—the ecstatic, frantic, intense union that can occur—is a symbol of the way in which we can be intensely involved with God. We most lose ourselves to another person in the sexual experience. We are totally open and vulnerable with each other. God would have us give ourselves to him with the same abandonment.

The concept that sexual union is an example of the way God would like to relate to mankind is further developed throughout the Old Testament.

God's Bride

Israel is frequently referred to in Scripture as God's bride. In Jeremiah 7:9 and 23:10, the terms "adultery" and "adulterers" are used to describe Israel's sin of worshiping other gods. Ezekiel 16 talks in great detail of how God's grace was demonstrated to unfaithful Jerusalem. It talks in symbolic terms of a lover preparing his bride. The passage refers to bathing, oiling, clothing, adorning her; and yet she becomes an adulterous wife, who takes strangers instead of her husband (v. 32).

The entire book of Hosea is an account of God's relationship with Israel, his bride. This symbolism is used regularly when God is trying to establish a relationship with his chosen people. When God began to make a covenant with his people, he said, "This is how I'm going to relate to you," and then he laid out the conditions. And the conditions included his steadfast love and mercy. God wants to have a loving relationship with his people. This is symbolized in the sexual relationship. Isaiah 62:5 reads: "As a young man marries a maiden, so will your sons marry you; as a bridegroom rejoices over his bride, so will your God rejoice over you."

Another interesting fact that confirms the symbolism is evident throughout the Old Testament. The Hebrew word meaning "to know," referring to sexual intercourse, is the same Hebrew word used when the Bible refers to man's "knowing" God. For example, Genesis 4:1 says, "Adam knew Eve his wife, and she conceived and bore Cain." Jeremiah 24:7 quotes the Lord: "I will give them a heart to know me."

Christ's Bride

We find the most explicit passage showing the symbolism of the church (the body of believers) as Christ's bride in Ephesians 5. It says, "Submit to one another out of reverence for Christ. Wives, submit to your husbands. . . . For the husband is the head of the wife as Christ is the head of the church. . . . As the church submits to Christ, so also wives should submit to their husbands in everything. Husbands, love your wives, just as Christ loved the church and gave himself up for her" (vv. 21–25). The writer, Paul, keeps interweaving the relationship of husband and wife with the relationship of Christ and the church. Then Ephesians 5:31 quotes Genesis 2:24, summarizing leaving mother and father, cleaving, and becoming one flesh.

The whole passage is basically saying that the sexual relationship is what best symbolizes the relationship between Christ and the church. In Revelation 19:6–7, the writer talks about Christ's bride, the church, coming for the celebration, the wedding supper. This is a constant theme throughout Scripture. We have to assume that this symbolism is telling us there is something more to sex than physical release, since our sexual relationship is a model of how we can best understand God's desire to have an intense relationship with us.

Husbands are to love their wives as Christ loved the church and gave himself up for her. Christ did not claim his rights but became like us, so we could know him and invite him into our lives.

Solomon is a great model of the husband loving his wife as Christ loved the church. Solomon affirms and connects with the personhood of his wife. In response, his wife invites adventurous sexual activity. Solomon is effusive in his adoration of his new wife: "How beautiful you are, my darling! Oh, how beautiful!" (Song of Songs 4:1). He describes in detail what he enjoys about her.

In response, she pursues him with passion: "May he kiss me with the kisses of his mouth! For your love is better than wine" (1:2 NASB). "On my bed night after night I sought him Whom my soul loves" (3:1 NASB). "Come, my beloved, let us go out into the country, let us spend the night in the villages. Let us rise early and go to the vineyards; let us see whether the vine has budded and its blossoms have opened, and whether the pomegranates have bloomed. There I will give you my love" (7:11–12 NASB).

A Mystery

On the full meaning of this symbolism we read: "This is a profound mystery . . ." (Eph. 5:32). When the word *mystery* is used in the New Testament, we understand it to mean that the purpose of the event or teaching is in the process of being revealed to us. What we did not understand at all before, we can, through Christ, grasp with some degree of enlightenment. And someday the same concept will be clearly understood by all believers.

One thing most of us can be fairly sure of is that we do not experience the impact of this symbolism in the process of lovemaking. It's not likely that a sexual experience will trigger great thoughts about our relationship with God. We are much more apt to be intensely aware of our own physical and emotional expressions and sensations.

We *do* believe that it is in this mystical union of two bodies that body and spirit come closest to a merger. Most of the time we let our minds control us. But in the moment of orgasm we are released from that control. Climax is a "total being" experience; everything about us enters into it. Perhaps this is how the sexual experience represents our relationship to God. In this total, intense fusion of body, emotion, and spirit, we are connecting with what it can be like to be totally one with God. This is, indeed, a mystery. One day we will understand it fully. Meanwhile, we can simply accept and enjoy the truth of it.

4 WHAT THE BIBLE SAYS ABOUT OUR SEXUALITY

SEXUAL PLEASURE—A BIBLICAL EXPECTATION

Sexual Pleasure Within Marriage Is Encouraged and Expected

Besides the command to become one and the instruction to be fruitful and fill the earth, with the emphasis on propagating the messianic line, another consistent expectation throughout Scripture is that the sexual experience is for the pleasure of the relationship. Sex is for unity, procreation, and pleasure.

The Bible endorses the concept of sexual pleasure and assumes a healthy passion. The sexual relationship in marriage reflects God's image. Animals, however, have sex in order to reproduce; they don't make love for the fun of it. They mate according to their hormonal cycles. Humans make love for pleasure. In fact, Scripture instructs believers to always be available to their spouses (1 Cor. 7:3–5), not just for making babies at the time of the month when that is possible. Therefore, we see sexual pleasure as superseding procreation.

The Song of Songs contains some of the most beautiful and erotic poetry ever written. This book is included in the Bible for our benefit. Here are some segments from the New American Standard Bible: "On my bed night after night I sought him whom my soul loves" (3:1). "My beloved is dazzling and ruddy . . . His head is like gold . . . His eyes are like doves . . . His lips are lilies, dripping with liquid myrrh . . . His legs are pillars of alabaster set on pedestals of pure gold . . . and he is wholly desirable" (5:10–16). "How beautiful are your feet in sandals . . . The curves of your hips are like jewels . . . Your belly is like a heap of wheat fenced about with lilies. Your two breasts are like two fawns . . . Your stature is like a palm tree . . . I said, 'I will climb the palm tree, I will take hold of its fruit stalks.' Oh, may your breasts be like clusters of the vine . . . Come, my beloved, let us go out into the country" (7:1–11).

These passages obviously don't encourage us to hold back our passionate feelings! Yet many people come to the sexual experience with the feelings: "I can't really let go." "It's not right for me to feel that strongly." "I couldn't face God again." "Nice girls don't behave that way." Yet as we understand God's message, it is his intention for us to enjoy the sexual experience and to let our feelings flow freely. The Song of Songs is loaded with erotic messages of two lovers enjoying each other's bodies fully. Nothing seems to be restricted.

Another affirmation of the biblical expectations of pleasure comes from looking at men and women of faith in the Old Testament. The assumption we arrive at when we look at a number of these Old Testament faith heroes is that human sexuality not only is representative of our relationship with God (which is a high and lofty concept), but is accepted as being an internal part of human nature. One can be a great hero of the faith and still be an intensely passionate person (people recognized for their faith in Hebrews 11 include Abraham, Jacob, David, and even Rahab the harlot).

We learn from this that human beings are accepted by God as beings with a sexual nature. God does not condone disobedience to his standards in the expression of our sexuality; but he does not condemn our sexuality itself, nor does he condemn us for being intensely sexual beings. He recognizes that the sexual part of us is a very powerful element of our being—a forceful drive. We can see the power of sexuality in the men and women who were chosen as models of faith. Our human sexuality is not something to be diminished as we become more "spiritual." It is part of us as spiritual, godly persons, and it is good. However, we do need to follow our Lord's instructions for the responsible use of this important part of ourselves. Evil comes from the misuse of sex, not from its mere existence or the pleasure it brings in marriage.

Proverbs 5:18–19 is also interesting: "Let your fountain be blessed, and rejoice in the wife of your youth. As a loving hind and a graceful doe, let her breasts satisfy you at all times; be exhilarated always with her love" (NASB). The teaching is that our feelings of sexual pleasure are permissible, and we are encouraged to enjoy them. If we are holding back on our sexual experience for religious reasons, that is a cop-out. From a biblical point of view, there is no reason to hold back.

We cannot overemphasize how important it is for Christian couples to understand the Bible's pro-sex message. To the degree that the church has been antisexual and antipleasure, it has failed to be consistent with our understanding of what the Bible has to say about sex within marriage.

MUTUALITY—THE GUIDING PRINCIPLE

The New Testament teaches that the barriers between men and women have been broken down because of Christ. No longer do women and men live by different standards. This teaching is a radical departure from the culture that surrounded the church in Old Testament times. The main view of that day was that women were clearly beneath men.

The New Testament also teaches the basic concept that men and women are equal—not identical, not necessarily the same in roles—but equal in terms of value, ability, and position before God. This concept of equality is important because a myth has been perpetuated within the church, community, and society that assumes a man has sexual rights a woman does not have. We see that mentality as completely contrary to biblical teaching. The woman has as many rights as the man has, or the man has as few rights as the woman. This is particularly clear in Galatians 3:28: "There is neither Jew nor Greek, slave nor free, male nor female, for you are all one in Christ Jesus." There are many similar passages.

Ephesians 2:13–22 is extremely relevant. It talks about Christ breaking down the human barriers, making people who were formerly divided and at war with one another into the one household of God. What we take it to mean for our sexual experience is that men and women are equal before God in their right to sexual pleasure.

We are expected to give ourselves to *each other* in marriage; this is a mutual command, not for wives only. "Let the husband fulfill his duty to his wife, and likewise also the wife to her husband" (1 Cor. 7:3 NASB). Or as the passage reads in the *The Message*:

> The marriage bed must be a place of mutuality—the husband seeking to satisfy his wife, the wife seeking to satisfy her husband. Marriage is not a place to "stand up for your rights." Marriage is a decision to serve the other, whether in bed or out. Abstaining from sex is permissible for a period of time if you both agree to it, and if it's for the purposes of prayer and fasting—but only for such times. Then come back together again. Satan has an ingenious way of tempting us when we least expect it.

Each passage in the New Testament that teaches about the husband-wife sexual relationship either begins or ends with a command for mutuality. Not only are husband and wife equal in God's sight, but they have mutual rights and responsibilities.

Even in Ephesians 5, which deals with submission, the section starts with a command for *mutual* submission (v. 21). Mutuality in sexual rights and responsibilities is a biblical principle that has made a significant positive impact on many couples' sexual relationship. As a woman accepts the fact that she has the right to have her own needs met, she may begin initiating or become more expressive about what brings her pleasure.

Love is the new guiding principle for sexual behavior in marriage. This is not to say that love was never a part of Old Testament marriage relationships. Certainly Isaac and Rebekah and many others demonstrated loving, caring relationships. There was concern when a wife was unloved: "When the LORD saw that Leah was not loved, he opened her womb, but Rachel was barren" (Gen. 29:31). However, love was not commanded or expected, because marriage was more of a business deal.

In the New Testament, however, the husband-wife relationship is to depict the kind of love we see Christ lavishing on the church. "Husbands, love your wives, just as Christ loved the church and gave himself up for her . . . In this same way, husbands ought to love their wives as their own bodies. He who loves his wife loves himself" (Eph. 5:25, 28). This was news to the people in New Testament times; love in marriage was not a part of their culture. It is a specifically Christian concept—another one of God's good gifts to his people, along with sex.

Love has to be the guiding principle for deciding what sexual behaviors are right and wrong for a husband and wife. We look to love as our criterion because the New Testament gives us no teaching on how to enjoy each other sexually. There are no "dos and don'ts." Though there are many restrictions regarding the person with whom one may be involved sexually, there are no obvious limitations on how one may enjoy oneself within marriage. Within marriage, we are to freely enjoy each other's bodies as long as the activity is mutually desired, loving, brings us closer together, and does not interfere with our relationship with God.

The Design:	Pleasure and Intimacy
The Method of Fulfilling that Design:	Mutuality in Marriage
The Model:	The Man Adores and Affirms and the Woman Invites

THE

PHYSICAL

DIMENSION

5 OUR BODIES

He never lets me see him. He just quickly slips into the shower after
he gets his clothes off.

Gary had grown up in a home where there was little openness. Now,
even after fifteen years of marriage and two children, he still could
not let himself be open with his wife. He was too fat, his penis was
too short, and he was simply too embarrassed. He knew his wife
enjoyed his body, but he couldn't. This attitude affected his freedom
and security and led to problems in their marriage relationship.

BODY IMAGE

How we feel about ourselves affects how we relate to another person,
particularly sexually. It has been found that preorgasmic women (those
who have not yet experienced orgasm) who feel unworthy and who
have difficulty accepting themselves as persons cannot be helped to
become orgasmic until they deal with these feelings of low self-
worth. When Christ gave the commandment to love your neighbor
as yourself, he was spelling out the principle that your feelings about
yourself affect your ability to love someone else. His command

assumes that we love ourselves—and to the degree that we love ourselves we are able to love our neighbors. We have a hard time giving to or caring for someone else if we feel we are not worthy persons and do not have anything to give.

Body image is the part of our self-image that deals with our attitudes about our bodies, especially our bodily appearance. There is a tendency in our culture to be dissatisfied with one's body shape. We all strive for that perfect figure or physique. Women are often concerned that their breasts are too big, too small, too flabby, or too whatever. A man may be concerned with the size of his penis, fearing that a smaller penis is indicative of being less of a man and less likely to be able to satisfy a woman. There are a number of myths to be dispelled to counteract this concern with penis size. One is that it is the duty of the man to satisfy the woman. The second is that this satisfaction is dependent on the size of the man's penis. The truth is that the woman has the organ of accommodation, that is, the vagina changes to accommodate any size penis. Therefore, penis size has little to do with sexual pleasure or satisfaction. We will deal with this more technically in the next chapter.

Another focus of body dissatisfaction for both men and women is one's weight. We are trying to either lose weight or gain weight—or to get our weight properly proportioned. Whatever the specific focus, often our feelings about ourselves, good or bad, are related to how we feel about our bodies.

We have talked about the dissatisfaction we frequently have with our bodies. What about the opposite dilemma? Can you place too much value on positive feelings about your body? If you see yourself as having the perfect figure, you may be in danger of depending on your good feelings about your body for good feelings about yourself in general. In this case, your self-esteem is totally dependent on your appearance. But what happens when illness or injury damages that beautiful body? You will have a hard time continuing to feel good about yourself.

Whether we devalue ourselves because of our appearance or feel worthwhile only because of our appearance, this kind of preoccupation with our bodies distorts our position as God's creation. We must look inside ourselves for other positive assets. What qualities do you have as a person that make you unique and special? What is your real value as a person, aside from your physical attributes? These are the important questions.

DEVELOPMENT OF BODY IMAGE

How does a person develop his or her body image? There are three factors that affect how we perceive and accept our bodies. These are the sensory experiences we had as children, the feedback we received from significant others as we were growing up, and the models with which we compare ourselves.

First of all, the development of our body image started with the sensory experiences we had as children. This included both internal feelings and external input. Internally, you may have experienced hunger or pain. You did not develop positive feelings about your body because it gave you so much pain or discomfort. It is difficult to do much about reversing the effects of these internal negative experiences, except to understand them.

External sensory experiences are those received from the outside world. The first input that affected us was the kind of touch we received—the tactile stimulus. Was it gentle, warm, comforting, and loving? Were we cared for as babies and growing children? Did we get a positive feeling about touch? The second external sensory input that affects how we value our bodies has to do with the kinesthetic sense— the kind of movement we experienced. This includes how we were rocked, picked up, and played with, whether we were handled gently or roughly, and whether the primary caretakers (usually parents) in our world were secure or insecure in the way they held us.

Another important area of input that affects body image is the verbal feedback received from significant persons in our lives when we are forming opinions about ourselves. Such persons include parents, relatives, and classmates. Sometimes children are teased and thus become self-conscious about aspects of their appearance that adults view as attractive. For example, our son tried to cut the curls out of his hair when he was in kindergarten because he was being called "curly head." Freckles can be a similarly disdained feature. "Fatty" or "skinny" are labels that may leave a person with a negative feeling about himself for the rest of his life. Even after "fatties" lose their excess weight, they may still view themselves as fat.

Negative labels can inadvertently be given to children by parents as well. Often we do not give little children credit for their ability to understand what adults are saying. We have heard parents openly discuss the fact that their daughter "just doesn't have it as far as looks are concerned, so we'll really have to work on developing her personality."

Other adults in the child's world may also give feedback that labels the child. More often these will be positive rather than negative, but not always. It is disappointing and amazing to find how easily teachers will label a child.

The daughter of some close family friends, who is a gifted child and an excellent student, was identified as "slow" in front of the rest of her class when she was in first grade. She was a perfectionist and had a creative imagination. This often kept her from completing her work as quickly as the teacher expected her to. Five years later she is still extremely sensitive to any suggestion that she is doing a task slowly. Recently, as she was being tucked into bed, she said, "You know, Mom, whenever anyone tells me to hurry or says anything that might mean I'm doing something too slowly, I get this terrible feeling all over me and I see the whole picture of what happened in first grade. It's just as clear as if it were happening right then. Miss Harris had reminded me several times to hurry with my work. She was helping the person in front of me. She looked back at me, and instead of writing I was thinking about what I was going to write next. In front of the whole class she said, 'I know what's the matter with you. You're a daydreamer and you're slow.'"

That example does not have to do with body appearance, but its effect on self-worth is the same.

Our daughter has received a more positive kind of labeling. From infancy on, she has received a considerable amount of feedback about her physical attractiveness. She is also aware that she was born breech—feetfirst instead of headfirst. One day, when she was about seven, we were driving along in the car and she said, "Mommy, I have figured out why I am pretty. It's because my face came out last. My feet might not look as good as others because they came out first, and they had all the pressure on them, but my face looks better than others." She had developed her own rationale for feeling set apart from the rest of her world because of excessive positive input about her appearance.

The third major influence on our self-image is the comparison of ourselves to others. The models we choose to compare ourselves with are critical. Cultures vary considerably as to what is defined as attractive. Most cultures have ideal male and female body images. What is your ideal? What has influenced the development of this ideal? Whom have you chosen as models? How do you see yourself in view of this ideal?

RESOLVING BODY IMAGE PROBLEMS

Body image problems occur when there is a large gap between how we view our bodies and what we define as the ideal body. When the way we would like to look is different from the way we think we do look, we will have difficulty accepting ourselves and will probably have difficulty being free with our bodies sexually.

How do we bridge the gap? How can we bring our view of ourselves closer to our ideal?

The first step toward body image enhancement is to *examine your view of yourself.* Is how you see yourself fairly consistent with how others see you? Maybe you are stuck with a childhood label that does not reflect who you really are. Get some honest feedback from your spouse and others close to you—hopefully, positive feedback.

When we were dating, the difference in how Joyce felt about herself and how Cliff viewed her became obvious. Cliff tells the story best: "I had selected Joyce as one of the prettiest girls in the freshman class, and so I pursued dating her. She had a poor image of her physical appearance. She saw herself as skinny, with a long nose and puffy eyes. The rest of her family had lighter complexions than she. So she had the fantasy that she must have been adopted.

"After we had been dating regularly for several months, we ended up in an argument about my feedback regarding what I saw as her beauty. I argued that I could not believe she really did not think she was pretty. I thought she was just fishing for compliments. She was frustrated with me because she didn't believe anyone could think of themselves as attractive. The evening ended with my telling Joyce that if she would go up to her room and look in the mirror, she would know she was beautiful—because all people, when they are by themselves and looking in a mirror, really believe they are good-looking. In her frustration she retorted, 'If you go up and look in the mirror, you will know you're not!'"

We have come a long way since then. We realize that there is a huge range of views people have of themselves. We have a mirror assignment for you that we recommend for married couples in seminars or in therapy. This assignment gives you a structured plan for looking at yourself realistically and getting some honest feedback from your spouse.

▊ EXERCISE 1

Body Image Assignment

Partner #1: Stand in front of a full-length mirror in the nude. Describe your body as honestly as you can to your partner. Start with general feelings about your body as you see it. Then talk about each specific body part, starting with your hair and working down. Talk about how your body feels and looks, ways you wish you were different, what you feel particularly good about. If this is impossible for one of you to do, talk about it! Then modify the experience so it can work for you (for example, cover parts of your body as needed or dim the lights).

Partner #2: Only listen and observe. Listen to both the words and feelings of your spouse as he/she talks. *Do not interrupt!* When your spouse is finished, feed back to him/her what you have sensed and heard.

Partner #1: Clarify or expand on what your partner has heard from you.

Partner #2: Fill in any positive messages you can give that will be constructive.

Partner #1: When you feel you have been understood accurately, reverse this process. You be the quiet observer and listen while your spouse describes his/her body.

Another area in which you may need feedback to enhance a realistic acceptance of your body is the sensory dimension. If the touch and movement you received as a child left you feeling uncared for and unaccepted, you are likely to need much more affirmation of your body through touch and holding—even though you may resist it. We hope you have a spouse who is willing and able to fill that need for you. If you are aware of a need for more touching, talk about this with your spouse. Talk about what feels good to you and what would be a comfortable way for your spouse to respond to your feelings.

The second step in bringing your own body view closer to that of your ideal is to *determine ways it is possible to change your body*. Joyce has become positive about her eyes since she learned to use eye makeup that distracts from her puffy eyelids. There are other ways in which women can learn to use makeup to hide the features they do not like and to accent those they do. Men might grow a mustache or beard or shave these off to vary some aspect of their facial features. Straightening or correcting faulty teeth is important for some people, whereas others accept such variations as part of who they are, something they would not want to change.

Additional ways a person may plan to change his or her body include losing or gaining weight, an exercise program, posture correction, or other body enhancement processes. Plastic surgery is an option when there is serious dissatisfaction with one's body or when there has been a traumatic disfigurement. Successful cosmetic changes can be made to almost any part of the body. We would recommend that you get some professional assistance in evaluating cosmetic surgery as an option before you pursue it as the solution to a body image problem. It is usually a big investment financially—and a rather permanent change that may or may not be the answer for your particular dissatisfaction. There may be other emotional barriers that hinder your acceptance of yourself. In such cases, the correction of one body part would only lead to finding dissatisfaction with yourself in other ways.

The third and final suggestion for bringing your ideal closer to your real view is to *reevaluate what you're measuring yourself against.* What kind of models have you chosen? Are you looking at the extremes held up by the media? How do these "ideal" images compare with the significant and valued people in your life? In other words, are your expectations so far out of reach that you will always feel dissatisfied? If that is the case, we recommend the following procedure: Commit yourself to one other person who will hold you accountable to get rid of the current ideals and to start selecting more realistic body models acceptable and attainable for you. If your new models are people with whom you can talk freely, ask them how they achieved their physical condition.

The struggle to feel good about your body is a process of becoming open with yourself and your spouse. It also includes honesty concerning your feelings about yourself, feeling comfortable being in the nude, caring for your body, and allowing yourself to receive affirmation through touch and verbal feedback from others in your world. A new sense of comfort with and acceptance of your body can bring increased freedom and pleasure to your sexual experience.

In all this, it is crucial to maintain a healthy perspective on where your value as a person is centered. Christ's message is loud and clear: "Man looks at the outward appearance, but the LORD looks at the heart" (1 Sam. 16:7b). We cannot disregard either part: the part that man looks at—the outside, nor the part God looks at—the heart.

6 DISCOVERING AND SHARING OUR BODIES

And God created man *in His own image, in the image of God He created him; male and female He created them.* (Gen. 1:27 NASB, emphasis added)

OUR BODIES ARE GOD'S WORK

Our bodies—including our sexual anatomy—are God's work. He created us with all our internal and external body parts; all our sexual organs were made by him. "And God saw all that He had made, and behold, it was very good" (Gen. 1:31 NASB).

Oh yes, you shaped me first inside, then out; you formed me in my mother's womb. I thank you, High God—you're breathtaking! Body and soul, I am marvelously made! I worship in adoration—what a creation! You know me inside and out, you know every bone in my body; you know exactly how I was made, bit by bit, how I was sculpted from nothing into something. Like an open book, you watched me grow from conception to birth; all stages of my life were spread out before

43

you, the days of my life all prepared before I'd even lived one
day. (Ps. 139:13–16 MSG)

Even our sexual parts are good. They were not added as a result
of sin. They were there from the moment of creation and are to be
enjoyed and discovered. The entire sexual anatomy is present in a
newborn baby. This was affirmed for us when each of our children
was born. It was amazing to us that each body part was there. They
were like miniature adults in their newborn bodies.

Self-Discovery

It is natural for children to discover their genitals. Even in infancy,
during the first year of life, a girl may find her clitoris and enjoy
touching it because it *feels* good. In the same way, the boy finds his
penis. These good feelings are God-given. They are natural and normal; they have not been conditioned by a sinful society. Rather, sexual feelings are God's gift to us, just as intellect or other abilities are.

If we accept this premise—that our sexual parts and feelings are of
God—then it would follow that, as with any other gift from God, we
should become familiar with them and develop them. A child will
naturally become familiar with sexual anatomy and feelings if allowed
the freedom to do so. Unfortunately, too often this is not the case.
Most of us have been brought up to believe that sexual exploration is
"bad" or sinful. Without really stopping to think about the biblical
teaching regarding our bodies, we automatically impose on our children the negative standards we learned. The constant repetition of
the warning to keep yourself pure from sexual play outside marriage
tends to affect both childhood and marriage. That is, we do not allow
children an innocent touching of their bodies; and we do not allow
ourselves the full freedom of sexual pleasure in marriage.

Most children between three and six years of age will engage in
self-exploration and discovery activities, as well as "playing doctor,"
or peer exploration, with children of the same and/or opposite sex.
When our daughter was four years old, Joyce walked into her bedroom after her bath. She found Julene sitting on the floor with her

legs spread apart, her head down as she tried to examine her genitals. When she heard Joyce enter the room, she remained in the same position and casually asked, "Mom, what is that hole in my bottom?" Joyce's first tendency was to respond with shock, but Julene's comfortableness made her stop and think. She remembered that just the day before Julene had spent a long time in front of the bathroom mirror, trying to examine and watch the uvula at the back of her throat. There was no difference in the child's intent in discovering her body. She did not think that while looking at her throat was fine, looking at her genitals was shameful.

Joyce got a hand mirror so Julene could see her own genitals better. She sat down with Julene and pointed to the various openings, the lips and the clitoris, and indicated their technical names. Julene's curiosity seemed satisfied, and she ran off to play.

You may be a woman who never felt free to sit down with a mirror and really find out what your genitals look or feel like. For men, this lack of exploration is unlikely, since a man's sexual anatomy is so externally evident. As a woman you may think of your genitals as the "doctor's area"—he's the one who examines you regularly—or maybe as your husband's territory to fondle, but you have never really thought of becoming familiar with your own genitals. You may be more familiar with the map of the world than your own sexual anatomy.

We encourage you to engage freely in a natural discovery of your sexual anatomy. You probably will not have the spontaneous feeling that a young girl would have, but you can think of it as something you missed in the development and understanding of yourself. It is something you need to do to have complete sexual freedom with your body. The more familiar you are with your own and your spouse's sexual anatomy and feelings, the less guessing will be involved in the sexual act. This obviously leads to greater confidence and freedom.

▪ EXERCISE 2

Women: Discovering and Knowing Your Own Genitals

Begin with clean hands and body. Using a hand mirror, examine your external genitalia. Become familiar with what is normal for you. There can be medical benefits from this also. Once you are familiar with yourself, you will be able to notice changes that may need medical attention. You can mention these to your physician long before your next gynecological examination.

When you use the hand mirror to examine your genitals, what you see will look something like Figure 1. The female's external genitals include the labia majora (the outer lips), the labia minora (the inner lips), and the clitoris.

The Labia Majora and Labia Minora

What you see when you look at your genitals before you open the outer lips (the labia majora) are the mons pubis, the soft part above the clitoris that is covered with pubic hair, and the thick outer lips, the labia majora, which are also partially covered by hair. If you have never given birth to a child, your outer lips probably meet in a closed fashion at the center or midline of your genitals, providing protection for the inner lips, the urinary opening and the vagina. In women who have borne children, it is common to find that the process of childbirth has interrupted the neat fit of the outer lips at the midline. This change in the midline makes a difference in the changes that occur when the outer lips spread apart during sexual arousal (refer to the following chapter, excitement phase).

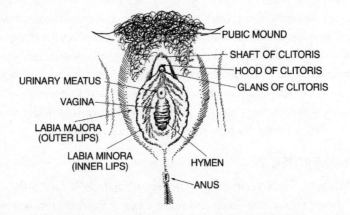

Figure 1: External Female Genitals (Front View)

The Clitoris

With a hand mirror in one hand, use your other hand to spread apart the outer lips to examine the rest of the external genitalia. Look for the clitoris (refer to the previous diagram). Even though the diagram points out the three parts of the clitoris—the glans, the hood, and the shaft—these may be difficult to identify specifically on yourself. The hood that covers the shaft flows down to form the inner lips.

The shaft is a miniature penislike cylinder located under the hood with the glans or head being the only part exposed. Even the glans may not be easy to locate. For some women the glans, or tip, of the clitoris may tend to hide under the hood, and the hood may seem like the point at which the inner lips join.

If you have difficulty visually identifying the clitoris, you may be able to find it by touching the place where you expect it to be. The tip of the clitoris is particularly sensitive to any touch. In fact, rubbing the glans may actually be painful to you. Many women report that the most pleasurable place to receive stimulation is around the clitoris, not directly on it. You may want to touch various points around and on the clitoris, not necessarily for the purpose of stimulation, but to learn where the best feelings occur for you. The discovery of where pleasure points are for you and where you tend to experience pain is crucial to communicate to your husband for the enhancement of your lovemaking. We will talk more about this later.

Intense pleasure and pain are closely related in our bodies. Those areas like the clitoris that are loaded with nerve endings are most receptive to pleasure and, for the same reason, most receptive to pain. As pleasure intensifies, susceptibility to pain increases (see graph below).

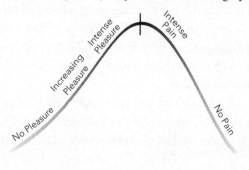

Your husband will not automatically be able to differentiate where to apply, how much, and what type of pressure feels good. He does not know this by instinct. If you learn this for yourself, you can show him and even guide his hand to demonstrate the most pleasurable pressure and touch (refer to Exercise 10 in Chapter 13). This can do away with much of his guesswork and add to your pleasure. Self-discovery comes first, before you try to show or demonstrate. Your husband's presence may introduce some level of tension and/or excitement, which may hinder the initial learning that needs to take place.

Before we move on to further self-exploration, we want to say more about the clitoris. This factual data will be particularly important if you think that men are by nature more sexual than women, or that God created men to have more intense sexual feelings than women. Maybe you have underlying feelings that a woman is to be the passive recipient of the man's sexual desire. Women were created with vaginas as a receptacle for the sperm and seminal fluid of the man, you may reason; should this not make the woman a passive receiver of the man's aggression, rather than an active participant?

The presence of the clitoris counters this attitude. The clitoris is the only organ in the human anatomy designed solely for receiving and transmitting sexual stimuli. Physiologically, that is its *only* function. The woman, not the man, was created with the clitoris. The penis is the equivalent organ for the man, in that it is composed of similar erectile tissue—tissue with spaces that fill with blood and become engorged when stimulated, making the organ larger and firmer. However, the penis serves many other functions. The fact that the clitoris in the woman is unique in its function of receiving and transmitting sexual stimuli is confirmation that God intended women to be intensely sexual beings, not just "vaginas" to receive the man's sexual expression.

This is an important concept to consider. It often affects how couples make love, how a woman feels about herself, and how the man relates to the woman sexually. We feel that the Christian community has assimilated society's "passive woman vs. aggressive man" mentality, which is sometimes translated into the wife's being submissive and passive in the sexual act. If you hold that view, we challenge you to study the New Testament teachings on sex in marriage (refer to Chapter 3).

The Urinary Meatus

Moving on with your hand-mirror exploration, let's talk about the location of the urinary meatus opening. The urinary meatus is not part of the sexual anatomy per se, but its proximity makes it important to locate. It is found right above the vagina or, for some women, it may actually be in the opening of the vagina. It may look like a little pimple. It is the opening to the urinary tract that leads to the urinary bladder and on to the kidneys. That entire system is sterile. When there is no infection present, it is free of microorganisms. It does not carry germs or transmit diseases.

The other two openings the woman has in the genital and perineal area are the vagina and the rectum. The vagina is the largest opening you see.

Women: Knowing What's Inside

Okay, now that you're familiar with your external genitalia, let's look at your internal sexual organs. Looking at the diagram of the front-view cross section of the internal female reproductive organs (Figure 2), you will see the ovaries, uterus, fallopian tubes, and vagina. The ovaries look like large almonds and are located one on either side of the uterus, below and behind the fallopian tubes. Some of the sex hormones that affect the whole menstrual cycle are produced by the ovaries. Primarily, however, they produce the ova, or eggs, for reproduction. The egg is usually released fourteen days before a woman's menstrual period. It is carried by one of the two fallopian tubes to the uterus, where it is implanted if it becomes fertilized. Or it is discharged from the body with the menstrual flow if it does not become fertilized. This process begins in puberty and ceases during menopause.

Figure 2: Internal Female Genitalia (Front View)

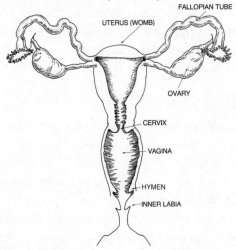

FALLOPIAN TUBE

UTERUS (WOMB)

OVARY

CERVIX

VAGINA

HYMEN

INNER LABIA

The Uterus

The uterus, or womb, is a pear-shaped organ located between the urinary bladder and the rectum, as you can see in Figure 3. In its normal position, the uterus is flexed toward the front of the body, pointing forward and slightly upward. If you have been told that you have a "tipped" uterus, this probably means the uterus is retroflexed or flipped back toward the backbone. Less frequently, a tipped uterus may be anteflexed or tipped too much toward the front of the body, putting pressure on the urinary bladder and thus causing the feeling of needing to urinate frequently. A retroflexed uterus is likely to cause momentary, intense pain upon deep thrusting during intercourse. When a woman comes to us complaining of pain during intercourse, we immediately want to know just where she feels this pain and when in the process of intercourse it is felt.

A woman complained that she was not enjoying the sexual experience. She did all she could to avoid her husband's approaches. Though she used to become very aroused, as time passed she was less and less responsive. From further questioning we learned that she was almost completely inactive after entry—because "It hurts!" The pain she was trying to avoid occurred when her husband was highly aroused and thrusting deeply. She confirmed that her physician had

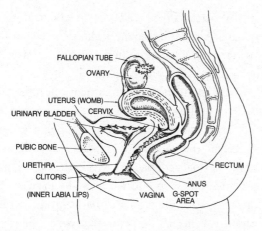

Figure 3: Unaroused Internal Female Genitalia (Side View)

told her she had a tipped uterus. By some shifts in positioning and exercising, she learned that this pain can be avoided. She was freed to begin to enjoy the sexual experience without pain (see Chapter 30 for more detail on pain).

The Vagina

In contrast to the urinary system, the vagina does have microorganisms present. The microorganisms present in the vagina are not disease-producing microorganisms (germs). Rather, their function is to ward off infection and to keep the vagina in a healthy state. Therefore, the vagina is considered a clean passageway when there is no infection present.

Some of us have tended to think of our genitals as dirty. That was also probably what we read into the message, "Don't touch." It might also be a response to the important and necessary sanitary practice of washing hands after toileting. It is important for us to note that the need for washing after going to the bathroom is not because of the possibility of the *genitals* contaminating our hands, but rather because of the rectum. The rectum is highly contaminated. It is loaded with potentially disease-producing microorganisms. When you wipe after toileting, it is important to wipe from front to back, from the urinary meatus to the rectum, to avoid contaminating the vagina and the urinary system. If you are a woman who tends to suffer from frequent vaginal or bladder infections, begin to note your wiping habits. You may be carrying disease-producing microorganisms from the rectum to the urinary bladder and vagina.

There are other facts about the vagina that may affect sexual attitudes and habits. In a healthy state, the vagina maintains its own acid-base balance. This is another mechanism that helps to fight off infections and enhances the process of impregnation. Because of these functions of the normal acid balance within the vagina, douching is not recommended unless so directed by a physician.

One more characteristic of the vagina is that it produces lubrication. This lubrication is a normal response that occurs shortly after birth and continues throughout life. It may lessen after menopause, in which case a woman may need to use a lubricant to enhance the comfort of entry. Lubrication is an involuntary response of the body. By that we mean it is something over which you have no control. Lubrication can best be described as beads of perspiration that appear along the walls of the vagina. Lubrication may occur when you are in a relaxed state, with or without any obvious sexual stimulation. For example, adult women lubricate every eighty to ninety minutes while asleep.

Now back to the self-examination of your genitals. To examine the vagina, we would encourage you to use a lubricant. There are many available including Astroglide, Probe, Replens, Intimate Moisture, and Long-Lasting K-Y Jelly. After lubricating your forefinger, insert it into the vagina as far as the second knuckle and slowly follow the wall of the vagina all the way around.

You might think of the opening of the vagina as a clock, with the top of the vagina, the point nearest the clitoris, as the twelve o'clock location. When you follow the wall of the vagina, start at some point on the clock and put varying degrees of pressure on the wall of the vagina with your finger at each point of the clock. As you do this, notice the sensation.

Identify any differences in feeling at the various places within the vagina. For example, identify any areas that are particularly sensitive to touch and seem to trigger either a painful feeling or a pleasurable feeling. In this process, some women for whom intercourse has always been painful locate a specific tear or irritation of the vagina wall that needs medical attention to promote healing. Alleviating the pain will enhance the intercourse experience.

Other women have found that a certain area of the vagina is much more responsive to sexual stimulation. This discovery can enhance sexual feelings during intercourse if a position is assumed that places the penis in more direct contact with that area of the vaginal wall. For example, some women find that stimulation at the twelve o'clock, four o'clock, and eight o'clock locations provides the most pleasurable vaginal sensations. Assuming the lateral position, with the top person straddling the legs of the person on the bottom, will allow the penis to provide more intense friction of the four o'clock and eight o'clock areas of the vaginal wall (see diagram, page 62). The woman-on-top position will typically allow the penis to stimulate the G-spot area at twelve o'clock.

▪ EXERCISE 3

PC Muscle Conditioning (Kegel Exercise)

The vagina is the most important anatomical structure for intercourse. It is often referred to as the "organ of accommodation"; that is, the vagina is a muscular passageway very changeable in size. It can tighten or expand to receive any size penis during intercourse. It can even expand to deliver a baby. This ability of the vagina to tighten or expand can be enhanced by exercise, and the same exercise will also increase the vagina's sensitivity to sexual stimulation and its responsiveness. The muscle to be exercised is the pubococcygeus (PC) muscle, which is also used to start and stop urination. Although the exercise should not be done regularly during urination, you can identify the correct muscle by sitting on the toilet with your legs spread apart. Start urinating, then stop urination for about three seconds, then start again. Do this several times before you finish emptying your bladder. If you can do it easily, you probably need to tighten and relax this muscle only about twenty-five times a day to keep it in good condition.

If this process is very difficult for you, however, it means that the muscle is sloppy and needs a great deal of work. We would recommend that you start with tightening it twenty-five times a day and work up to two hundred times a day. When the muscle is sloppy, it may take a great deal of concentration to tighten and hold for three seconds before relaxing. As it develops better tone, you can do the exercise anywhere at any time, and no one will even know (unless you get a little smile on your face!). It's often helpful to associate tightening the PC muscle with some other daily activity, such as waiting at the grocery checkout counter, stopping at red lights, ironing, washing dishes, taking notes at the board meeting, working at the computer, watching your son's Little League game, or whatever happens to fit your lifestyle.

Experiment with tightening and releasing the PC muscle during an actual intercourse experience as well. This will be particularly helpful if you are not aware of feelings in the vagina after entry. We will give more explicit instruction regarding this particular enhancement exercise when we talk about increasing the responsiveness of the preorgasmic woman.

This concludes the self-discovery exercises for women. If this has been difficult or uncomfortable for you, we would encourage you to repeat the process several times in the future until you have a sense of being at ease with your genitals. If you find that your genitals are distasteful or ugly to you, or this whole exercise seems like something wrong that would be condemned or frowned upon by God, we suggest that before you enter into this self-discovery experience you read the Song of Songs in a modern version or paraphrase such as *The Message*. Then, as you explore your genitals, thank God for creating each part and for its function in your body. If you found the self-discovery exercise to be comfortable, we would still encourage you to take time to thank God for your genitals, for what you have learned about yourself, and for the good feelings this part of your body brings you.

▓ EXERCISE 4

Men: Knowing Yourself

Now, if you are a man, knowing yourself genitally probably will not be a new or difficult task. Somehow, little boys grow up automatically familiar with their genitals—maybe because the male's genitals are so obvious. It is not uncommon for a mother to hear her little two- or three-year-old giggling because he has just discovered it feels good to touch his penis. This type of self-discovery is typical for most boys sometime during their growing-up period. This tends to be true whether or not the home environment has been open to allowing genital exploration. If your home environment condemned touching yourself genitally, you probably have guilt associated with the good feelings. This guilt associated with good feelings in your body may play havoc with your sexual experiences in marriage. You may find yourself having difficulty really enjoying the pleasure of your body even when this is a condoned, expected part of being a husband. Since you learned to associate bodily pleasure with something wrong, you did not automatically associate sexual behavior with marriage after the wedding ceremony.

Whether your self-discovery as a child was positive or guilt-related, you probably are familiar with what it feels like to touch or stimulate your penis and scrotum. You may not, however, be familiar with all the various parts of your genitals and what they are called. You will need this information when you learn, in Chapter 8, how your body responds during a full sexual experience.

The Scrotum and Testes

The scrotum is like a pouch that holds two small, ball-like glands called the testes (see Figure 4). The testes, which you can feel moving around when you press on the scrotum, are the primary sex organs in the male. They are similar in function to the ovaries in the female. The testes produce the sperm that unite with the female egg to begin a new life. In addition to producing the sperm, the testes also produce a portion of the semen or seminal fluid that carries the sperm from the testes through a series of ducts and out through the penis. The seminal fluid containing the sperm is called the ejaculate. The third function of the testes is totally unrelated to the duct system; it is the production of the male hormone testosterone, which is secreted directly into the bloodstream.

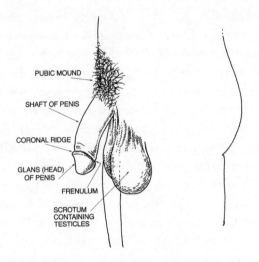

PUBIC MOUND

SHAFT OF PENIS

CORONAL RIDGE

GLANS (HEAD)
OF PENIS

FRENULUM

SCROTUM
CONTAINING
TESTICLES

Figure 4: Circumcised External Male Genitals (Side View)

Testosterone. Testosterone is what causes the changes in puberty that transform a boy into a man. These changes begin to evidence themselves about three years after testosterone begins to be produced in the boy's body. The production of testosterone gradually increases from that time until it reaches its peak around twenty years of age. It maintains that peak level of production until forty years of age and then gradually declines. The decrease in testosterone after age forty does not need to affect a man's sexual pleasure or sexual functioning (see the section on aging and impotence in Chapter 27). This hormonal function of the testes is an internal function that is not something you can examine on your body or identify on a diagram.

Sperm. We would like to guide you into becoming more familiar with the first two functions of the testes, the production and secretion of sperm and seminal fluid. Once the sperm and seminal fluid leave the testes, there is a series of ducts through which they travel. This process can be identified on Figure 5. The epididymis begins this duct system. The epididymis is housed within the scrotum and then connects to the seminal ducts, which carry the seminal fluid and sperm to the inside of the body; there the sperm connect with the ejaculatory ducts and pass through the prostate gland, which is doughnut-shaped. The prostate gland supplies additional seminal fluid to the ejaculate. The ducts that carry the ejaculate from this point are short tubes that end almost immediately and join the urethra. The urethra is the tube that carries the urine from the urinary bladder out through the penis. Given this whole setup, you can see why swelling of the prostate gland, which can occur in older men, would cause difficulties. This swelling is usually detected when the man begins to experience difficulty urinating or pain upon ejaculation. A vitamin/mineral/herbal supplement is often recommended for men to promote prostate health. Speak with a healthcare professional or check a health-food store for a recommendation.

The Penis

The ejaculatory system, as you can see in the diagram, joins the urinary system and leads into the penis. The penis is the obvious essential organ for sexual intercourse in that it is the means by which the ejaculate is introduced into the female vagina. The penis is composed of erectile tissue. This tissue has a lot of spaces called venous sinuses. When there is sexual arousal, blood rushes to these sinuses, causing the penis to become enlarged, firm, and erect. This makes possible the penis's entry into the vagina.

Figure 5: Unaroused Internal Male Genitalia
(Side View)

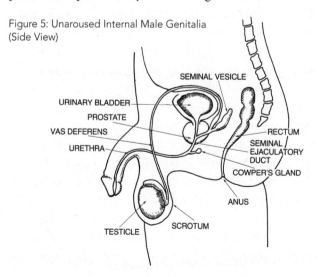

The penis has various parts. There is the glans or bulging tip of the penis with the coronal ridge. If a man has not been circumcised, the glans is covered with a loose skin called the foreskin. This can be pulled back from the glans; it is important for the uncircumcised man to pull back the foreskin and wash underneath it during his daily showering to promote cleanliness and to prevent infection. The penis head (glans) of a circumcised man is exposed. The shaft of the penis is the whole cylindrical structure that responds most pleasurably to being stroked. The loose skin around the shaft of the penis forms what looks like a seam down the backside of the penis. This is called the frenulum and for some men is the part of the penis they find most responsive to caressing. You might note if that is the case with you.

Fallacies About Penis Size. Many fallacies regarding men and their sexual anatomy and responsiveness have been perpetuated by locker-room or construction-crew jokes and comparisons. Frequently these relate to penis size. The assumption that the larger a man's penis, the better he will be able to satisfy a woman, just isn't true.

First of all, most women don't gain the majority of their sexual satisfaction from the penis being in the vagina, no matter what size the penis. Women tend to be most responsive to general sensuous caressing of the body and stimulation of the breasts and external genitalia.

Second, the unaroused (flaccid) penis size does not relate proportionately to erect penis size. A small flaccid penis, upon sexual stimulation, enlarges to a greater extent than does a larger flaccid penis. In their erect state there is not much difference in size between one penis and another, even though they may differ significantly in size when they are not aroused.

Third, as we will describe in more detail later in this chapter, the primary contact the penis has with the walls of the vagina during intercourse occurs in the lower one and a half to two inches. During sexual arousal the vagina changes from a collapsed, cylindrical passageway as the inner or upper two-thirds expands and the lower third thickens and tightens due to vasocongestion (blood rushing in to fill up the tissues, similar to a man's erection). This lower third, which is one and a half to two inches into the vagina, becomes highly responsive to sexual stimulation and is the only area of contact the vagina has with the penis. In our seminars we often teasingly tell the men that if they have two inches that's all they need to please a woman!

Fourth, just as the length of a man's penis has little or nothing to do with his effectiveness during sexual intercourse, contrary to the many ads on the Internet and radio, neither does the circumference or thickness of his penis have much importance to sexual performance. The woman's PC muscle can tighten so as to completely close the opening of the vagina; therefore, a thin penis can still have firm sensation and pressure on the vagina.

If a woman's PC muscle is sloppy, she may need to keep her legs together to help with the pressure until her exercises have enhanced the quality of that muscle. The muscular nature of the vagina is also such that it can expand to allow the passage of a newborn baby, so there is no need to worry about a penis being too large, either in length or in circumference. If you are a new bride having painful intercourse because of the circumference of your husband's penis, you may need to use dilators to stretch your vaginal muscle.

If you have had concerns about penis size, we trust these facts will reassure you and allay your self-consciousness in the sexual experience. We would encourage the two of you to talk about the facts just presented regarding penis size and sexual functioning. What feelings have each of you had? How have these affected your sexual experience or feelings about yourselves? Affirm each other when you can honestly do that. For example, if you as the woman are hearing for the first time that your husband has had feelings of inadequacy because of his penis, but his penis size has never been a problem for you, reassure him of this fact. Continue to explore these areas of concern with each other.

SHARING YOUR DISCOVERIES WITH EACH OTHER

Many couples have had full sexual experiences with each other for years, but these may have been "quickies" that have occurred at bedtime, in the dark, under the covers, and possibly with nightclothes on. Or even if the sexual experience hasn't been that "covered," there may not be a sense of freedom with each other's bodies. For certain, most couples are not very familiar with each other's genitals. Many have the feeling that they would not want such familiarity—that it would take away the romanticism by removing the mystery. We cast our vote for the removal of that kind of mystery. Mystery or unfamiliarity does not enhance the sexual experience. In fact, most couples who have been functioning within a closed sexual relationship soon lose romantic enjoyment of each other and fall into a humdrum, routine sex life.

We have found that the process of becoming familiar with each other's genitals may be an incredibly difficult task for some couples. Yet when this hurdle is conquered, the communication may open up a whole new dimension of freedom and enjoyment with each other that they never have had, or at least have not had for years.

What we would like to guide you through is an "I'll show you mine, if you'll show me yours" kind of sharing time. You might think of it as being very similar to children playing doctor. It is basically a repeat of your self-discovery experiences except that now you are in it together. This may feel awkward. Talk about any uncomfortable feelings before you begin. What fears, concerns, or embarrassments does each of you feel? What could make the experience more comfortable without taking away from the openness? Often, sharing our hesitant feelings with each other makes moving into the exercise less difficult. Once you both have communicated your feelings, read the assignment together. After gathering the necessary equipment (a light, a hand mirror, lubricant, and tissues), you may proceed as outlined below.

▓ EXERCISE 5

Sharing Your Genital Examination

Step 1: Shower or bathe together; suds each other's bodies and enjoy the pleasure of relaxation and of touching each other in that process, not for purposes of arousal.

Step 2: In a private, well-lit room, with the diagram of external male genitalia, identify all the specific parts of the penis and testes. Wife: Join in the exploration by touching the various parts as your husband identifies each. Particularly note the coronal ridge and the frenulum or seam on the backside of the penis. After exploring the various parts of the genitals, talk about what kind of touch feels good. Husband: Talk about any stimulation of the genitals your wife has given you in the past that you would like more of and any stimulation and handling of the genitals that have been unpleasant for you. Wife: Talk about ways you enjoy pleasuring his genitals and/or feelings of discomfort you have with male genitals.

Step 3: Wife: Assume a comfortable position with legs spread apart, light focused on genitals, the diagram of external female genitals within view, and hand mirror between legs so the genitals can be seen clearly. Look at how the outer labia come together. Then spread the outer labia and identify the inner labia. Find the clitoris and note how the labia form a hood over the clitoris. See if you can feel the shaft of the clitoris, almost like a hidden, small penis up behind the tip of the clitoris. Touch the tip or glans of the clitoris and then the areas around it, and talk with your husband about what kind of touch feels good and where it feels good. Husband: Join in exploration and touching as is comfortable. Identify the urinary meatus, vaginal opening, and any other points of interest. Wife: Talk about what genital stimulation your husband has given you in the past that felt good, what you would like more of, what touching has been negative, and how stimulation of your genitals might be enhanced.

Step 4: Husband: With closely trimmed nails and the wife's invitation, gently insert your finger into the vagina to the second knuckle. Then gently press on the wall of the vagina. If you think of the opening of the vagina as a clock, start at the twelve o'clock position and then slowly move around the wall of the vagina, pressing or stroking at every hour. Try varying degrees of pressure and types of touch. Wife: Feed back what sensations you note. Particularly be aware of any points of pain or pleasure.

Wife: After this exploration is completed, tighten the PC muscle while your husband's finger is in the vagina. Talk about how that feels to each of you. Husband: Now, with your finger in the vagina and the PC muscle tightened, move your finger just below the inner/upper ridge of the PC muscle to explore the G-spot area (refer to Figure 6 on page 73, which shows aroused internal female genitalia). Explore that area with various degrees of pressure and stroking while the wife notes and talks about the sensations she feels in the vagina.

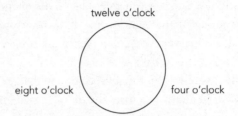

Step 5: Talk about the experience: What felt good, what you each learned, what was uncomfortable about it. You may want to spend some time just holding and affirming each other.

This is a clinical learning experience, not for the purpose of arousal. If arousal should occur, it is okay. Enjoy the feelings, but do not focus on the arousal.

7 HOW OUR BODIES WORK

Now that you have progressed through self-exploration and have shared your discoveries with your spouse, let's take a look at how you function: the impact of the physiology of human sexual organs on sexual functioning.

SEXUAL FROM BIRTH

All sexual parts are present at birth, and involuntary sexual responses begin shortly after birth. A baby boy has his first erection within five to ten minutes of birth, and a baby girl lubricates vaginally within twenty-four hours of birth. These responses are not accompanied by the sexual feelings that occur once puberty begins, but they are involuntary sexual responses that confirm our design as sexual persons.

SEXUAL DEVELOPMENT THROUGH LIFE STAGES

Even though all the sexual parts are present at birth, much of the development and functioning of these parts do not occur until puberty. About three years before any obvious developmental changes take place, the sex glands begin to secrete small amounts of sex hormones. This hormonal activity may be signaled by increased emotional fluctuations in the seven- to ten-year-old child.

Males and females have the same sex hormones, only in different proportions: estrogen, progesterone, and testosterone. For simplicity, we like to think of estrogen as the happy hormone, progesterone as the relaxation hormone, and testosterone as the drive hormone.

From Girl to Woman

In the young girl, the hormones (primarily estrogen and progesterone) gradually increase, promoting development of breast tissue, broadening of hips, hair growth in the genital area, and other changes that are indicators of a maturing body. When the hormones are first secreted they are very irregular. Within several years of the beginning of these changes, the girl's sexual cycle starts with the first menstruation. After the girl has been menstruating for a year or more, the changes in the level of hormonal production establish a monthly rhythmic pattern. The effects of these changes on the woman's emotional state and/or sexual responsiveness vary from one woman to another and in the same woman from time to time.

Sometimes early developmental changes in a little girl may elicit surprise or even panic. It is not unusual for the mother of an eight- or nine-year-old girl, especially if it's her first daughter, to take her to the doctor with concern that the girl might have a growth under one nipple. A nipple popping out early in the process is one more sign that hormones are being secreted. It is comforting to know that this early sign does *not* mean she is going to quickly develop into a physically mature "woman."

Most girls' breast development occurs very slowly. If the girl's nipples have budded at around age eight or nine, she may not have enough breast tissue to warrant wearing a bra until she is twelve or older. Some girls become self-conscious about their nipples showing through their clothes and others seem to be unaware that anything has changed. Either reaction is normal. Ideally, parents can help most by accepting the child's feelings either way; that is, parents should *not* lead the child to become self-conscious and cover up, nor should they put the child down for being self-conscious. Allow her to wear vests, fuller tops, thicker sweaters, or whatever happens to be acceptable attire at the time.

Make sure the child recognizes the parents as her advocate. Confirm the feelings of the child verbally, and actively participate in finding clothes that provide comfort, yet genuinely affirm the attractiveness of her developing body. Sometimes it's also helpful to discuss how other girls at her stage of development are dressing and how she feels about their choices. The child may have become so focused on herself, she thinks she is alone in this new adventure. When she looks around and sees that Heather, Allison, and Rebecca also have little bulges under their T-shirts, she may relax.

It is most important for children this age to sense that they are a part of the norm, that they are not unique. When they begin to develop earlier or later than their friends, they begin to ask the question: "Am I normal?" They need accurate facts and reassurance from their parents. Reading a book together or attending a class on changes of puberty will normalize the child's experience.

The woman's cyclic hormonal process continues for about thirty years from puberty until menopause, except during pregnancy and breast-feeding, when the cycle is interrupted. The bodily changes associated with pregnancy, breast-feeding, and menopause are likely to affect sexual functioning. Menopause causes a lessening of vaginal lubrication and a thinning of the walls of the vagina, which are best handled by using a lubricant during sexual intercourse, exercising the vaginal muscles, and using hormonal replacement therapy as directed by the physician.

From Boy to Man

What about the increasing production of hormones in the young boy? Testosterone in boys increases gradually for about three years before puberty and then takes some big jumps, causing the commonly recognized changes of deepening voice, growing beard, broadening shoulders, and so on. The genitals also become larger and are surrounded by hair growth. Some boys may have a nocturnal emission of seminal fluid, or what is more commonly referred to as a "wet dream." The boy should be made aware that this is a normal happening, but it is not necessary as a sign that he is developing. It occurs for some, not for others. Just as there is nothing wrong if a wet dream does occur, there is also nothing wrong if it doesn't.

The secretion of testosterone in the male reaches its peak in the early twenties, levels off, and then begins to diminish after age forty. Men sense these changes in their bodies and may become concerned that their sexual functioning will be affected. There are several effects of a decreased testosterone level on sexual functioning: There may be a decrease in frequency and urgency of desire for sexual involvement; the man may need direct penile stimulation to get an erection; the erection may not be as firm; ejaculation may take longer; or there may not be a need to ejaculate with each sexual experience. None of these need affect sexual enjoyment—nor are they causes for lack of response unless, of course, anxiety about these changes sets in. Aging slows down all body processes. A sixty-year-old man cannot run around the block as fast as a twenty-year-old. When it comes to sexual functioning for men, fast isn't equivalent to better. In fact, many women are pleased with the man's after-forty changes. These may be the couple's best years together.

SEX DRIVE

Why do some men and some women have much more interest in sex than others? Or why might the same person have higher interest at certain times of life and in different situations?

The miracle of God's creation is clearly evidenced by the intricate interaction of our minds, emotions, hormones, and physical well-being. Not only our unique creation, but also the experiences we have had throughout life and the physical condition of our bodies will affect our sex drive.

Our sex drive is triggered by hormones. Testosterone is the primary hormone responsible for sex drive in both men and women. It gives us the energy to get things done in life and is also the base for sexual desire, arousal, and release.

When men and women come to our offices reporting problems with desire, arousal, and release, most often we will ask that their testosterone levels be evaluated. It is important to know that both the total and the free (or bioavailable) testosterone levels need to be assessed. The bound level may be high enough to make up for a low free testosterone. The free is necessary for sexual functioning. When the free is low, we partner with the client's physician and recommend that women use a testosterone cream applied to the vulval area and that men either use a testosterone patch applied to the scrotum or a gel applied to their chest and upper arms.

We lead groups for men who struggle with sexual issues and for women with sexual difficulties unique to them. In leading groups for women with past sexual abuse or incest, we have found these women typically have low free testosterone levels. It is our belief that mind and body work in sync. When violated as a child, the woman shuts down on her sexuality, which affects her hormones. We are complex beings.

The endocrine glands produce hormones (including sex hormones) that stimulate the nerves to carry messages to the brain. The brain then sends messages back via the nervous system to our muscular and vascular (blood vessel) systems. This process produces sexual arousal and response. In turn, this response stimulates the glands to produce more hormones, which again send messages to the brain via the nerves, and thus the cycle tends to be self-perpetuating. Because of the building nature of our body's interaction, the more sexual arousal and satisfaction, the more drive. The reverse is also true: When one of the bodily systems interferes with or inhibits this naturally building cycle, arousal and/or response may be difficult.

SEXUAL AROUSAL

The autonomic or involuntary nervous system has two branches that affect sexual arousal: the sympathetic nervous system (SNS) and the parasympathetic nervous system (PNS). These function without our willing them or even being conscious of them. They affect our bodies' responses in exactly opposite ways. Thus, together they can either increase or decrease the activity of our bodily organs. The PNS has an upbuilding effect on the body. It is in action when we are relaxed and more passive. The SNS is our "fight or flight," that is, our energy system. It goes into action when we are anxious or intensely aroused emotionally and has more to do with release than arousal.

Sexual excitement or arousal is controlled by the PNS. When we are aroused, blood and fluid rush to the genitals, producing the erection in the male and vaginal lubrication and swelling in the female. This is an involuntary response. Men have erections and women experience vaginal lubrication every eighty to ninety minutes during sleep. Likewise, when we allow ourselves to soak in sexual pleasure through what we touch or hear or see, our PNS will automatically cause us to become sexually aroused. This involuntary arousal will cause a man's penis to become erect and a woman's vagina to swell and lubricate.

Neither of these responses will occur as easily if a man or woman is *trying* to get aroused or watching themselves to see if arousal is occurring. When we are trying, our brain or head is in control and, again, interferes with the involuntary control of the PNS. We have found it helpful for some men and women with arousal problems to think of "getting with" their parasympathetic or getting out of their heads and into their penises or vaginas—going with the sensation of the moment. Another way of saying this is that we have to let our bodies respond without letting our brains get in the way.

Just as arousal is controlled by the PNS, the muscular contractions of the orgasmic response for both the man and the woman are primarily an SNS function. Our bodies shift from PNS dominance to SNS control just as we are approaching orgasm. The SNS is the dominant involuntary nervous system when we are active rather than passive. Therefore, the orgasmic response can be actively enhanced or inhibited by behavior. Our complicated brain centers trigger the sympathetic nerve system to produce the orgasmic reflex. What we do with our bodies, not our thoughts, can enhance this response. Thus, men can learn ejaculatory control by becoming more passive and women can learn to actively go after an orgasm, not by tensing up and trying to make it happen (brain action) but rather by engaging in behaviors (SNS action) that will trigger this normal bodily reflex.

Several days after leading a seminar in a church, we received a call from Laura, who had been in attendance. She was calling to thank us for helping her respond sexually. When we inquired what had been so helpful, she reported that in her first four years of marriage she had not been able to allow herself to let go and have an orgasm. After hearing us talk about the nervous system, she had gone into her next sexual experience telling herself to let her body respond—or, as she put it, "to get with her sympathetic." In this experience when her arousal became intense, she got active and triggered her first orgasmic response. We don't tell this story to suggest it as the easy answer for women who have orgasmic difficulties, but rather to illustrate the importance of letting our bodies fulfill their God-given potential.

The orgasmic response can be actively pursued by the woman who has difficulty letting go, or can be delayed by the man who ejaculates prematurely. This is true because, even though these are reflex responses, they are triggered by messages that come through the sympathetic nervous system, the intense energy branch of our involuntary nervous system.

An analogy might help us understand this process. When the doctor is performing a physical examination, he taps the patient's knee to check his/her reflexes. The tap on the knee is a voluntary action that produces the reflex of the lower leg jerking. In the same way, when we engage in certain sexual behaviors (breathing, moving, stimulating the clitoris), and we don't stop the natural bodily responses, the muscular contractions of the orgasm will occur as a reflex response. One can stop his leg from jerking even if the knee is tapped. Even so, we can stop an orgasm from occurring when the necessary stimulation has taken place, but we cannot cause or will a leg jerk or an orgasm.

8 OUR BODIES' SEXUAL RESPONSE

To help us understand the physical aspects of sexual response, Masters and Johnson were the first to define the sexual response pattern in four specific phases. These are the excitement, plateau, orgasm, and resolution phases. Although sexual experiences usually begin with sexual desire that precedes the excitement phase, desire is mainly an emotional response and hence will be dealt with in Chapter 9. The four phases of the sexual response cycle we will be discussing here are not distinct in terms of how we experience them. There is no "click" as we move from one phase to the next (see graph on next page). Physiologically, the intricate details of men's and women's sexual responses confirm God's masterful creative work.

1. The excitement phase has to do with our initial arousal. It is most clearly evidenced by an erection in the man and by vaginal lubrication in the woman.
2. The plateau phase, which is ideally the longest phase of the lovemaking process, is the period of love play during which arousal intensifies in preparation for the sexual release.
3. The orgasmic phase, the briefest, most intense, and most internal phase, is the release.

4. Finally, there is the resolution phase, during which the body returns to its unaroused state.

The specific physical changes that occur are basically the same from one woman to another and from one man to another. However, every person differs from one experience to the next, and there are certainly differences from one person to another. These differences primarily occur in timing, intensity, and feeling.

The responses that occur—the changes in the body—may be as a result of sexual intercourse, manual or oral stimulation, self-stimulation, caressing, deep kissing, fantasies, dreams, or visual input. Sexual intercourse is not necessary for a full sexual response, nor does intercourse ensure a full sexual release.

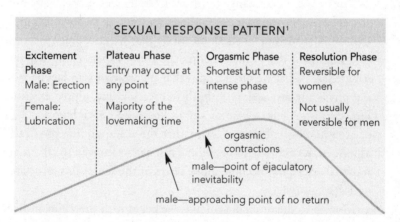

SEXUAL RESPONSE PATTERN[1]

Excitement Phase	Plateau Phase	Orgasmic Phase	Resolution Phase
Male: Erection	Entry may occur at any point	Shortest but most intense phase	Reversible for women
Female: Lubrication	Majority of the lovemaking time		Not usually reversible for men

orgasmic contractions

male—point of ejaculatory inevitability

male—approaching point of no return

EXCITEMENT

The Female Response

Let's begin by looking at what happens to the woman during the excitement phase. Excitement can result from either physical or emotional stimulation. When this stimulation is received and enjoyed, sexual arousal produces external and internal changes. First, in the external genitalia, we note that the clitoris is probably the most important organ during the excitement phase. As you will recall, the clitoris is a unique organ in the human anatomy in that its only purpose is the receiving and transmitting of sexual stimuli. With arousal, the clitoris becomes engorged or enlarged, just as the penis becomes erect. The clitoris increases two to three times in length and size. Hunger for clitoral stimulation may result. Most women report that the caressing of the general area around the clitoris is more desirable than having the head, or glans, of the clitoris directly manipulated.

Other changes that occur in the external genitalia during the excitement phase are in the lips, both the inner and the outer. The outer lips, or the *labia majora,* spread out flat as if opening up in preparation for receiving the penis. The inner lips, or *labia minora,* increase in size, extend outward, and become slightly engorged, forming a funnel shape. (To identify clitoris, inner lips, and outer lips refer to Figure 1 on page 46.)

The breasts, too, change during the excitement phase. They usually enlarge, becoming more rounded and full, with obvious nipple erection. This is one of the indications that we encourage a couple to watch for if the woman reports she is not experiencing any sexual arousal. What we often find is that the woman is in fact becoming physically aroused, with both lubrication and nipple erection. However, she is not aware of any feelings and hence reports a lack of arousal. As she becomes aware that she *is* responding physically, at least in the excitement phase, she can be encouraged to affirm her responsiveness and become more aware of the sensations associated with her arousal.

Moving to the internal genitalia, we begin with the vagina, which responds by lubricating within ten to twenty seconds after stimulation is received. Although lubrication has been thought of as the sign of readiness for entry, entry is not likely to be desired or recommended until much later. The lubrication that occurs can be understood by thinking of it as perspiration—little beads of lubrication that form along the walls of the vagina (see Figure 6 on the next page). Their simple function is to reduce friction and enhance the pleasure of the penis in the vagina.

The cervix, which is situated at the back of the vagina, is the opening to the uterus. As the uterus elevates with increased arousal, it begins to pull away from the vagina so as not to be in the way of the penis during thrusting (see Figure 6). When the woman happens to have a tipped or retroverted uterus, this pulling up and away of the cervix is less likely to occur because the uterus cannot elevate as it is supposed to. Thus, the woman with a tipped uterus may experience pain upon deep thrusting. A change in position during intercourse can lessen the likelihood of the penis striking the cervix. Exercises and help from the physician may be necessary to correct a tipped uterus.

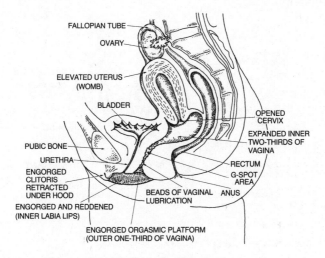

Figure 6: Aroused Internal Female Genitalia (Side View)

The Male Response

The penis, like the clitoris, is the receiver and transmitter of sexual feelings. The main male response during the excitement stage is penile erection (see Figure 7 on page 74). To define it simply, the unstimulated or flaccid penis becomes erect as the man receives stimulation, either physically or emotionally. The erection occurs as a result of the blood that flows into the penis and is held there in the veins by valves that keep it from flowing back out as long as there is arousal. Erections can be maintained for extended periods of time without ejaculation, if the man is not anxious, and when the stimulation is varied, both in terms of its type and its intensity. Note that the intensity of the erection will tend to fluctuate over a period of time and may be lost and regained during extended love play. The only factor in the way of regaining an erection would be anxiety about the loss of the erection, or some external event that may have interrupted the sexual experience. Erections are emotionally tenuous. An erection can be stopped very easily when some nonsexual event occurs such as the telephone ringing, a knock on the door, a change in the lighting, or any other interruption. Even a sharp critical comment can make the erection diminish.

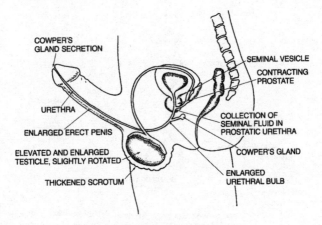

Figure 7: Aroused Internal Male Genitalia (Side View)

The other change that occurs for the man during sexual excitement is the thickening of the skin around the testicles. This is believed to occur in order to increase slightly the temperature of the seminal fluid as it is prepared for expulsion and fertilization of the egg.

About 60 percent of men also experience nipple erection. However, since a man's breasts are less prominent, the nipple erection is usually not as noticeable in the man as it is in the woman.

Sex Flush

One other bodily change that may take place in both men and women during the excitement phase is called a sex flush. It is a blushing or reddening that occurs over the upper third of the body—the chest, neck, face, and forehead. It is more likely to occur in a room where the temperature is slightly elevated and in situations of extreme anticipation. This is observable in some men and women and not in others. It is not fully understood why the flush occurs for some people; it may be the result of complexion differences. We would hasten to add that it is not a matter of concern whether one does or does not experience the sexual flush; this may simply be an additional sign for some that sexual arousal is taking place.

PLATEAU

The Male Response

In the male, during the plateau phase the coronal gland or head of the penis deepens in color, due to greater engorgement, and continues to enlarge. During this time of extended love play, a small amount of pre-ejaculatory fluid seeps from the penis. (This fluid contains live sperm that can impregnate the woman. Because of this, withdrawing the penis from the vagina before ejaculation is *not* a safe method of birth control.) The skin of the scrotum continues to thicken, and the right testicle pulls in closer to the body and rotates about a quarter of a turn during the midpoint of the plateau phase. There is also a significant increase in the size of the testicles (see Figure 7).

Internally, the seminal fluid begins to collect in the area around the prostate gland. As the man moves through the plateau phase toward the point of orgasm, he begins to feel that he is reaching ejaculatory inevitability, or the point of no return (see Sexual Response Pattern graph on page 71).

The Female Response

During the plateau phase, the woman continues to enjoy stimulation. Some prefer a brief time of pleasuring while others prefer a longer period of love play. This is one of those needs or desires that seem to vary from one person to another, and in the same person from one time to another. It is important to recognize that many women experience their building sexual arousal in a way that might best be described as waves. There is a peak and then an ebb or diminishing of the intensity of feelings—and then a new wave of sexual arousal. If a woman lets herself ride the waves, the peaks will tend to intensify. However, if this wavelike diminishing of sexual feelings is thought to be the end of her arousal, the woman may become anxious and stop her response from occurring in its natural wavelike pattern. The anxiety fulfills her fear. It, then, *does* end her arousal.

The signs of breast engorgement and the sexual flush, which were noted in the excitement phase, continue. Most of the changes take place in the internal genitalia. There are a few changes that should be noted externally first. The inner lips become bright red and increase in size. This occurs about one minute before an orgasm. The clitoris continues to be enlarged, but draws up or retracts under the hood and, as the arousal continues, becomes more difficult to locate. It is often extremely sensitive to being touched directly.

Internally, a number of significant changes take place. The uterus becomes fully elevated or pulled into position ready for the orgasm, with the cervix being pulled away from the thrusting penis (see Figure 6, page 73). The most important changes take place in the vagina. Blood rushes to the outer third of the vagina, causing it to become densely engorged and contract, forming what is called the orgasmic platform.

It is as if God designed the vagina for both pleasure and procreation. In terms of the reproductive purpose, the upper, inner two-thirds of the vagina balloons out and forms a pool to keep the seminal fluid containing the sperm inside the vagina. As the woman responds, the uterus, which lifted up and away earlier, now falls into the seminal pool, and the cervix of the uterus opens so the sperm can travel up through the cervix into the uterus for fertilization. For the pleasure purpose of intercourse, the tightening of the external third of the vagina functions as an extra stimulation to the penis and the vagina. This outer portion of the vagina thickens, contracts, and produces a grasping effect, holding the penis firmly in the vagina. It is important to note again that since this orgasmic platform includes only the first third of the vagina, or about an inch and a half to two inches, the preoccupation with penis size is of little real consequence. The most important part of the vagina for penis contact is this orgasmic platform area, which at the most is two inches in length and can tighten or expand to any width.

ORGASM

This is the phase that elicits the most attention. It is the most intense phase of the sexual experience, yet it lasts the shortest period of time and is experienced mainly internally and individually. The orgasm does not focus on the relationship. This is often the phase talked and written about as the ultimate and central part of the whole sexual experience. Yet we have talked with many couples who, although they have little difficulty with orgasm, are very unsatisfied with their overall sexual experience. So as we begin the discussion of the orgasmic phase we want to look at it in proper perspective.

We see the orgasm as an essential ingredient when there is intense sexual arousal. It is important, but not something that is to be focused on to the exclusion of all the other phases. Some women, particularly more passive or low-key women, find pleasuring and affirming more necessary than release. Men over age forty may end a sexual experience feeling fulfilled without an orgasm. The orgasm is a reflex response. An orgasm is not a response that we can will, but if we allow the right kind of stimulation, we can expect that the reflex of the orgasm will follow (see Chapter 17).

The Female Response

As a woman moves into the orgasmic stage, various changes happen within the body. The clitoris and inner and outer lips remain basically the same as they were at the end of the plateau phase. The genitally centered feelings of the orgasm (see Chapter 17) are due to the strong vaginal contractions in the orgasmic platform. Masters and Johnson have measured three to five contractions for a mild orgasm and eight to twelve contractions for an intense orgasm. These contractions occur at intervals of eight-tenths of a second. This is true for all women and is the same as the spacing of the contractions in the man. As the outer third of the vagina is contracting, the inner two-thirds is expanding even farther to form a place for the seminal fluid.

Women have two centers of orgasmic response. The orgasm is experienced not only in the vagina but also in the uterus. The uterus undergoes contractions similar to the first stages of labor. Some women have reported that they experience a dull pain in their lower abdomen. This may be due to the uterine contractions that occur. Once a woman's fears have been allayed through the explanation that this is a normal response, she learns to enjoy the intensity of those contractions rather than to experience them as painful.

We knew a highly intense woman who was very responsive in the initial phases of the sexual experience, but then, as she moved into the orgasmic response, she would draw back from further stimulation to avoid the lower abdominal discomfort. This had been true of the first eight years of her married life and was particularly noticeable when she was extremely aroused. As she learned to relax and let herself enjoy the abdominal feelings, her experience shifted from sensing the contractions as pain to experiencing them as intense pleasure. This confirms the close relationship of pain and pleasure in our bodies. Just as a very intense pleasurable sensation can easily shift to being painful (refer to graph on page 47), a painful sexual feeling may change to intense pleasure.

While the centers of the orgasmic response are in the vagina and the uterus, the sensations that grow out of this center cover the whole body. It is analogous to dropping a rock into a pool of water. The most intense reaction is at the center where the rock is dropped, but the reaction continues to move out in wider and wider circles.

These total-body responses occur in both men and women. Many of these begin during the plateau phase and reach their peak with orgasm. Let us enumerate them. The heart rate increases up to 180 beats per minute. The blood pressure often rises measurably. The breathing intensifies, becoming deeper, faster, and noisier (hyperventilation). There may be a great deal of involuntary muscular movement—thrusting of the pelvis and spasticlike contractions of the face, arms, legs, back, or lower abdomen. There is a specific response that occurs in the foot called a carpopedal spasm, which is a straightening out of the foot in a clawlike contraction, where the toes curl downward and away from the body (hyperextension). These are all involuntary responses that are orgasmic triggers.

Many times the contractions of the face, particularly the mouth, are of great concern to women. Some women like to make love with the lights out because they do not want to be seen making these "unladylike" responses. In the face, the contracting muscles sometimes give the appearance of a frown, scowl, or grimace. The mouth may open involuntarily with a gasping kind of reaction that often includes some involuntary sounds or words. Once a woman can accept the fact that all these reactions and noises are a natural part of the sexual response, it may become easier for her to let herself be responsive with her husband. Many women are surprised to find that rather than turning off their partners, these bodily responses will usually heighten a man's arousal.

Vaginal vs. Clitoral Orgasm. Much has been written and many misconceptions have been passed on about various kinds of female orgasm. It is important to understand the background of these myths. When Freud was developing his psychoanalytic theory, in some of his writings he defined the woman who had achieved orgasm only through external or manual stimulation as an "immature woman"—in fact, a little girl. He said that as a woman matured into full womanhood she would obviously have her orgasm in the "normal" adult manner: that is, as a result of vaginal penetration through intercourse. These concepts have been disseminated throughout the Western world and used to put pressure on women to experience orgasm during sexual intercourse. The research of Masters and Johnson has proved Freud's theories to be physiologically inaccurate, and thus has diminished the potency of Freud's argument from a psychological perspective.

Masters and Johnson found that there is only one kind of orgasm a woman can experience. All orgasms, regardless of the source of stimulation, are exactly the same in terms of their physical components. When a woman has an orgasm, whether it is the result of her thoughts and fantasies, self-stimulation, breast stimulation, manual stimulation by her partner, or intercourse, exactly the same things happen to her body as were just described. There is the formation of the orgasmic platform, the contractions in the outer third of the vagina, the contractions of the uterus. All the bodily responses occur regardless of the source of stimulation.

Since Masters and Johnson's research, women have reported a difference in sensation between an orgasm from internal, vaginal stimulation and one from external stimulation. The reports on G-spot-stimulated orgasms indicate that those are different from orgasms resulting from external stimulation.

The G-spot, an area named after Dr. Ernst Grafenburg, was written about in medical literature in the early 1940s but then left unnoticed for forty years. This area is located on the upper inside of the vagina just beyond the upper, inner edge of the PC muscle. When a woman is aroused and the G-spot area is stimulated by her husband's penis or finger, she may respond with a very intense orgasm that tends to feel like a bearing down sensation. For some women, this intense response is accompanied by a release of fluid called a flooding response or female ejaculation.[2]

Some women who have experienced orgasm from both external and internal stimulation report that they find these two to be different on an emotional level. For them the orgasm during intercourse is more fulfilling than the orgasm brought about by external stimulation. This is a matter of personal preference for a woman. There is nothing wrong with striving for an orgasm during intercourse, unless that becomes an inhibiting effort. There is also nothing wrong with being satisfied having an orgasm as a result of external stimulation. In fact, some women report a more intense response when the penis is not in the vagina.

Many times the pressure on a woman to experience orgasm during intercourse is a serious deterrent to full satisfaction. This pressure may come from a husband who feels he is less of a man because he can't get her to have an orgasm during intercourse. It is as though his worth is dependent on achieving this goal. This mentality is in contrast to our suggestion that each person be responsible to pursue his or her own sexual desires as long as it is not at the expense of the other.

The Male Response

We have said that during the excitement and plateau phases the man's penis becomes erect, the skin of the scrotum thickens, the right testicle rises and rotates toward the body, and the seminal fluid begins to gather. The male orgasmic phase can be described as having two stages:

Stage 1: As a man nears the end of the plateau phase and moves into the orgasmic phase, he begins to notice that some changes are taking place. He senses that he is getting ready to ejaculate. Most men can identify when this occurs, though they usually do not know what is happening to their bodies. They are approaching the point of no return.

A number of changes take place during this first stage of the orgasmic response. Contractions in the prostate gland occur at intervals of eight-tenths of a second. The outlet (sphincter) from the bladder closes off so none of the seminal fluid will be pushed back into the bladder nor will any urine escape during ejaculation. Most men are aware that immediately before or after an ejaculation it is almost impossible to urinate. This is because the opening from the bladder has been closed in preparation for the ejaculation. Another change now takes place. The left testicle pulls up toward the body and rotates about one quarter of a turn (the right testicle elevated during the plateau phase; see Figure 7, page 74). All these changes take place in a few seconds. They are warnings to the man that he is about to ejaculate. In addition to these warnings, the seminal fluid gathers near the base of the penis in readiness for expulsion during the contractions that occur in the second stage of the orgasmic phase.

Stage 2: When a man reaches the point of no return, or ejaculatory inevitability, the ejaculation *will* take place. He can try to stop, the phone can ring, or a bucket of water can be dumped on his head, but he *will* ejaculate! The ejaculation consists of contractions along the seminal duct system and the penis, which force the seminal fluid out the end of the penis. In younger men the force is more intense, causing greater spurts. The force of the ejaculation decreases with age. The contractions of the penis and seminal duct system are eight-tenths of a second apart. Men usually experience five or six such contractions, with the second and third usually the most intense. The expelled seminal fluid contains between 150 and 350 million living sperm, which will stay active within the vagina up to ten hours after expulsion.

Differences Between Male and Female Response

With every discussion of male/female differences, there will be exceptions. You may be one of those. As you read what is typical for women or what is typical for men, you may be saying, "But that isn't true for us." If the findings we report here don't fit the two of you, use this information to define your uniqueness and difference as a husband and wife. When we understand and embrace our differences as men and women, we minimize conflict and false expectations and maximize the enjoyment of our orgasmic response.

Differences between men and women in their orgasmic response:

- For women, the orgasmic response is a total-body experience with a flood of warmth throughout the body, whereas men tend to have primarily intense genitally focused sensations during release.
- Women vary in their orgasmic expression. They vary from one woman to another and from one time to another. Men seem to be more predictable and consistent in their expression of an orgasm.
- Women have the potential to respond indefinitely—with multiple and sequential orgasms. Not all women desire or feel the need for more than one response, but some do. In contrast men, except for about 1 percent, need a refractory period of at least twenty minutes. Usually it is several hours before they

can regain arousal, erection, and release. Although, the authors of *The G Spot* say men can learn to have multiple orgasms, we would be hesitant to encourage that as a goal lest it become a demand.[3]

- A woman's orgasm can be interrupted at any point; once the man starts his ejaculatory response, he will ejaculate! Nothing can stop his ejaculation. Men can control their actions and they also can learn to control their response *before* they reach that point of ejaculation.

- The longer the time between sexual experiences with release, the wider the gap between men and women in their eagerness and responsiveness. If a sexual experience is the first in a long time, a woman will be less aware of her need for sex and tend to be slower in her arousal and have more difficulty letting go. A man's felt need for sex intensifies and he will tend to move quickly to arousal and release. Because of this tendency for men and women to go in opposite directions, we believe we were created to have sexual release regularly. The biblical teaching in 1 Corinthians 7: 3–5 affirms the importance of coming together on a regular basis.

- Women experience more difficulty with and pressure to have an orgasm. Men experience little difficulty with having an orgasm, but more with controlling the timing of their orgasms. Their pressure is to get and keep an erection and delay ejaculation.

RESOLUTION

The Female Response

For the woman the resolution phase varies significantly, depending on whether or not she has had release. If she has had an orgasmic release—whether this has come about as a result of manual stimulation or intercourse—the body goes into a rather quick period of tension loss. Everything moves in the reverse of what has occurred throughout the excitement, plateau, and orgasmic phases. The whole genital area is relieved of tension and congestion. That is, the extra blood flows out of the area. The woman may feel a tingling sensation as this happens. The vagina, cervix, and uterus move back into their prestimulated stage, and the woman's whole body is relaxed.

If the woman has not had an orgasmic release, the resolution phase takes much longer. Some doctors have reported that the engorgement can last well beyond several hours. Many women will experience a significant amount of tension during this extended resolution period. A woman may cry, thus providing the physical and emotional release denied her by the lack of orgasm. Her crying may cause her to turn away from her husband in shame. This turning away is just the opposite of what both she and her husband need: warmth, affirmation, and reassurance. The human body is designed for sexual release; if arousal takes place without release, it is likely to cause discomfort. That discomfort can best be handled through mutual expression of care and affirmation.

If you are a woman who consistently experiences arousal without release, it is crucial that you share this with your husband. Let him know what your body feels like so the two of you can move closer together. There can be some relief just in being reached out to. He needs to know what you need.

What about multiple orgasms? A woman's body is designed so that she can have another orgasm at any point of the resolution phase. It can be five seconds, five minutes, or fifty minutes after the previous orgasm. There is no waiting or rest period necessary before she is physically capable of experiencing another orgasm if the stimulation is continued or renewed. Her body does not need to return to its prestimulated state before it can be responsive again. This is not to say that having more than one orgasm is better, or that sexually "together" women will desire this. The point is that, physically, if she desires it and can allow it, the woman's orgasm can be repeated indefinitely.

The Male Response

After orgasmic release, the man returns rather quickly to the prestimulated state. His erection may not decrease completely, but the penis is usually somewhat flaccid and the testicles lower. There is a loss in the tension buildup and in the intensity of feelings. Some men report that the glans or head of the penis becomes very sensitive to touch after an ejaculation and because of this, they want to quickly disengage from their partner. The man may not have told his wife this because he feels uncomfortable or embarrassed about it. It is important to know that a significant number of men feel this postejaculation pain. If you experience such discomfort, it is crucial to share this with your partner so she can be sympathetic and understanding rather than taking your withdrawal as rejection.

It is rare for a man not to experience orgasm. However, there are some men (especially older men) who do not need an orgasm and do not feel frustrated without one.

GRAPHING THE SEXUAL RESPONSE

Throughout this chapter, we have described what happens to men and to women in each of the four phases of the sexual response cycle. The graphs for men and women on the following pages demonstrate these phases.

The curved graph on the top of the next page that summarizes the sexual response pattern of men's bodies to positive stimulation represents a composite of responses rather than any individual man's response.

The male sexual response pattern might look more like the chart at the bottom of the next page.

There is not much variation among men in the intensity of the response they experience. There is considerable variation, however, in the amount of time each phase might take. Thus the graph might be spread out more or it might be compacted into a briefer experience, but the height of the intensity in each phase would tend not to vary much.

Just as the curved graph for men is a composite of all men, so is the women's graph on page 87. However, women vary infinitely in both the amount of time each phase might take and in the intensity of the response.

Using four simplified patterns, we have represented the possible ways a woman might respond. These closely represent most of the

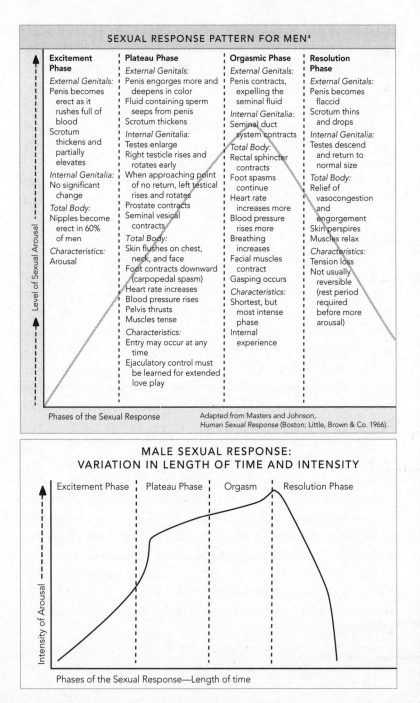

SEXUAL RESPONSE PATTERN FOR MEN[4]

Excitement Phase	Plateau Phase	Orgasmic Phase	Resolution Phase
External Genitals: Penis becomes erect as it rushes full of blood Scrotum thickens and partially elevates	*External Genitals:* Penis engorges more and deepens in color Fluid containing sperm seeps from penis Scrotum thickens	*External Genitals:* Penis contracts, expelling the seminal fluid	*External Genitals:* Penis becomes flaccid Scrotum thins and drops
Internal Genitalia: No significant change	*Internal Genitalia:* Testes enlarge Right testicle rises and rotates early When approaching point of no return, left testical rises and rotates Prostate contracts Seminal vesical contracts	*Internal Genitalia:* Seminal duct system contracts	*Internal Genitalia:* Testes descend and return to normal size
Total Body: Nipples become erect in 60% of men	*Total Body:* Skin flushes on chest, neck, and face Foot contracts downward (carpopedal spasm) Heart rate increases Blood pressure rises Pelvis thrusts Muscles tense	*Total Body:* Rectal sphincter contracts Foot spasms continue Heart rate increases more Blood pressure rises more Breathing increases Facial muscles contract Gasping occurs	*Total Body:* Relief of vasocongestion and engorgement Skin perspires Muscles relax
Characteristics: Arousal	*Characteristics:* Entry may occur at any time Ejaculatory control must be learned for extended love play	*Characteristics:* Shortest, but most intense phase Internal experience	*Characteristics:* Tension loss Not usually reversible (rest period required before more arousal)

Level of Sexual Arousal

Phases of the Sexual Response

Adapted from Masters and Johnson, *Human Sexual Response* (Boston; Little, Brown & Co. 1966).

MALE SEXUAL RESPONSE: VARIATION IN LENGTH OF TIME AND INTENSITY

Excitement Phase | Plateau Phase | Orgasm | Resolution Phase

Intensity of Arousal

Phases of the Sexual Response—Length of time

SEXUAL RESPONSE PATTERN FOR WOMEN

Excitement Phase	Plateau Phase	Orgasmic Phase	Resolution Phase
External Genitals: Clitoris lengthens Outer lips spread flat *Internal Genitalia:* Vagina lubricates (within 10–20 sec.) Uterus elevates *Total Body:* Nipples become erect Breasts enlarge *Characteristics:* Arousal	*External Genitals:* Clitoris retracts under hood Inner lips turn bright red and enlarge (about 1 min. before orgasmic response) *Internal Genitalia:* Inner 2/3 of vagina expands Outer 1/3 of vagina thickens and contracts, forming orgasmic platform *Total Body:* Skin flushes over abdomen, chest, etc. Foot contracts downward (carpopedal spasm) Heart rate increases Blood pressure rises Pelvis thrusts Muscles tense *Characteristics:* Entry may occur at any time Majority of love play	*External Genitals:* No noticeable change *Internal Genitalia:* Outer 1/3 of vagina contracts 3 to 12 times *Total Body:* Rectal sphincter contracts Foot spasms continue Heart rate increases more Blood pressure rises more Breathing increases Facial muscles contract Gasping occurs *Characteristics:* Shortest, but most intense phase Internal experience	*External Genitals:* Clitoris returns to normal size Inner and outer lips return to normal size and position *Internal Genitalia:* Cervix opens slightly and drops into seminal pool Uterus drops back toward front of pelvis Vagina collapses and thins *Total Body:* Relief of vasocongestion and engorgement Skin perspires Muscles relax Breasts and nipples return to prestimulated appearance *Characteristics:* Tension loss Reversible

Level of Sexual Arousal

Phases of the Sexual Response

responses graphed by women who have attended our seminars. To see these patterns, refer to the graphs on the following two pages.

The first graph pictures the woman who is quickly aroused. She experiences her arousal building in peaks followed by short dips, and with effective stimulation moves rapidly to an intense orgasmic release. As her buildup is rapid and her release intense, so she also returns to her prestimulated state (resolution) rather quickly. The woman with this intense response pattern may feel satisfied with one release, as the graph depicts. A few women may have the drive to pursue more love play with repeated arousal and response.

The second graph is a description of the woman who enjoys extended love play before she goes after the intense arousal that

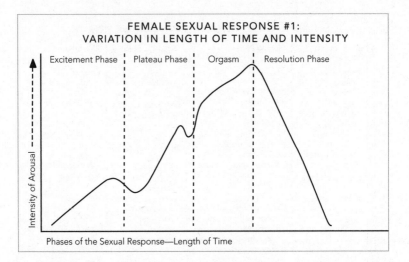

FEMALE SEXUAL RESPONSE #1:
VARIATION IN LENGTH OF TIME AND INTENSITY

would trigger an orgasm. Her arousal may intensify upward rather steadily, as the graph demonstrates. One variation may follow the same general pattern, but the woman may experience her upward intensity in waves that have flowing dips, as the dotted-line graph would indicate. As the sex drive and tension build, whether steadily or in waves, this woman experiences an orgasmic release with very little tension loss, and she is quickly stimulated to the point of another orgasm. This may happen twice, as the graph shows, or as

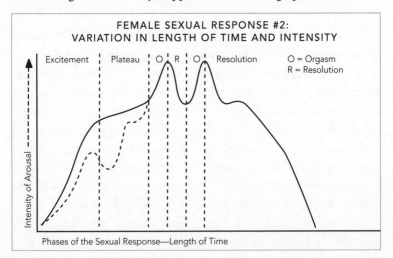

FEMALE SEXUAL RESPONSE #2:
VARIATION IN LENGTH OF TIME AND INTENSITY

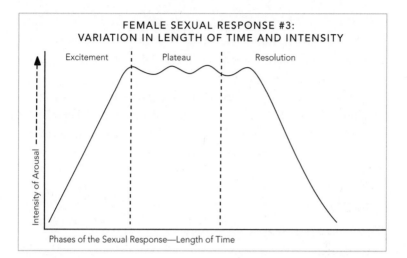

FEMALE SEXUAL RESPONSE #3:
VARIATION IN LENGTH OF TIME AND INTENSITY

many times as she desires and her spouse is willing. The orgasms may be pursued in rapid sequence or there may be more letdown and relaxation between orgasms. When she feels satisfied, she allows her body to relax and return to its prestimulated state.

The third graph represents a discouraging dilemma for many women. For them, arousal comes naturally and easily. They hit the peak of the plateau phase, feel intensely aroused, experience waves of arousal, but stay pretty much at the same level for an extended

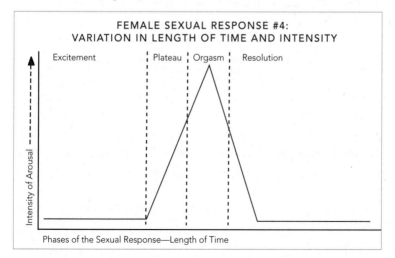

FEMALE SEXUAL RESPONSE #4:
VARIATION IN LENGTH OF TIME AND INTENSITY

period of time. It is as if they cannot quite make it over the hill. Finally, they give up and let down. Because there has been no orgasmic release, resolution takes several hours or more. They often are left feeling unfulfilled and wanting.

The fourth graph pictures what some women experience who were raised in alcoholic or emotionally chaotic homes. These sexually ambivalent women have serious difficulty letting themselves feel aroused—but once they do get aroused, they respond very intensely. As soon as the orgasm ends, the resistance returns.

▨ EXERCISE 6

Graphing Your Sexual Response

Using the graphs on pages 86 through 89, which summarize the primary male and female bodily responses during the four phases of the sexual experience, and the variations just described, we would encourage you to graph your own sexual response pattern. You may choose the graph closest to your experience and then vary the graph line according to your individual situation. After drawing the graph, fill in your bodily responses in as much detail as is available to you.

If you are a person with a sexual problem such as lack of arousal, difficulties with erections, or others, identify at what point your response or arousal stops. What are you aware of happening at that point? What are your thoughts or feelings? What is going on between you and your spouse? What do you sense needs to be different to allow your response to accelerate rather than stop?

We suggest that you and your spouse complete your graphs individually. Then read each other's and have the other person explain his or hers to you. When you are the listener, work hard at sensing what your spouse experiences rather than defending yourself or describing what you experience. When you are the one relating what you feel, concentrate diligently on talking about your feelings, not on blaming your spouse. This sharing experience is an important step to understanding each other in a way that can bring enhancement to your sexual experience.

THE

TOTAL

EXPERIENCE

9 GETTING INTERESTED

You are pushing your grocery cart down the pet food aisle when you become aware that the song playing on the music system is making you feel bouncy.

You lie down in the warm sand at the beach, and the warmth seems to radiate up through your body. You feel good all over.

As you pay for lunch you see the picture of your spouse in your wallet. You get that yummy feeling inside that makes you want to be with him or her. Desire is being stirred.

How does the desire for sexual involvement get started for you? There can be many sources of sexual arousal in your world. You may or may not be aware of responding to these. You might not even notice what stimulates or decreases your sexual interest. Following are some suggestions of things you can do that will have a positive, direct effect on your sexuality.

ATTEND TO EXTERNAL AND INTERNAL STIMULI

Many kinds of outside stimuli serve to get you in touch with your body. For some people such stimulation includes listening to certain kinds of music, reading a sexual or intimate book, watching a romantic movie or television show, being in a setting that feels romantic, or even seeing someone who may be a friend or a stranger.

Sensuous input may also come from within. Perhaps no particular event or setting stimulates your sexual desire; instead, your sexual awareness may grow out of a relaxing, body-oriented time. You might be exercising, bathing or showering, relaxing in the sun, or oiling your body. When "getting interested" is not a problem, sexual desire may be triggered spontaneously by natural internal sex drives.

ALLOW COUPLE TIME

Spending time with your spouse is likely to get you interested sexually. This is particularly true if your sexual experiences are fulfilling and free of anxiety. We find that working together or playing together tends to draw us in that direction. This is one of the advantages of writing a book together. As we become one emotionally and mentally, the physical response is automatic. This is particularly true if the times together are not burdened with stress or high expectations.

We recommend that all couples plan regular times to be together. These times must be free of demands such as expectations for sexual intercourse, obligations regarding children, pressures from work, and distractions by other external involvements. Come together without restrictions or preconceived ideas, so you can create something special and unique for your time together.

CONSERVE ENERGY

Having sexual energy available to you is necessary for sexual desire. Sexual desire is different from sexual arousal. Arousal is your body's response to stimulation. The four physical phases of sexual response as described in Chapter 8 have to do with sexual arousal—release. This is a process of physical change that occurs in the body.

On the other hand, sexual desire is a manifestation of our sex drive or libido. Some use this sexual energy for creative production such as establishing a new business, being submerged in musical achievement, or focusing on sports. When creativity requires a great deal of energy, the person will have little sex drive left. Therefore, this person will feel less desire for sexual involvement. This lack of desire can be helpful for singles, but it can be detrimental to a marriage relationship. Stress is likely to develop when one spouse is burning up energy in nonsexual pursuits and the other wants more sexual involvement.

In addition to being used up for creative production, the sex drive may be burned up by emotional stress such as anxiety, depression, or conflict. A person suffering from this sort of stress may have little or no sexual desire.

Since sexual desire is an outgrowth of sex drive or the energy available in the body, nutrition, exercise, sleep, and hormonal cycles affect the energy available for sexual involvement. Thus, making certain that your body is well nourished, hormonally balanced, properly exercised, and adequately rested should enhance your sexual desire.

ADDRESS PROBLEMS

What if you're not particularly aware of getting interested sexually? Perhaps your sexual energy is not accessible to you. Chapter 26 addresses problems with sexual desire. If you have a chronic lack of interest—more than just a temporary reaction to your life being too full and not having enough space—refer to that section.

CLEAR OUT DISTRACTIONS

For those who live complicated, busy lives, there may never be a natural time to feel sexual. To correct this problem, you must start by clearing out distractions. Begin the process by making a decision about the television. Many people have the TV on most of the time when they are home together. It is a constant distraction. You may need to turn it off and spend some time alone together. We often recommend moving the TV out of the bedroom. Sometimes putting it in the garage for a month nudges a change in patterns.

Outside commitments often interfere. Many of us are busy because of community and church involvements. If those commitments crowd our lives so much that we have no relaxed block of time to spend together as a couple, those involvements probably are not advantageous. Whether you are a Young Life leader, a pastor, a PTA president, or an involved community person, your time commitments to organizations cannot replace your time commitment to your marriage. Marriage is a God-ordained institution that does not function effectively when it is not given enough time or priority. Just as a car does not continue to perform at a maximum level if it is not serviced routinely, a relationship cannot maintain its maximum effectiveness if it is not given regular, focused attention.

Children can be a distraction. Mothers with preschool children frequently find that their sexual desire has lessened considerably. Their energy is being burned up. Any mother with a toddler and an infant will need to have some relief from the responsibility of caring for the needs of two almost totally dependent children. Even a mother with just one child in either of these age groups will probably feel the need for some time in which she is free of demands. A child with health problems or a behavioral disruption can cause so much stress for the parents that they find themselves having little sexual interest in each other. Very often, getting away from the stressful situation for several days will help the couple revive their physical desires.

IDENTIFY AND SET POSITIVE CONDITIONS

In addition to clearing out distractions and, in that process, allowing opportunity for one's feelings of desire to surface, it is important to spend some time identifying what works for you. Think back on your life together. When have you felt the most interested in your sexual relationship? Where were you? What kind of setting was it? What was going on in your life at that time? Was it in response to something you did for or with your spouse, or something he or she did for or with you?

Sometimes there may be a specific action you need from your spouse. For example, one man has a problem with lack of desire. If he and his wife ever do get involved sexually, he has no problem with arousal (getting and maintaining an erection), and he has learned to control ejaculation. But he rarely thinks about sex, and he experiences his wife's suggestions as demands. Thus, they might have intercourse every two or three months. Yet he was very aware of his sexual desire before marriage when sexual intercourse was ruled out because of their standards. Then there was no demand, so there was no anxiety to burn up his sexual energy.

As this man explored his problem, he remembered that his first panic hit when his bride took off her panties on the wedding night. The female genitalia were an unknown, and they represented a demand for performance. He was sure he could not measure up; thus his anxiety blocked his desire. It would have been helpful to him if his wife had left her panties on until he could cope with the problem, but he did not feel comfortable communicating this to her. His wife would have been willing to cooperate with him had he shared his need.

Think about your own situation. Is there something, however small, that would reduce your anxiety and increase your desire to be together with your spouse in a sexual experience? Communicate this to your husband or wife. Set aside a special time for this sharing—a time each of you knows is designated for talking about your sexual activity. The individual with the need should assume the responsibility for initiating such a talk time.

When couples work to identify needs in order to feel sexual desire, they normally discover that although each person knows his or her individual needs, there is a reluctance to communicate these to the spouse. Often they think, *If I am that blunt about what I would like, it'll take all the fun, spontaneity, and mystery out of it.* There is the idea, particularly among women, that the man should intuitively know what the woman needs. This is somehow a sign of his love. "If I tell him that his bringing me a gift, a flower, or something special turns me on, then I don't think it will work anymore," one woman reported. The fact that *she knew* that *he knew* what she wanted would destroy her response to his action.

We meet separately to talk with wives and then husbands at our weekend seminars for couples. The wives usually have messages they would like us to tell the husbands about what would make their sexual experience more positive. This occurs at the end of a twelve-hour time that has provided regular, structured communication experiences focused on enhancing the couple's sexual relationship. Some women seem to think it is okay if their husbands are informed about what they desire, but the messages cannot come directly from the wives. Such openness evokes a fear of destroying the mystery or the romance. It is ironic that these are usually the relationships in which sex has little or no romantic quality or spark to it.

Keeping secrets from your spouse about what you desire is a *barrier* to sexual fulfillment, not an asset. Let's destroy the mystery. Humans are unique individuals with emotions that vary greatly from one sexual experience to another—and this fact provides the possibility of continually making new discoveries. The more you know about yourself and about what you desire, and the more you communicate those wishes to your partner without placing demands on him or her, the more enhancement you can expect.

Identify it, communicate it, then practice it. Above all, if you're the one with the need, *you* take responsibility for getting that need met. When it's something you can provide for yourself, do that. If it's something you need from your partner, work it out with him or her so that it is not experienced as a demand. For your need *not* to be received as a demand, it must be clearly communicated as *your* need and not something inadequate about your *spouse*.

ASSUME RESPONSIBILITY

The concept of taking responsibility for oneself is central to sexual enhancement and critical for reversing sexual problems. We will refer to this concept throughout the book, so this is a good place to explain it.

Many who have been raised in the church have come to marriage with the idea that their responsibility as a Christian spouse is to *please* the other. Somehow the biblical concepts of love, mutual submission, and giving of ourselves have all taken on the meaning of doing the things that will make the other person happy or pleased. There is nothing wrong with our being pleasing to our spouse and bringing him or her happiness. In fact, that is likely to be the *result* when we are loving, giving, and mutually submitting. However, when our goal (rather than the result) is to please and make the other person happy, we are likely to be anxious. This anxiety will cause stress instead of pleasure and happiness.

Because of this tendency to translate being loving into pleasing, and thereby causing anxiety and stress in relationships, we advocate that you take responsibility to know, communicate, and pursue the activities that will meet your sexual needs, without placing demand on each other. The sexual response is something that happens in your body. It is personal and loaded with emotions. Each individual differs from every other individual, and each individual differs from one experience to another. You can't count on all women wanting to have sex "this way" or men "always wanting . . . ," or even this particular woman or man responding to the same thing in the same way every time. Because of the beautiful and complicated creation you are, there is no way your spouse can consistently guess what would please you. However, *you* usually know what you like, so you should take the responsibility to go after that desire, but never at the expense of the other.

When a spot on your back itches, you have to tell someone exactly where it itches and how you'd like to have it scratched. There is no way someone else can automatically know exactly where you itch and scratch it just right. Similarly, no one can read your mind to know exactly what will give you the most pleasure sexually at *this* time, in *this* experience.

However, there are some general things you and your spouse can learn about each other's likes and dislikes that you can automatically incorporate into your lovemaking—just as you may know that one

likes to be scratched with fingernails while the other prefers fingertips. Taking responsibility for your own pleasure includes honoring
your partner's preferences.

This leads to a second point. In addition to taking responsibility
for identifying, communicating, and pursuing your own sexual
desires and needs, each spouse is responsible to communicate and
redirect when the other is doing something violating or negative.
This ensures that going after your own pleasure will not take place
at the expense of your lover. Chapter 12 gives suggestions for non-
threatening ways to redirect your partner.

To summarize this concept of responsibility, you and your spouse
will be most relaxed together in your lovemaking if each one pursues
the pleasures that give him or her the most enjoyment *so long as* you
know these will not be negative experiences for your spouse.

Sexual desire or interest is not something someone else can provide for you. It is something already in you by creation that you have
to allow to surface. There may be conditions, as we have discussed,
that are necessary for that to happen. Your spouse must be cooperative with those, but not responsible for them. Desire is not something to be added on or gained. You don't have to *learn* how to
desire. All of us have been designed with sexual urges. If you don't
freely and spontaneously have sexual interest, there is some distraction, hormonal imbalance, anxiety, or barrier blocking its free
expression in you. You need to uncover and correct the problem to
free the natural desire that is in you.

10 HAVING FUN

Sometimes I just want to cuddle but don't particularly want to make love. Doing this gets my husband aroused—then he wants to make love. What can we do to work this out?

When a couple is dating and getting to know one another, they usually play and touch, tease and laugh together. Once they are married, this physical playfulness may diminish. It's easy to get in the habit of rushing through all the fun and getting down to "real" sex. The cuddling and affection are lost. The playfulness is not fulfilling but is designed to lead to fulfillment. We even often call it foreplay, as if it is not part of the whole experience. When we can freely and creatively enjoy one another without demand or expectation, our loving takes on a new dimension.

AFFECTION WITHOUT EXPECTATION

We were giving a seminar at an evangelical church in our community. The message we received from the surveys of a number of the women were typical of what we regularly hear. "How can we have fun together, be affectionate and caring, without sexual intercourse?"

"It seems the only interest my husband has in me is to have (get) his sexual goodies. I wish we could take more time to talk and be affectionate."

It seems that men in our culture have been conditioned to sexual release rather than to total-body pleasure and emotional intimacy. After some time of living with a husband who is focused on only the physical dimension of the sexual experience, a woman feels used and devalued.

A great resource for understanding boys in our culture is the book *Bringing Up Boys* by Dr. James Dobson. Boys learn two things that prepare them to be men who seek fast physical release. The first is that boys are *not* to be tender and emotional. Recently at a swim meet we observed a father with his four-year-old son. This father was affectionate and used expressions like "honey" in addressing his son. The woman sitting next to us mentioned how unusual and beautiful it was to see a father and son interacting with the tenderness one would expect of a mother and daughter. This father is a psychologist, which may contribute to his ability to break out of the traditional role interaction. Or it may be that as a boy he experienced the same emotional tenderness from his father. Whatever the case, boys need more modeling of tenderness from fathers and more encouragement of the expression of feelings from all the significant adults in their world if they are to grow up to be men who can relax and enjoy sexual pleasure and emotional intimacy.

The second message that affects boys is this: The sooner you reach your goal, the better you are. This is true of most sports. In addition, most teaching or modeling of success in business has reflected this attitude. *The focus has not been on enjoyment of the moment, but rather on reaching the goal quickly.*

Girls continue to be given more opportunity for sensuous enjoyment through music, ballet, and other girl-dominated extracurricular activities. In these activities the focus is on the good feeling of the movement and the control and expressiveness of the body. As we have observed in our own children, this is very different from the challenge of getting the ball into the goal area or running to home base with one hit.

Experiencing affection without intercourse is an essential part of marriage. As we mentioned in the theological discussion in Chapter 3, this dimension of our humanness, our potential for relationship, sets us apart from the rest of the animal world. We are made in God's image; thus, our sexuality is in the image of God.

Cuddling and holding and caressing, without expecting or fearing they will lead to intercourse every time, are essential to the well-rounded sexual relationship. If this possibility is not present, the one needing to cuddle will draw back from any affection for fear that it will lead to intercourse. Traditionally it has been the woman who draws back from touch because she is not free to go with what she feels. Often the man pushes for more because he expects resistance from the woman. When both partners are free to let the play go in the direction they mutually desire, knowing that the hesitant one will not be violated, cuddling without demand becomes natural. On occasion, the man or the woman may be left aroused but unfulfilled, but as long as that does not become the usual pattern, it need not be a problem.

FREEDOM AND CREATIVITY

A sense of freedom and a desire to be creative are necessary elements of a couple's being able to play and have fun together. But a person will not experience freedom and creativity in the relationship if he or she encounters demands. These may be internal demands or demands the spouse imposes. In either case, if the person is concerned about doing it the right way (pleasing one's partner), "turning on" the other person, or having a sexual response, he or she is not likely to have much free, enjoyable sexual play.

If either or both of you are aware of these pressures or demands, you need to discuss and deal with them before you attempt to add fun and creativity to your sexual experience. (You will find suggestions for such discussions in various chapters of this book. For example, if you are experiencing demands in the area of initiation, refer to Chapter 11 for help in overcoming those demands.)

How might you as a couple bring about freedom and creativity in your sexual relationship? Even if you are not experiencing any particular demands or stress, your sexual times may lack spontaneity. They may have become routine. Maybe you tend to get together at the same time and in the same place, and you both behave in much the same way. The script is written before the first kiss.

INITIATING CHANGE

When things have become humdrum, you need to start with both of you recognizing the need to change. The next step would be talking together about how each of you would like to change. This conversation will be more productive if you talk about yourself, rather than the changes you desire in your spouse. If you start outlining desired changes for the other person, you inhibit freedom rather than encourage it.

It is important, too, that the discussion about changes in your sexual relationship occurs away from the bedroom. If you read this section and get the idea you'd like to start talking with your spouse about enhancing your sexual times, it would be best to plan a special time to do this. If you mention what you have read the next time you crawl into bed to make love, it will probably cause a hassle and end that lovemaking attempt. Your ideas will be much less threatening if you say, "I've been reading a book about sexual enhancement and have some ideas that sound neat and fun for us. I'd love to take you out to tell you about my thoughts and hear your ideas."

Once the two of you agree that you'd like to have more playful fun together sexually, the door is wide open for ways to make it happen.

A good place to begin is to change the location and the setting or atmosphere of your sexual encounter. The *location* is the room or area of the house (or the place outside the house) where you get together sexually. The *setting* or *atmosphere* involves what you do to modify the location. For example, you can vary the lighting; you can reverse your position in the bed by putting your feet at the "head" end; you can use a comforter on the floor or by the fireplace instead of having your sexual experience in bed.

It will add spark to your relationship if you and your spouse take turns choosing the place and creating the atmosphere. This idea provides newness and an element of surprise. (The next chapter provides additional suggestions.)

Sometimes it takes some struggling together to come up with alternate locations and provide the privacy both of you need. One couple, Marilee and Bob, had six children ranging from two to seventeen years of age. The little ones awakened early in the morning, while the teenagers stayed up later than their parents at night. Marilee and Bob found that they were rarely getting together sexually. And when they did, they were under pressure to hurry in the morning or be quiet in the evening. Without a conscious awareness, they had developed a routine that took about three minutes. It was entirely predictable from start to finish. Sexual intrigue had left their relationship soon after their second child was born sixteen years before.

Finding new locations and creating new atmosphere took some problem-solving creativity. They organized Marilee's craft and sewing room so they could add a hide-a-bed and keep the room tidy. This provided an alternate location to the bedroom. The teenagers were enlisted as part of the plan. Marilee and Bob told them that Mom and Dad needed some special nights together. From the little smiles on the kids' faces, you could tell they had caught on. There's an example of a great job of modeling by parents!

The plan they worked out was as follows: After nine o'clock two nights a week, the teenagers were limited to the family room, the kitchen, and their own bedrooms. In exchange for some favors, they were asked to be responsible to get up with the younger children on Saturday mornings. This gave Bob and Marilee three blocks of time each week free of interruption, thus assuring privacy. They now had two possible locations that alleviated the need to be quiet and provided the framework they needed to experience some new life sexually. It worked!

When there are no children or other people in the home twenty-four hours a day, any location in the house that is comfortable, free of distraction, and private is an option for creating a new setting. Your van, pickup camper, or private backyard are other alternatives.

The atmosphere can be varied rather easily. This can be done with lighting. The variations might include no light, candlelight, dim light, or bright light. You might find the visual enjoyment of each other's bodies is enhanced by varying the placement of a candle or lamp. The sheets, blankets, or comforters can be varied. Some couples enjoy the smell of incense burning. Others enjoy the use of perfumes or colognes. Others may prefer the smell of a natural, freshly bathed body.

In addition to having fun experimenting with the setting for playing together, you can enjoy many other areas of experimentation. Clothing can be varied. If you have tended to start fondling each other with nightclothes on, crawl into bed some night and let your spouse discover you in the nude. On the other hand, if you are a couple who are in the nude during most of your physical touching time or getting-ready time, you may find it much more arousing to use clothes to add new intrigue. Try a suggestive nightgown or nightshirt, a T-shirt, bra and panties, briefs, or a "fig leaf." When nudity is a threat to one or both of you, covering can be used in a fun, playful way to distract from the blatant exposure that triggers anxiety.

You can have fun with using different ways of covering the body to avoid being threatening. It's not necessary to make an issue of trying to overcome an inhibition about nudity. Instead, you can work with it; you can be creative and have fun with it; you can distract from it so it doesn't get in the way. One couple worked around the wife's inhibitions by developing fun ways to circumvent the problem. For example, she might wear something that covered her and yet was sexy, such as a sheer nightgown. Another idea is to tie scarves around the appropriate places. Try anything—the more fun and the sillier the better—that will help you get past a problem with nudity. Then, if you do want to learn to be more comfortable with your own and your spouse's nudity, you can try some of the exercises in Chapter 6. That is work, however, not fun and games. The work you put into the exercises will lead to more freedom with each other, but is not a creative experience in itself. Creativity may follow when you gain added freedom.

Nudity can be enjoyed in many ways. One young couple really enjoyed playing in the nude—playful pinching, poking, and caressing—but the man panicked if they were together in the nude to have sexual intercourse. We encouraged them to engage in nude play that involved more and more total-body involvement without any expectation for intercourse. We had them go home and roll together in the nude, embracing and interlocking their bodies. They also learned to make some use of coverings that they could have fun with. And that allowed him to be more comfortable. Nude swimming in the privacy of one's backyard pool is enjoyed by many couples. There are limitless possibilities.

Other ways to have fun and to play together with or without leading to sexual intercourse include the *teases that enhance*. It's critical that the teases do not carry a jab or put-down, or pick on a sensitive issue. Rather, the tease has to be for the fun of it and must not carry a hidden loaded message.

Resisting in a fun way is a tease that can enhance. This is the message that says, "Come on and try to get me," or "See if I'm available." Just pulling away slightly can be particularly evocative when used by the person who has tended to be the aggressor. It is not suggested for the person who has been the resister in the relationship, since it might be taken seriously.

The man needs to be as active as the woman in creating new ways to tease and in preparing enjoyable surprises. One man came running out of his bathroom without any clothes on. He leaped over the bed on which his wife was lying, and then asked her to guess what Bible verse he was acting out. The verse was, "Listen! My lover! Look! Here he comes, leaping across the mountains, bounding over the hills. My lover is like a gazelle . . ." (Song of Songs 2:8–9). They've had fun with that ever since.

Whatever variation you use—however crazy it might seem—if it creates fun and laughter and does not have to lead to intercourse, you have a good start on keeping alive your total sexual expression with each other.

11 INITIATING

My husband wants me to initiate sex sometimes, but I just feel so self-conscious and awkward—it seems that he should initiate.

WHO INITIATES?

It is not uncommon for a woman to be frustrated, crying, and complaining that nothing is happening sexually between herself and her husband. As we gather data and put together a total picture, what emerges is rather interesting. After she describes her husband's excessive involvement in his career and lack of sexual approach to her, we will usually ask, "What keeps you from approaching him sexually, since you're the one wanting sex and he apparently doesn't have the drive?" The response is often a blank look or a stumbling for words. Finally, the answer comes: "I just never thought of it." She may have given all sorts of subtle hints and become upset because he did not respond. The husband usually didn't even catch on that his wife desired sex. Perhaps she mentioned that she'd like to go to bed, or she wore a special nightgown, or she was waiting up for him when he came home late at night. But she never let him know the *real* meaning of these symbolic, subtle expressions of her sexual desire.

Breaking Down Stereotypes of Male-Female Roles

The stereotype is that the man *is* and *should be* the sexually aggressive initiator. The woman is to use somewhat manipulative tactics to get him to approach her. For some couples this works. But there are many marriages for which these expectations are disruptive.

Here again, you may need to have a frank discussion with your spouse in which you examine the initiation pattern in your sexual relationship. What percentage of the time do you see yourself initiating, and what percentage do you see your spouse initiating? Often there are discrepancies in how each partner answers the question. The husband may see himself as initiating 90 percent of the time; whereas the wife may feel that each one initiates 50 percent of the time. If you discover that your views are quite different, don't try to settle whose view is accurate. Each person's experience and perceptions are his or her own; therefore, the way *each* of you feels is accurate. What is important is to try to "get under the other person's skin" to discover the other's view. Maybe the differences lie in the way each of you defines *initiation*. For example, the "90 percent" husband may not be conscious of his wife's cues, so he doesn't realize how often she has communicated a subtle message intended to cue him.

After you've each discovered how you would define the frequency of your initiation pattern, talk about your feelings concerning that pattern. Is it working for the two of you? How much stress or anxiety does each of you experience around the issue of getting sexual times started? Work through the exercise Resolving Initiation Problems described later in this chapter.

APPROACH-AVOIDANCE GAMES

One typical problematic initiation pattern that develops is the approach-avoidance game. One person sees it as his or her responsibility to get sexual activity going, so he makes frequent approaches to the other—using sexual overtures, dropping hints, or making direct suggestions. He feels as if he has to mention it eight times if it's going to happen once. So he is anxiously suggesting sex far more often than he really wants it. His wife would like him not to bother her and feels that she never even has an opportunity to suggest getting together sexually because he wants it all the time. She feels bombarded and unable to get in touch with her desire. So she resists or avoids his approaches. You can see how the pattern perpetuates itself: The more she avoids, the more anxious he becomes, so the more he makes advances. This increases her feeling that demands are being placed on her that don't allow room for her desire to build, and so the pattern continues.

This approach-avoidance pattern may have developed as a result of varying levels of sex drive, interest, or desire for frequency. It may be that one of you has an intense sex drive, but after a sexual time with your spouse, you have a sense of release and satisfaction for quite some time. Your partner may be the opposite. The release may not be as complete, so there is more ongoing desire, or a satisfying experience may serve to heighten interest for one of you.

If you are a young mother with several preschoolers you're probably tired most of the time. Sexual encounters sound like a good idea, but by the time of day you're available for such activity, you feel exhausted. Therefore, your interest rarely has an opportunity to be expressed. Your husband is probably young and full of sexual energy and can't understand what's wrong with you. This very real difference in sexual interest may lead to an approach-avoidance pattern if the two of you do not talk about the dilemma and plan ways for you to be rested and available.

You may be a thirty-five-year-old businessman or professional at the peak of establishing your career. Your sex drive is so used in pursuit of your vocation that your frequency of desire for sexual activity has decreased significantly. In contrast, your wife finally has time for herself, and so her frequency of desire has increased. The children are in school. She has time to bathe leisurely, manicure her nails, and play tennis; she is much more in tune with her body. You may experience her constant state of readiness for sexual encounters as a demand that makes you feel inadequate.

You walk into the house exhausted. You're late for dinner. Your mind is still going a mile a minute, thinking about the decisions of the day. She is beautiful, well rested, and in her negligee. The children are in bed. She has a beautiful candlelight dinner set up for the two of you. Instead of feeling appreciative, you think, *Oh, no, not again. I'm just not up to it tonight.* But you feel guilty for thinking that, and you try to express appreciation for her caring intention.

After many such events, you experience more and more tension about the demand you feel being placed on you. You either start coming home later or you blow up over the smallest conflicts with your wife. And so another form of approach-avoidance has developed. Talking about your feelings at a time away from the event is the only way to break the pattern.

There are many other versions of this same dilemma. If you have fallen into such a problem, what is your version? How can you break into the situation? You need to take decisive action.

EXERCISE 7

Resolving Initiation Problems

Here are steps you can take to resolve an initiation problem:

1. Have a casual time together in which you decide you both want to talk about your sexual initiation patterns. If one of you is the initiator in suggesting there is a problem, do not blame your spouse for it! Rather, *own the problem* yourself. This means that you use "I" statements rather than "you" statements. You might say, "I've been desiring intercourse more frequently." Avoid a statement like, "You never seem interested in intercourse anymore." Tell how the situation affects you and what you bring to the situation, rather than what your partner is doing wrong. For example, "I end up being afraid to take the lead because I don't want to be rejected again."

2. Plan a time to work on the difficulty. During that planned time, follow the next steps:

a. Each of you spend at least an hour alone writing out how you experience the dilemma. What do you see happening between the two of you? How do you participate in this problem—what is your role in perpetuating the difficulty? What feelings does the entire experience trigger for you?

b. Plan a two- to three-hour block of time for the two of you to be together when you won't be distracted or interrupted—preferably when you are both at your best, and not when either of you is exhausted. A breakfast or lunch date usually works best—at a restaurant, having a picnic, or staying at home without children and with the telephone off the hook.

c. During the allotted time, start by reading each other's writings from step *a* above. In reading, focus on what the other person is saying about himself or herself. Try to really step into the other person's shoes and feel how he or she experiences the difficulty. This may take concentration. The more natural response is to see what the other is saying about you, and then to become defensive or start arguing or attacking him. The latter reaction will stifle progress.

d. Apply active listening skills (see Chapter 12) to feed back to your partner what you have understood about him or her from the writing. Work hard on reflecting how you sense your partner experiences the sexual initiation situation.

e. Partner: Clarify and expand on what your spouse has learned from your writing (e.g., "Yes, and another way I sense that is . . ."; or "I know that's what I said, but when I hear you say it I realize what I really meant was . . ."; or "If that's what I said, it isn't what I meant; let me try again").

f. Repeat steps *d* and *e,* reversing roles.

g. Agree on the need for change.

h. Make a plan that reverses the old pattern. That is, the approacher will not make sexual suggestions, just be affirming. The avoider will be responsible to initiate an agreed-on number of sexual encounters within a designated time frame.

EXAMPLES OF PLANS TO REVERSE INITIATION PATTERNS

Problem: The Man Always Initiates

After discussing what the situation feels like for each of you and deciding on the need for change, you might make a plan similar to this:

1. Set a time span (for example, one week or slightly longer than your usual time lapse between lovemaking events).

2. Rules for this time span:

For husband: Back way off—no sexual approach, not even a hint—don't bring up the topic. Be affirming of wife—warm, loving, but make no sexual advances.

For wife: Be responsible to initiate intercourse once during this period of time. Be free to initiate by any method that is possible for you. If you want to initiate but are having a particular difficulty, you may bring up the topic and discuss your feelings and anything that might be helpful to you.

3. At the end of the time span, set aside a minimum of two hours to talk about what happened or didn't happen, and what it felt like. If the designated time elapsed and the wife didn't initiate, discuss a plan for the next time span. Or perhaps she initiated, but he didn't catch on. Maybe she sat down close to him while he was watching TV. She snuggled up to him and rubbed his neck in an attempt to get something started, but he just kept on watching TV. Discuss what sort of behavior each of you perceives as sexual initiation.

Problem: Fatigue (for One or Both of You)

Before you get into a plan for breaking an old habit, start by defining how each of you sees the problem.

1. Look at your reasons for fatigue. Are you a mother of small children, getting up at night with a baby? Are you a husband who arrives home late and must get up early for work or other responsibilities? Are you depressed? Or is fatigue your way to escape involvement? If the cause is one of the last two (depression or escape), you need to work with a therapist or counselor. If it's a lifestyle problem, then proceed to the next step.

2. Agree that time together each week or every other week is a priority. This together time must occur when neither of you is tired.

3. Schedule specific time to be spent together: an evening, two hours at lunchtime, two or three hours in the morning, a weekend or day away every now and then.

4. Make sure this time is free of interruption—telephone off the hook, kids at friend's house or down for the night, the two of you away at a motel—whatever it takes.

5. Plan for adequate rest on a regular basis—have a baby-sitter come in one hour a day so the wife can nap; the husband may cut down on commitments, and so on.

Once both partners are free to express sexual desires when they feel them, most couples enjoy mutual and spontaneous initiation. Mutuality means that both feel equal freedom and responsibility to initiate when the desire is there. It can also mean that the desire grows mutually out of contact with each other. That is, instead of sexual desire starting in one person and that person approaching the other, the feelings grow spontaneously between two people. This may happen while working together, playing together, or just being together. When the old, demanding pattern is broken so that each of you is free of the negative feelings, the good feelings flow. However, be alert to difficulties creeping in. Plan for correction before negative patterns are formed again. Obviously the most relaxed style is the ability to feel free with your own sexual desires and to be accepting of your spouse's. That way either one can express desires as they are felt, without causing conflict.

WHEN "WHEN" IS A SOURCE OF DIFFICULTY

The same flexibility and spontaneity that are the goal for who initiates are also ideal for when sexual encounters are initiated. It is helpful if neither of you holds rigid stereotypes of when it is appropriate to enjoy lovemaking. You may always have associated sexual activity with going to bed at night. Once the lights are turned out and you have both crawled under the covers, you will roll over to your spouse and start fondling with the intention of proceeding to intercourse. That's the only time you envision as a lovemaking time. This clearly does not allow for flexibility and spontaneity.

If you are in a rut, you will need to make clear plans to open the door to sexual encounters at other times of the day. Flexibility doesn't usually happen just by recognizing the need or the desire for it. Start by talking about how your limited concepts about when sexual activity should occur developed. Then plan some times together that are different from your usual times. It's best if planned times are designed primarily for sexual pleasure, with the option of intercourse if that is desired by both.

Little children in the home may limit flexibility. Plan around their schedules, or find ways to be free of them periodically. Maybe you can get away from home or have the children cared for out of the house. It will be more difficult to allow spontaneous initiation if you have young children or anyone else present in the house.

There are other ways in which the "when" of initiation can cause tension. Timing can sometimes be used to sabotage the relationship. This usually happens when anger has built up in the relationship or when there is anxiety about performing sexually. The way timing manifests itself varies. It may be that the woman is most alert and responsive in the morning, but the man always initiates sex at night when she is tired. Or he has his fullest erections and is most sure of his responsiveness in the morning, but she says she's just not a morning person, and then complains when he's not responsive in the evening. One partner may insist that sex always has to occur before a certain time.

Whatever the reason, they never seem to be able to get on the same timetable. We will talk about other forms of sabotage in Chapter 20.

To reverse problems with timing, try scheduling times agreeable to both partners. This may involve compromise, perhaps alternating with each other's preferred time. Or it may be that neither time is used, and several new, mutually agreeable times are selected. Again, it is important to make sure that your planned time together will be free of interruptions and pressures. The time period should be long enough so that neither of you feels rushed at either end of the experience together. The goal of the time together must be enjoyment and pleasure, without demands for response or intercourse. Allow each sexual experience to be what it will be!

WHERE—CREATIVITY WITH SENSITIVITY

Finding new and fun places to enjoy each other's bodies can give new spark to a rather "ho-hum" sexual relationship. This is one of the ways to create an ever-changing mood that allows each experience to be a new one. The variety in itself is a delight.

There are really only two limits on where you might plan a sexual nest. One is that the place chosen provides the privacy needed by both of you. For example, your backyard might be an option for you but would make your spouse feel very uncomfortable. If it's not comfortable for both, it's not a possible place. However, if you're the one who has always been hesitant about feeling private in the backyard, and you decide you'd like to push yourself a bit, that's fine.

The second limit is that your choice of a place must respect other people. You may be totally uninhibited but your neighbors need to be protected from your sexual activities.

It can be fun to plan a new place. You can plan together or surprise each other. In all situations, remember to be sensitive to each other's need for privacy. A lock on the door of the chosen room usually relieves anxiety about being interrupted. Taking the telephone off the hook prevents fear of intrusion. Closing windows, doors, and drapes can encourage freedom from noises. A secluded yard or area is necessary for outdoor play. Once the privacy needs have been cared for, let your minds run free. The swimming pool at night has been a fun variation for some. A new room in the house, a different bed, a love nest in the family room or living room are all options. Or you may want to be so different as to take your pickup camper to the grocery store parking lot!

HOW—SYMBOLIC MESSAGES AND
DIRECT INVITATIONS

Different people initiate sexual activity in different ways. Some individuals tend to express themselves with direct physical activity. This may be a combination of kissing, fondling, hugging, caressing, or rubbing bodies together. For these people, their bodies express their desires more easily than words.

Others are direct with verbal messages of initiation. "I'm really feeling turned on. Let's go to bed and make love," for example.

Then there are others who are much more subtle and indirect in their initiation. In our culture this has tended to be true of women more than of men. However, we are finding that the trend is changing, and women are becoming more direct. For some men, a woman's increased directness stimulates a tendency toward hesitancy and timidity.

If you are a subtle initiator, it is important that you take responsibility to make certain your desires are clearly communicated to your spouse.

As long as both spouses are clear about the message being communicated, subtle, symbolic methods of initiation can add spark and intrigue. You might use pet phrases, fix a love nest, come to bed in the nude, prepare a romantic dinner for the two of you, light a candle, bring flowers; or, as you get totally free with each other, you may have fun with more ridiculous messages. One man appeared in the bedroom with a bow tied around his penis. Another man took everything off except his white shirt and tie and came in carrying his briefcase and a rose. One woman pasted hearts over the appropriate spots on her body. It's fun to be creative. Remember, within marriage the Bible has no restrictions on your behavior, as long as it's loving. Being sexy with your marriage partner is a plus, not a negative!

In summary, it's important to reduce stress concerning who initiates sexual play and when, where, and how that initiation takes place. Then initiation will assume a healthy role in the total sexual picture, rather than presenting a barrier or being a source of tension. Initiation can also be cultivated to enhance a merely adequate sexual relationship where more spark is desired. The needed ingredients are removal of demands, freedom within oneself, and unconditional acceptance of each other.

12 MESHING YOUR WORLDS

The production line broke down at the plant, two team managers called in sick, and you almost ran out of gas on the way home from work. At home, your wife has had her own management problems: Your eight-year-old son punched the neighbor girl, the toilet flooded, and the baby has an eye infection. Now, plan a loving time for the evening.

A TOTAL-PERSON RELATIONSHIP

Getting in tune with each other or meshing each other's worlds is a total-person process. It is becoming "one flesh" as the Hebrews saw it—uniting spirits, emotions, and bodies. All three are necessary to a satisfying relationship. Sex that is just a union of physical bodies cannot be a satisfying communion experience. God intended sexual intercourse to be much more than just physical release. When total togetherness is missing, trouble usually ensues!

Spending time together enables two people to mesh. Having been together, you will be more likely to have a sense of each other's feelings. Meshing takes more effort, care, and tenderness when you have come from separate and consuming outside places. You may need to spend time chatting—catching up with each other's worlds. If you have concerns that are difficult to put aside, it might help to share these concerns with each other and in prayer with God. Together praising God for joys, accomplishments, and excitements of the day is a way of being one. What you have experienced in your day will affect the time and effort needed to feel together in each sexual experience.

Eliminate Barriers

Tackle any barriers that prevent the two of you from feeling free with each other. Perhaps one of you has some negative feelings toward the other that have not been resolved. You need to talk these over.

Oftentimes aesthetic or physical barriers also stand in the way of true togetherness. Many people are repelled by bad breath, bodily odors, or certain aspects of the partner's appearance, yet they find it difficult to discuss these barriers. If there is something physical about your partner that makes it difficult for you to feel one with him or her, it is best to share it.

When possible, a physical barrier that is a sensitive topic should be discussed at a time other than the actual meshing time. For example, if bad breath really turns you off and your spouse has bad breath every time he eats onions, pick a comfortable time to talk about how that bothers you. Then the two of you can come up with a loving way to discuss the situation so it does not interfere with your meshing process. Develop a prearranged symbolic message that will communicate the need to do something to reverse the interfering negative situation. Something like, "I think we need a mouthwash break," or "A mouthful of peanut butter would help things a lot right now." The message will be better received if delivered in a lighthearted and nonoffensive manner.

Vaginal odors or infectious discharge can certainly get in the way of sexual togetherness. Keep freshly washed. Try wearing all-cotton underwear, which gives the vaginal area more opportunity to air out. Sometimes blow-drying the external genitals or the use of a heat lamp after baths or showers can help keep the vaginal area dry and free of discharge. (Naturally, you will need to be careful not to burn yourself.) If these precautions don't correct the situation, see your gynecologist for assistance.

If being freshly washed is important to you, but it is not important to your spouse, take the responsibility to let your need and desire
be known. Don't play the game "If he loves me, he will remember."
It probably has nothing to do with his love or lack of it. It is simply
a difference in what is aesthetically important to each of you. Avoid
placing demands on your spouse to remember what is important to
you. It will make the atmosphere much more relaxing if a system has
been prearranged in which the one who remembers has a humorous
way to remind the other to bathe, or whatever is needed.

It is best if each of us can realize that our spouse *will* sometimes
forget the messages we have communicated about what we like.
Usually that is not an indication of lack of care. Rather, it is an outgrowth of the fact that sexual pleasure and satisfaction are internal
experiences. In the process of learning about her sexual needs,
Suzanne discovered that having her breasts stimulated when she was
lying on her back felt repulsive. She had always assumed that all
breast touching was negative, but found that she really enjoyed having her breasts fondled and kissed when she was on top of Jerry.
During one positive pleasuring experience, Suzanne and Jerry were
lying side by side on their backs. They were relaxed and enjoying
each other. In this comfortable state, Jerry reached over and started
expressing his warm, affectionate feelings by caressing Suzanne's
breasts. He was not thinking of her previous request, nor did he
intend to violate her in any way, yet she became irate because he did
not remember such a specific request. To Suzanne, it was a clear
message that Jerry did not value her. She felt violated. Her reaction
placed incredible pressure on Jerry. The message he received was that
he'd better be vigilant and on his toes at all times.

If Suzanne had been able to incorporate this attitude, she could
have responded with: "Let me get on top of you so I can enjoy your
touching me," or "Right now I do not feel like moving into a more
comfortable position for breast play, but I would love to have you
roll over and we could just hold each other."

Having taken care of aesthetic barriers, you can start at your present positions and then move together. This tends to create a new

mood for each experience. Each time of coming together has discovery in it. Sometimes it may evolve into fun—silly, giggling events. Other times might be sad but close, or tender with much vulnerability. Intense, passionate expressions will occasionally predominate your lovemaking; some of your times together might seem like raw erotic expressions. Then there will always be times that seem rather functional. That is, one or both of you need the physical or emotional closeness and release, but you experience little more than that. These functional sexual experiences are acceptable and need not be seen as a negative sign about your relationship—so long as they don't become your primary sexual expression.

Communicate

What role does communication play in the whole meshing process? Effective verbal and nonverbal communication can enhance the process of becoming one. To feel one with each other, it is critical that each partner feel heard by the other. This requires empathy, which is a major part of active listening. Empathy is more than a mechanical technique. It is the ability to enter into another person's feelings instead of defending your own. In addition, it is the ability to communicate with the other person in such a way that he or she feels you are in tune.

It takes discipline to practice empathy and active listening, to achieve an awareness of our own feelings and reactions. We discipline ourselves to acknowledge our own feelings, to be real about them, but not to let them interfere with hearing and being with the other person. The more emotionally difficult an area is for us, the more disciplined our practice of empathy has to be. The best way to practice empathy is to reflect and clarify. Reflect what you have heard and sensed from the other. Listen and observe with all your senses. Sort out your own reaction and set it aside. Then feed back what you've heard and seen. After that invite the other person to clarify and expand the original communication.

It is most difficult for us to remain nondefensive and be in tune with the other person when that person is talking about us. Following is an example of how you might practice empathy even when the message is about you:

Bill: You've gotten so much better—you used to want to have sex right when you felt like it. If it couldn't be right then, and if I didn't get an erection right away, then you'd pout.

Linda: You're feeling less demand from me. (Good reflection and focus on his feelings rather than on what he is saying about her.)

Bill: Yes, it seems we've both learned that if one of us isn't turned on, we can enjoy cuddling and that's okay.

Linda: So there is more relaxation in realizing our pleasuring times can be an end in themselves, rather than having to lead to intercourse.

Bill: That has really made me want to get together with you more often.

With Linda's consistent reflection of Bill's feelings, he was able to move from talking about her to talking about himself. For many of us, being an active listener when we are hearing negative messages about ourselves is not easy.

This disciplined, effective, verbal communication does not work well once sexual excitement begins. So this work has to occur before or apart from sexual arousal. We do not hear as accurately when we are aroused by intense sexual feelings. Getting with the sexual process is really flowing with your own internal experience, so it is contradictory to work on empathy once you are into a sexual experience. This does not mean that you switch to being cruel, selfish, or insensitive at the expense of your spouse. Rather, you focus on the enjoyment and pleasure of the moment, respecting the guidelines previously established about what is violating to your partner. We will build on this principle in the next chapter.

Because verbal communication is not at its best during sexual excitement, sexual decisions must be made away from the lovemaking event. In the process of making decisions about what is best for each of you sexually, it is helpful to develop a *nonverbal* signal system. This can then be used during sexual experiences to follow through with decisions made previously.

Here's an example of how this might work. One common discomfort for women is the man's tendency to manually stimulate the clitoris too directly, too intensely, and for too long a time. Usually the man has no idea that what he is doing is uncomfortable or painful for the woman. After she has shared that she frequently experiences discomfort from manual stimulation, the man will still need ongoing guidance to know what does feel good. You can have an instruction time where the woman shows the man and talks about it. But once you are into a sexually arousing time, that type of instruction will tend to kill the sexual feelings. Instead, use a prearranged nonverbal message that can flow with the feelings of the moment. For example, the woman might gently lift the man's hand to reduce the pressure, or move his hand to another location that feels hungry for touch. This is much easier for a man to take than the verbal message, "You're doing it too hard again."

When there is a particular kind of touch uniquely negative to you, you might decide that a tap on your spouse's shoulder is a reminder that those negative feelings are occurring. One man experienced his wife's touch as ticklish. Another woman could not stand to be kissed on the neck, yet when her husband was enjoying himself he might forget. Both of these people developed mutually accepted methods of signaling a need for change.

A positive, nonverbal cue can ask for more of a specific action that feels good. A woman might push her pelvis toward a point of stimulation that is bringing her pleasure. A man might move the woman's buttocks when she is in the top position if he needs more movement to keep his erection, or he might stop her movement to control ejaculation. There are many ways we can communicate with each other without using words. The important ingredient is that both the sender and receiver attach the same meaning to the nonverbal message. When positive nonverbal systems are developed within a couple's sexual relationship, the meshing of your worlds can be a beautiful, harmonious process.

13 PLEASURING

My sexual relationship with my husband leaves me unfulfilled.
He gets, I give. What are some positive steps to being able to enjoy
mutual pleasure?

THE RIGHT TO PLEASURE

So husbands ought also to love their own wives as their own
bodies. He who loves his own wife loves himself; *for no one ever*
hated his own flesh, but nourishes and cherishes it, just as Christ
also does the church. (Eph. 5:28–29 NASB, emphasis added)

Bodily pleasure is a biblical expectation. God created us in his
likeness with the capacity to enjoy our bodies. This is analogous to
the enjoyment that he finds in his body, the Church (see Chapter 4).
Yet not all people can receive pleasure.

Morally rigid persons may tense up rather than relax and enjoy sensuous feelings. A woman may tell herself, "Nice girls don't do such
things." A man may rush past sensuous feelings to arousal and release.

A person who was raised in a rigid, antisexual setting may associate bodily pleasure with being fleshly and sinful. People who con-

nect bodily pleasure with sin cannot allow themselves to receive pleasure and feel good about it. One woman is not able to enjoy sex on a Saturday night because she will be going to church the next day, and she is unable to associate God and sex. For others, the sex act must occur quickly and in the dark. The man or the woman rushes their sexual times. The wife becomes very active with intense thrusting. Thus she brings her husband to ejaculation quickly because that is the only way she can allow herself to experience the sex act: in and out quickly. Unfortunately, both spouses are left frustrated and unfulfilled.

It may be that a person with the religious association of sex and sin can enjoy the sexual experience only when there are risk and guilt involved. For one couple, any sexual involvement they had before marriage was wild and exciting. However, those intense sexual feelings seemed to dissipate soon after marriage, and they began to doubt their attraction to each other.

At a time of deep disillusionment about their marriage and sex life, the wife happened to be working with a warm, caring male. She found herself incredibly responsive to him, and she even confided in him regarding her marital doubts. The outside relationship incidentally and unintentionally built until they became sexually involved. Her guilt about her wrong choices built even as the sexual pleasure and enjoyment with this other man intensified. She left her husband for the new man in her life. A divorce ensued. She married the man who had swept her away, and would you believe it, shortly after her second marriage, her sexual feelings for him faded. Sex was no longer enjoyable. This is usually the point at which the person or couple come for help and discover that the association of sexual pleasure with sin is interfering with the ability to enjoy sex in marriage.

Difficulty expressing emotions may also interfere with pleasure. This seems to be more commonly due to the cultural impact on men that says, "Big boys don't cry." Boys are not expected or allowed to be as emotional as girls. Thus, when a boy grows up in a home where either or both parents control their emotions and will not allow emotional expression, he is in double trouble. Not only does he have the cultural input, but also the emotional vacuum at home.

This man will usually not have had sexual intercourse before marriage. His avoidance of sexual involvement has been based on his own unrecognized fear of emotional intensity rather than biblical standards. When he has his first sexual experience with his new wife, if she is wildly and intensely expressive, he feels somewhat overwhelmed and a little frightened by the whole experience. He starts avoiding, suggesting sightseeing rather than lovemaking. She is confused and feels he does not want her. Since he is not used to negative emotional expression, her tears of rejection make him feel anxious. He experiences her sadness as a demand he cannot live up to. And so their downward spiral begins. Sex is now a demand, not a pleasure.

THE ABILITY TO RECEIVE PLEASURE

The acceptance of the right to pleasure is essential to experiencing all of what God intended for us sexually. In addition to being able to *accept* pleasure, we must be able to *receive* pleasure. The feeling that you are a worthy person is central to being able to receive sexual pleasure. You must have the sense that you are valuable and that you deserve to have good things happen in your life. Good, pleasurable sensations in your body are to be enjoyed. You can relax and know that your spouse is enjoying the experience. When this feeling of self-worth is missing, you will feel uncomfortable with sexual pleasure. You may feel embarrassed or guilty about allowing responsiveness. On the other hand, your lack of feelings of self-worth may take the form of anxiously checking with your partner to make sure he or she is being pleased. You experience no pleasure of your own, only satisfaction that your partner is having a good time. "Who am I to expect a good time?" A sense of worthiness is necessary to the pleasuring process.

FREEDOM FROM DEMAND

In addition to an attitude that you have the right to pleasure and a feeling of self-worth, freedom from demand is essential to the ability to pleasure for pleasure's sake. Anxiety due to demand interferes with the sexual experience. Because of this, we teach couples a process of giving and receiving pleasure without demand.

Demand-free pleasuring experiences are simple to talk about but not always easy to practice. Each lovemaking time is to be entered with this anticipation: I am here to enjoy myself and my spouse. But I will not enjoy this experience if I demand any of the following: that as a man I have to get or keep an erection; that I have to do a certain thing in a certain way; that as a woman I should get aroused and/or be orgasmic; that I should please my partner; or that I must perform in a certain way if the experience is to be satisfactory.

We recommend that you don't even expect intercourse as a necessary part of having a loving, touching get-together. The only criterion is that what you do must be pleasurable to both of you.

TAKE RESPONSIBILITY FOR PLEASURE:
A TWO-WAY SYSTEM

Enjoying each other's bodies and letting each event take on its own character is most possible when each person feels comfortable pursuing his or her own desire for touch. Each of you takes responsibility to go after your own desire for pleasure. This is not at the expense of your spouse. Rather, each of you will develop your awareness and knowledge of what is negative for the other. You will exclude those negatives from your range of options until the other person's perception of that aspect of pleasuring changes from negative to positive. (The idea of going with the conservative partner is found in Chapter 23.) There are usually unlimited possibilities for pleasure without violating your partner.

This is a two-way system. The first part, which we have just described, involves taking responsibility for yourself in the pleasuring experience. The assumption behind this is that you please your spouse the most when you are not preoccupied with pleasing, but are fully enjoying yourself sexually and focusing on soaking in pleasure and enjoying your spouse. This may sound more selfish than pleasing, but we find it the reverse. When you are concerned about doing what is best for the other person rather than enjoying yourself, you become performance-focused. This creates anxiety and tension. Your partner will sense this tension, and it will interfere with his or her pleasure as well as yours.

There is nothing more positive sexually than for both persons to take responsibility for themselves, to truly enjoy their own and each other's bodies for personal pleasure. This cannot work, however, without the second part of this system: Each person in the relationship must agree that he or she will not allow anything to continue that is negative. This agreement means you take the responsibility to redirect your spouse away from anything that feels negative and toward something pleasurable. That way, you and your partner can relax and enjoy yourselves, not worrying about whether the other is feeling good about the experience. You can trust that getting into your own feelings is not at the expense of your partner but rather for his or her pleasure.

This two-way contract is incredibly freeing, and yet it is most difficult for some couples to accept. We have been conditioned to believe that as spouses, it is our duty to determine what is most pleasing to our partners and then work hard to do everything just right. You can see how that can interfere with pleasure for both. Let's look back at the verses we started with. Ephesians 5:28–29 implies that the best guide for pleasing our partners is to find out what pleases ourselves. The only expectation is that we are not to withhold ourselves from our spouses (1 Cor. 7:5).

What plan might you set in motion to act on the attitude suggested above—the change from pleasing to pursuing pleasure? The remainder of this chapter will give you some ideas.

GOING AFTER GOOD FEELINGS

How can you pleasure for your own enjoyment and know that this will be the best way to give yourself to your spouse?

When you realize and believe that you will please each other most when you fully free yourselves in the sexual experience, then you will be most able to enjoy yourselves and each other. Going after pleasure will work only if this is a mutual commitment. Both of you have to be convinced, and both must cooperate with the plan. You also need mutual trust in each other's commitment. Once the basic verbal communication has been worked out, then it's best to practice some very simple pleasuring exercises. Start with a foot and hand caress. These are the parts of the body farthest from the genitals; therefore, you are less likely to experience any of the anxieties or demands previously associated with your sexual experience.

Following are the steps for the foot and hand caress. This is one of the early assignments we give to couples in sexual therapy. The pleasuring exercises can significantly enhance a couple's sexual relationship whether or not there are any specific sexual problems or patterns of relating sexually that need to be reversed.

EXERCISE 8

Foot and Hand Caress
Underlying principles:
   • Receiving and pleasuring for your own pleasure:

Receiver: Your only task is to soak in pleasure and to redirect the pleasurer when the touch is not pleasing. Check out your concern if at any point you question whether or not your partner is enjoying himself or herself.

Pleasurer: Lovingly and tenderly touch your partner in a way that feels good to you. Think of radiating warmth through your fingertips and taking in or sensing the warmth and pulsation of the part of your partner that you are touching. Trust your partner to redirect you if what you are doing is not pleasurable. Express your concern if at any point you become anxious rather than enjoying your partner's body. Caress slowly. Take time to enjoy.

   • No experience at all is preferable to an experience by demand:

   When you feel that an experience is a demand—stop doing it, share your feelings, and shift the place or person being pleasured. If the demand still continues, talk about the feelings and reschedule the experience, modifying the setup to accommodate the needs of one or both partners in order to eliminate demand feelings.

• Varying the setting keeps the experience interesting:
Select a setting different from that of your usual sexual experiences. The receiver should be seated or reclined in a comfortable, upholstered high-backed chair or couch. The pleasurer should be positioned to have easy and comfortable access to the body part being enjoyed.

• Focus on pleasure:
Sexual arousal is not the expectation of this experience. If arousal should occur, this is an acceptable, involuntary response, so enjoy it. But do not become concerned if there is no arousal. The purpose of this experience is to learn to enjoy the giving and receiving of bodily pleasure. This is not to be a therapeutic massage to get the kinks out, but rather a sensuous touch that communicates warmth.

Steps:

1. *Both:* Bathe or shower, individually or together. Wear comfortable clothes or robes.

2. Decide who will first be the receiver and who will first be the pleasurer.

3. You may or may not use body lotion or oil. If using lotion, warm it in your hands first.

4. *Receiver:* Get comfortable in the selected chair or couch. Lie back and close your eyes. Breathe in deeply and exhale slowly several times, letting your body sink into the chair or couch as you do. (If your feet are ticklish, you may be highly responsive, thus making it difficult to receive the sensuous touch. Focusing intensely on the sensations you are feeling should help relieve the ticklishness and increase the pleasure.)

5. *Pleasurer:* With or without lotion, warm your hands. Start caressing your partner's foot. Get to know his or her foot through touch. Slowly explore the toes, arch, top of foot, ankle, and so on. If your touch is ticklish, try a firmer touch with the total palm of your hand. Maintain uninterrupted contact with the body part being caressed and inform your partner before you move to the next part. Caress one foot then the other. Next caress the hands, enjoying all surfaces and parts of each hand. Inform your partner when you are finished.

6. *Both:* Reverse roles and repeat steps 4 and 5.

You may want to repeat this experience at several different times in new settings. Change who begins the caress, and vary the location and the additions to the environment—music, fire in the fireplace, comforter, animal-skin rugs, candles, incense, lights on, dimmed, or off, and so on. When choosing accents for the setting, the *pleasurer* may choose the ingredients he or she would enjoy. This follows our basic attitude of pleasuring for one's own enjoyment. For example, if I'm going to pleasure my spouse and I like soft music, I will choose soft music unless I know my spouse finds it to be negative. In that case, I need to choose something that will enhance my involvement in the experience without being unpleasant for my spouse. When a couple's likes and dislikes are far apart, this takes a more loving effort.

Once the two of you feel free of demand and anxiety and can enjoy the foot and hand caress as both receiver and pleasurer, then you may want to move to the facial caress.

The purpose and guidelines for the facial caress are basically the same as for the foot and hand caress.

EXERCISE 9

Facial Caress
Steps:

1. *Both:* Bathe or shower individually or together. Hair should be clean, dry, and away from face. Man should be cleanly shaven.

2. *Together:* Reread underlying principles for foot and hand caress.

3. *Receiver:* (a) Position yourself comfortably on a bed or couch, with or without pillow, with your head near the unobstructed edge of the bed or couch. (b) Let yourself relax with eyes closed. Breathe in deeply and exhale slowly a few times, letting your body sink into the bed or couch.

4. *Pleasurer:* (a) Sit in a comfortable chair positioned for easy access to your partner's face. (b) Using a facial lotion or cream, close your eyes and focus on the sensation of touch as you explore your partner's face. Pleasure and explore as if you are a blind person getting to know your spouse through touch. Find eyebrows, eyes, all aspects of the nose,

cheeks, forehead, chin, lips. Gently, sensuously, and lovingly enjoy the warmth of your partner's face. Inform your partner when you finish.

5. *Both:* Reverse roles and repeat steps 3 and 4.

GIVING AND RECEIVING: WHEN THERE ARE BARRIERS

The barriers that usually surface in these early pleasuring experiences involve giving and receiving. Often it becomes clear that there are two givers and no receiver. Both partners have difficulty believing and feeling that they have the right to receive. It is difficult to let go, relax, and soak in the pleasure. It feels selfish and uncaring. Each imagines that the other is unable to enjoy the pleasuring process. One will think, *I know he's not enjoying himself.* Behind that thought is usually a feeling of low self-esteem: *He couldn't enjoy touching me.*

Sometimes one spouse can enjoy pleasuring and the other one receiving, but the opposite is not true. Then the giving is no longer a two-way proposition. The underlying principles we have proposed will not work as well in this situation. The one spouse may experience receiving more as a chore than as a delight, while the other experiences giving as the chore. If either giving or receiving is difficult for you, we would encourage you to practice the role that is most difficult. Go at it gradually. Talk about your difficulty with either receiving or giving. For the one who has difficulty pleasuring, performance anxiety could be getting in the way. He cannot focus on what feels good because he is so preoccupied with not measuring up—not doing it right—not being able to please a woman. Very often it *is* the man who has this difficulty. A man who has trouble pleasuring is often one who has grown up with a mother who continually expressed negative messages about the father. The son clearly learned that men are inadequate in making women happy.

The woman is probably the one having difficulty receiving. Usually this is a trust problem. She confirms the man's fears of inadequacy because she has learned, "You can't trust a man." She can pleasure him and enjoy his body since she is in control. To be in the receiving role raises all her anxieties about relying on someone else. The man's performance anxiety and the woman's inability to trust enough to receive will probably show up in other areas of the relationship, too. Therefore, besides practicing the roles that are most difficult for each of you, you need to watch for similar feelings popping up elsewhere in your lives. Awareness is a major starting place for breaking emotional barriers.

COMMUNICATING LIKES AND DISLIKES

After learning to touch and be touched for your own pleasure, a more complicated step is learning to incorporate the likes and dislikes of your partner. To pay attention to those likes and dislikes may feel like getting back to trying to please. That is why it is essential that you feel confident of your ability to give and receive pleasure for your own enjoyment before you move to this step. Then you can go after your own pleasure with an awareness of your partner's likes and dislikes. Often it will be more enjoyable to do something you know is particularly pleasing to your partner. If total-body caressing is delightful to your partner and positive for you, why not choose it even if there are activities you enjoy more? In this case, it is for your own pleasure that you might like to pursue the activity your partner enjoys most. *The motive is not trying to please, but rather mutual enjoyment.* As you become comfortable with pleasure for pleasure's sake, mutuality of expression will develop.

If you are going to incorporate each other's likes and dislikes into the pleasuring process, you need to talk about those likes and dislikes at a time separate from the pleasuring experience itself. Each of you probably has likes and dislikes you have never told the other. Using the instructions for positive verbal communication from Chapter 12, set aside a talk time. This talk time is just the beginning. Communicating sexual likes and dislikes is an ongoing process.

INSTRUCTING EACH OTHER IN POSITIVE TOUCHING

Nonverbal communication about what is pleasurable is another effective tool for learning each other's likes and dislikes. Nonverbal instruction does not carry the demand verbal instruction can sometimes impart.

Another step can be added to the facial caress to make it a nondemand instruction exercise. While the pleasurer is caressing the receiver's face, the receiver reaches up and gently, lovingly places his or her hands over the pleasurer's hands. (This must be an expected part of the experience so the pleasurer is not taken by surprise.) The pleasurer responds by relaxing his or her hands and letting the receiver guide them. The receiver then uses the pleasurer's hand to caress his or her own face. Another way of describing this step is that the receiver guides the pleasurer to demonstrate what kind of touch feels best. The pleasurer's task is to relax and get a sense of where and how the receiver likes to be touched. This can actually relieve anxiety for persons who are anxious about doing it right or who feel that the ways they touch are never right.

This experience may be followed by a more involved nondemand touching exercise that includes the whole front of the body.

▨ EXERCISE 10

Nondemand Touching

Step 1: Read these instructions together and clarify to each other what you are to do.

Step 2: Bathe or shower together in a way that brings relaxation and enjoyment of each other's bodies.

Step 3: The woman starts the actual experience by sitting in front of her husband in the nondemand position (see Figure 8). Then she places her hands over his hands and uses his hands to pleasure her face, breasts, abdomen, and genitals. The purpose of the exercise is for the wife to guide her husband's hands to demonstrate what kind of touch she really likes. The husband's job is to let his hand muscles be relaxed and limp, and to attend to the kind of touch he is being directed to give. He can learn what his partner really likes. This is a particularly good time for both to do a lot of experimenting and communicating about the kind of genital touch that brings pleasure. It is not likely to be an exciting or arousing experience, but more of a clinical and teaching time.

When the man guides the woman's hands to discover and teach the touch he enjoys on the upper front of his body, he may need to slide down and use a modified version of the upper diagram of the

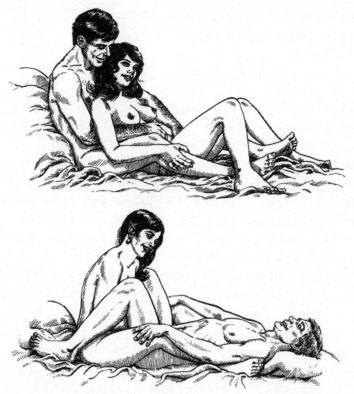

Figure 8: Nondemand Positions

nondemand position; for example, he may slide his head into his partner's lap. When the man is guiding the woman in pleasuring his lower body, especially the genitals, we encourage the use of the position shown in the lower diagram.

Step 4: Talk together about what you learned in this experience as well as in any other touching experiences you have always enjoyed, or that have always been painful or difficult for you.

Once you as a couple are comfortable with guiding each other's hands as a means of instruction, guiding hands can be interjected into any pleasuring, lovemaking time as a way of ongoing communication. When something feels particularly good you can guide your partner's hand to show that you would like more of the same. Your partner's hand can also be guided to communicate your need for readjustment of the touch when you are taking responsibility for your own pleasure as the receiver.

VARIETY IN SENSUOUS TOUCHING

When using hands as the pleasuring agent, it is important that the hands be free to communicate inner feelings. The hands become the instruments of loving, caring expression. For this to happen, there are some conditions that are helpful. It is better if nails are not rough or sharp so the receiving person doesn't have to worry about being jabbed. The pleasurer's hands feel best to the receiver when they are smooth, soft, and warm. Touch is most sensuous to both giver and receiver when the hands continuously touch the other's body. This unbroken contact provides a sense of continually being in touch with each other's vibrations. Men tend to touch in straight lines. Most women enjoy being touched in circles. If the man experiments with making the change from straight strokes to circular caress, the woman's pleasure may be greater.

The hands are not the only instruments through which we can sensuously enjoy each other's bodies. In fact, many couples find it most enlightening and exciting to vary the parts of the body used to enjoy each other. The forearms, lips, and breasts are particularly sensitive to touch for the pleasurer. Using one of these parts is a positive distraction for the person who has a difficult time pleasuring because of performance anxiety. The hair is a fun sensation for the receiver. Toes can add a spark. The tongue is very sensuous. Light stroking with fingernails is positive for some and negative for others.

A pleasuring exercise many couples find to be fun is one using no hands. All other parts of the body may be used. Try following the steps outlined below; you may find it challenging or hilarious.

▨ EXERCISE 11

No-Hands Pleasuring

Step 1: Together read these instructions and the underlying principles for the foot and hand caress. Tell each other what you understand the assignment to be.

Step 2: Bathe or shower together in a way that brings relaxation and enjoyment of each other's bodies.

Step 3: One of you start the actual pleasuring by following previous underlying principles for bodily pleasuring, *except* this time you may use any part of your body except your hands. Make it an experimental and fun time of discovering what parts of your body you really enjoy using to touch your partner. You might use your hair, nose, eyes, tongue, ears, forearms, breasts, genitals, feet, or whatever. When you have thoroughly enjoyed your partner's total body, reverse roles and your partner will pursue the discovery of using various parts of her or his body to pleasure you. Each of you stop when you feel you have thoroughly enjoyed your partner's total body. (A variation may be simultaneous enjoyment of giving and receiving.)

Step 4: Talk about the experience. What felt particularly good? What new things did you discover about yourself? About your partner? What got in the way of maximum enjoyment?

FLOWING WITH THE FEELINGS

Whatever part of the body you are enjoying, the key is to let yourself flow with your inner feelings. When we take a couple through a total body, general pleasuring experience (Chapter 28, Exercise 14), we encourage the pleasurer to start by placing his or her hands on the receiver's back. Rest there awhile. The pleasurer is to sense the warmth and vibrations of the other's back and begin to move in response to those feelings. Movement is best when it flows from within the person rather than being a mechanical exercise of making sure every inch of the receiver's back was touched.

You will learn sensuous touching as you are free to flow with the pleasure from your inner self, and as you are open to learning to touch in a way that is pleasurable to your partner. These two factors, plus the ability to allow variation and experimentation, can keep a relationship exciting for a lifetime.

14 SPECIAL TREATS THAT ADD PLEASURE

It was a warm summer day in California. John had been away on a business trip, and Michelle was anticipating his return. She felt herself getting aroused as she thought about being with him that evening. Yet the bedroom was hot and uncomfortable. In addition, she knew that she and John would need to spend some time getting back into each other's worlds after the time they had spent apart. How could she plan something enjoyable that would meet her sexual desire and yet respond to John and his probable need for unwinding from business pressures?

A creative plan emerged. Listening to her inner spark, she balanced it with the need to give John room and not push herself on him. She decided to prepare a simple, light but elegant candlelight dinner and to play their favorite music while they were relaxing and eating. These were treats she knew they would both enjoy.

What about the hot bedroom? Michelle decided to try a new setting that did not have any past demands or expectations. The family room was the coolest room in the house. How about a love pit? With cushions and comforters, she had a delightful time preparing a place where they could comfortably chat, touch, make love, or sleep. All were possible options.

In planning these special treats, Michelle was focused on mutual pleasure. It was not an anxious attempt to please, with insecurities about whether or not it would be received. On the contrary, the whole plan was an expression of her own sexuality that left room for John to enjoy what he could. She did not need him to be excited about what she had done, for she already felt fulfilled in her own creation. Therefore, her preparation did not come across as an anxiety-producing demand but rather a true expression of herself.

Unfortunately, we all are not always in touch with our own desires. Nor are we as secure in expressing them without making a demand to have them affirmed. Sometimes it is hard to be sensitive in allowing space for our spouse. Michelle's efforts provide a beautiful example of the way special treats can be developed to add to pleasure. In addition to learning to enjoy pleasuring and receiving, there are little extras that make a difference. Three extras we have found enhancing to general pleasuring are setting the atmosphere, sharing sensuous surprises, and expressing thoughtfulness.

SETTING THE ATMOSPHERE

When we think about setting the atmosphere, the old wedding cliché comes to mind: "something old, something new, something borrowed, something blue."

"Something Old"

A sense of warmth is expressed by including in the pleasuring setup some feature that has a positive history for both of you. For example, we light a candle by the bed when we are anticipating getting together for sexual pleasure. This has positive associations for both of us. Also, we use the candle to symbolically communicate with each other that we desire sexual contact.

Providing what we already know is positive makes a great start. For the two of you it might be a special sheet or blanket, a flower, music, a fire in the fireplace, oil or lotion, or perfume. There are unlimited possibilities.

"Something New"

If everything about the experience is old and familiar, regular repetition of that atmosphere will soon cause it to lose its spark.

Experimenting with new places, positions, methods of stimulation, or accouterments adds excitement. If you are not used to adding newness to your sex life, it may be difficult to start. You may feel awkward and your spouse may wonder what has happened to you. We suggest starting with a planned experience. You might find the steps of the following exercise helpful.

▦ EXERCISE 12
Creative Pleasuring

Step 1: Together read these instructions and the "Underlying principles" section in Exercise 8, Chapter 13. Tell each other what you understand the assignment to be.

Step 2: Bathe or shower together in a way that brings relaxation and enjoyment of each other's bodies.

Step 3: Each of you bring to the experience one or more items to use to pleasure your partner. Think of things that would feel pleasing and sensuous against the skin (a piece of fabric, fur, silk, hair, brush, feather, and so on). Let these items be a surprise.

Step 4: One of you start the actual pleasuring by having your partner lie on his or her abdomen. Gently stroke his or her back with the accouterment you chose for this event. If you and your partner both enjoy the feeling of the item you chose, continue pleasuring his or her entire body. When you feel finished, reverse roles. The other partner now does the same thing with the accouterment he or she chose. Each one should stop when you have thoroughly enjoyed your partner's total body.

Step 5: Talk about the experience. What did you enjoy? What would you have liked more of? What other kind of object could you imagine enjoying? What did you learn?

Another way you might vary this exercise is by taking turns setting the atmosphere. For each spouse's turn, that person would be responsible to add something new and sensuous to your lovemaking setup.

"Something Borrowed"

This phrase reminds us of an attitude of openness to ideas from others. This may come from talking with a friend, reading a book, or attending a class. Through some outside exposure, you acquire information that can be incorporated into your lovemaking experience. The borrowed idea enhances your situation.

"Something Blue"

The blue garter at a wedding speaks of tradition. Creating traditions that are special for the two of you provides continuity and invites anticipation. Sometimes traditions for a sexual setting are incorporated as part of a special event such as an anniversary. Perhaps the husband always buys roses for his wife, or they always go out for an extra-nice dinner. These are fun, familiar experiences that may enhance your sexual encounters.

If you are the one planning the setting for your next time together, think through these four areas—"something old, something new, something borrowed, something blue." It can provide a framework for creativity.

PLANNED SURPRISES

The entire event Michelle planned in anticipation of John's homecoming was a surprise to John. Planned surprises are often more fun for the doer than for the receiver. The person who is managing the surprise has time to get into the details of the event. He or she also enjoys all the positive feelings of anticipation. The person to be surprised misses the fun of preparation and anticipation, and may not feel ready when the surprise comes. Nonetheless, the right kind of surprise can be a pleasure.

To be sensuous, a surprise does not have to include physical touching. You may want to plan a hike in the mountains, a barefoot walk on the beach, a drive through the country, an afternoon at a cultural event, an evening at the movies, a special dinner. There are many sensuous, nontouching events that promote intimacy and arousal for many couples. It can add a new zing to your relationship to plan such an event as a total surprise for your spouse. Perhaps there is some activity you've really been wishing the two of you could do together. For some reason, you have not done anything about it. Maybe you're expecting your spouse to take responsibility for the plans. Why not take charge and make the arrangements yourself? Turn it from, "I wish he would think of things like that," or "I wonder why she isn't making those plans?" to, "If it's something I'd like to have happen, why don't I plan it as a surprise?"

Just as sensuous events are fun to plan as surprises for each other, so are total sexual experiences. Occasionally it is refreshing for one spouse to take over the entire plan for a time together. For example, say Thursday evening next week is an evening set aside for the two of you. Let your spouse know that you will be in charge. Then plan creatively. Think of setting the atmosphere as we just outlined. You might also become creative in what you do with each other. If your sexual relationship has been limited to intercourse experiences, you might enjoy planning some time for the two of you to be together in an atmosphere that's conducive to chatting and being affectionate without the necessity of intercourse. Make the entire plan an expression of yourself that takes into account your spouse's likes and dislikes.

If you don't have the energy or interest to plan a total experience surprise, you might consider adding one small surprise to an already planned or anticipated experience. This could be something creative to pleasure with, some sensuous addition to the atmosphere, or a new activity focus. Maybe you both have been wanting a new bedspread. If you both are clear on what the other likes, one of you could buy it and save it for a surprise.

SPONTANEOUS SURPRISES

Spontaneous surprises also add excitement. Spontaneity grows out of being aware of one's own inner sexual desire and being in tune with each other. A fun surprise we enjoy giving each other is to go to bed nude. We usually wear bedclothes at night, so it is a delightful surprise to find a warm, nude body in the bed. Spontaneous surprises that grow out of the moment give the other person the message that you are desiring him or her—that you are excited about your relationship.

THOUGHTFULNESS THAT COMMUNICATES CARE

Thoughtful expressions have much the same effect as planned or spontaneous surprises. For many individuals, it is important that their partners show they care enough to prepare their bodies. This might involve shaving the face for the man or the legs for the woman. It usually includes having a clean, fresh-smelling body. What is important varies greatly from person to person. This is a sensitive area in which people often do not feel free to communicate their needs.

One woman found herself sexually repulsed by her husband. They always made love in the evening. His work caused him to perspire profusely, and he did not like to shower after work. To her, he was smelly and uncomfortable to touch. He felt her avoidance of him but never knew what it was about. The communication process took some hard work. He was not very open to changing his ways. He saw her as fussy, and she saw him as stubborn and uncaring.

Sometimes just talking about the problem eliminates it as a barrier. Other situations may require more investment in the problem. Usually a person is happy to do whatever is needed to correct a negative odor or to prepare in a way that is important to one's partner.

Another exercise of thoughtfulness involves having supplies ready for a spontaneous or previously planned sexual encounter. This might include birth-control devices, tissue, lubricants, a pillow, or special sheets. Some couples have prepared a lovemaking kit. Either this kit is stored where it is easily accessible or both partners share the responsibility of remembering to bring it to their together times.

Preparing the setting is an expression of thoughtfulness even when it is not done as a surprise. Just the idea of taking time to turn on the electric blanket, warm the room, lock the door, dim the lights, or clean the bedroom is an expression of caring. The sexual relationship between you and your spouse is important and special to you.

Treating yourself and each other adds to sexual pleasure as long as treats do not become demands. Plan a treat because you enjoy doing it, not because you expect a response. Otherwise, you will develop anxiety and tension that detract from rather than add to your pleasure. Treats can also get in the way if you start expecting or demanding that your partner provide them. Keeping score also destroys the pleasure: "I surprised her last time. It's her turn now." Keep it fun, free, and an expression of *your* sensuousness.

15 STIMULATING

I know how I'm supposed to be able to turn her on, but she's different. She doesn't work like the books said she would.

STIMULATING VS. PLEASURING

Why a chapter on pleasuring and one on stimulating? What is the difference? Pleasure may or may not be stimulating. Sexual arousal and stimulation *may* occur in response to pleasurable touch, but they may *not*. Sexual stimulation should be pleasurable, but that is not necessarily the case. The extreme situation is rape. A woman who is raped may actually experience physical sexual stimulation, but her feelings are of fear and pain rather than of pleasure.

CREATIVE VARIETY VS. MECHANICAL MONOTONY

The mechanical approach to stimulation carries with it several myths. The three-push-button approach assumes that the man is responsible to produce a response in his wife. If the man pushes the right buttons in the correct order, he will turn on a woman. The myth is that if he kisses her, fondles her breasts, and rubs the clitoris, she'll be ready to go.

The manual we studied before our marriage in 1963 described it this way:

> The husband must always delay and control his impatient desire, until he has carried his wife through an adequate period of preparation . . . The most complete response is likely to be evoked if caresses follow a definite sequence, beginning with the lips and neck, then the breasts and finally the sex organs, but women differ and the husband must learn the preferences of his wife instead of relying on theory.[1]

Mechanical prescriptions for stimulation lead to monotony. Positive sexual stimulation is most likely to occur when two people are free to enjoy each other's bodies with creativity and variety. Any part of the body is responsive to sexual stimulation. Rubbing each other's skin anywhere can be a turnon. Indeed, a change is often more intensely erotic because it is a new sensation. There is no one standard for what will work. The door needs to be wide open to new discoveries.

INDIVIDUALITY VS. PREDICTABILITY

Creative variety forces us to recognize and allow for individual differences. This includes differences between men and women, from one woman to another, from one man to another, in the same person from one experience to another, and from time to time within the same experience. "Doing it" the same way every time does not account for individual variation. That is why a mechanical routine soon gets boring.

Let's talk about allowing differences from one person to another. Just because a certain kind of touch is stimulating to you does not ensure the same will be true for your spouse. Each person needs to be his or her own authority on what is pleasurable or stimulating. That is why it works best for each person to go after his or her own desire. It takes the guesswork out of the experience.

Another way we can get ourselves in trouble and not allow individuality is by imposing lessons learned in a previous situation on our spouses. If you were sexually involved with someone before your spouse, it is easy to expect the same response. Many couples have had difficulty resolving their sexual tensions because they imposed such expectations on their current situation.

The scenario may go something like this: The woman had been involved sexually as a teenager. Those sexual experiences were exciting and full of vitality. Her partners were usually somewhat older men who swept her off her feet and turned her on. After that she became a Christian. Guilt about her past experiences and her current intense sexual desire plagued her. She resolved never to be promiscuous again—or even to be sexual. By that decision, she chose to turn off her sexual feelings. Then she chose a husband of deep faith. He was most unlike her lovers of the past, yet she expected him to display the kind of charming and aggressive traits he would never possess. She also expected in herself (a now turned-off person) the same responsiveness she had experienced before. Not surprisingly, she was disappointed! It took a time of intensive work in therapy to free her God-given potential so that she was again able to be responsive, this time to her husband.

In another case, a man remarried after his first marriage ended. His first wife was quickly aroused and intensely orgasmic. His second wife had experienced sexual trauma as a child and so could not allow herself to freely respond orgasmically. She experienced a great deal of conflict about her sexual responsiveness. Though she would become intensely aroused, she fought the arousal and therefore showed strain and frustration. The man read this as a message about her feelings for him. He had difficulty comprehending how orgasm could be difficult for his second wife when it had been so easy for his first wife.

Besides respecting differences from one person to another, it is important to expect that the same person will change from one experience to another. This is reported more frequently by women than by men. Generally, men report feeling more consistent about what they find stimulating. Women tell us that one time kissing may be highly arousing and the next time they do not even want their lips touched. For the man who believes it is his responsibility to turn on and please his wife, this can be very frustrating. Just about the time he thinks he has figured her out, she changes. This is another example of why it works best for each person to take responsibility to recognize and go after his or her own pleasure. When a woman is very changeable, the only way she and her spouse can experience freedom and relaxation in lovemaking is for her to take responsibility for what she needs. There is no way her husband will be able to decide for her what is going to be stimulating.

This is true, too, for changes that occur within the same sexual event. Again, women seem to be more changeable than men. Hormonal fluctuations and the complexity of how women are designed affect these fluctuations.

A common dissatisfaction women report is that the man will find a responsive spot and stick with it "until he wears it thin." This approach of finding the correct button does not allow for change.

How might the two of you develop a system that allows individuality and variation? The most effective guidelines we can give are in the chapter on pleasuring. It is particularly important to learn the two-way system. That is, each person takes the responsibility to go after his or her own needs for stimulation; and each person takes the responsibility to communicate in some way when he or she wants a particular activity changed. If you learn some nonverbal communication signals (see Chapter 12), you will probably have a flexible system. The nondemand exercise in the nondemand position is an effective way to learn for yourself and to communicate to your partner what is stimulating for you. In this experience, you guide the other person's hands to teach what feels good to you. Even though what you have communicated may vary from time to time, you can learn some basic awareness of each other's tendencies. Then, the same guiding of hands can be incorporated into your sexual stimulation as a way to communicate your changing desire.

STIMULATING TOUCH VS. IRRITATING TOUCH

Touch has the greatest potential for eliciting sexual stimulation when the person doing the touching is relaxed and enjoying the other person's body. The less anxiety and stress, the more likely it is that stimulation will occur.

Anxiety and tension are communicated in the vibrations we send through sexual touching. This can cause the touch to feel irritating.

Also, individual differences in how people touch can affect one's touch perception. For example, if you get most aroused with a firm touch, you are likely to touch your spouse firmly. Your spouse may actually be much more responsive to a light touch. Unless you have talked about this and done some nondemand instructing, each of you may find the other's touch to be irritating rather than stimulating. Too much or too little pressure can make a major difference in your response to being touched. Guiding your partner with your own hand to adjust the touch to meet your needs is an effective means of ongoing flexibility (Chapter 13, Exercise 10).

When stroking and caressing flow, they are more likely to be arousing than when abrupt and jerky. Abruptness usually is indicative of discomfort in the pleasurer. Maintaining continuous contact with the other person's skin helps counteract the tendency for abruptness and promotes a flowing touch. For example, even when the pleasurer is obtaining additional lotion, it helps to keep one hand on the partner's body.

Lubricants can add to the stimulating quality of the touch. This is true for general pleasuring of the whole body as well as for genital caressing. Putting a lotion on your hand before stimulating your partner's genitals can be a great feeling for both of you. For men, it feels most like being in the vagina and is very arousing. For the women, it reduces irritations and can add greatly to arousal. The only persons we have found for whom the use of lubricants is not a positive experience are men and women who do not like messes. For them natural genital secretions have been negative, so to add a lubricant that feels similar to these natural juices is a turnoff. We encourage such people to work to desensitize this negative response because it interferes with their sexual pleasure—not just with the positive use of a lubricant.

Certain types of problems with giving and receiving touch are more deeply based, such as forceful, controlling touch and ticklishness.

Forceful, controlling touch is often used by a person who needs to dominate or who is angry. In either case, the person may be too passive to express the need directly. Therefore, it comes out in the way he or she touches during sexual play. The partner often experiences the touch as smothering and as limiting his or her own sexual expression.

Ticklishness is thought to be indicative of intense erotic responsiveness that is blocked. In other words, the extremely ticklish person feels the partner's touch intensely, but instead of perceiving the touch as arousing, the erotic feeling is blocked and the ticklish feeling is substituted.

Jeff had this difficulty. He and his wife came to us because of his impotence. We discovered that during the foot caress his ticklishness interfered with the pleasure of the caress. We had him focus intensely on the sensation of the feeling, at the same time being aware that he was not allowing himself to take in the sensuous touch. With practice, he was able to allow himself incredibly sensuous responses to foot caresses. The same thing surfaced as Jeff and his wife, Susan, went through the nondemand instruction for positive genital stimulation. We learned that Susan had stopped touching Jeff's penis years before. There was no way she could provide him positive genital stimulation without tickling. No wonder he was unable to get an erection! First we worked through some emotional barriers that had never allowed him to feel anything intensely. Then the couple practiced some experiences that allowed Jeff to focus on and receive sensuous stimulation. As anxiety about erections was reduced and stimuli received, erections became a regular response.

Kissing

Kissing is a part of stimulating touch that is often not addressed. We have been surprised to find individuals and couples who have never kissed passionately. Their kissing would not be considered stimulating; it is a friendship peck. It has been a challenging experience to teach couples how to kiss! When a couple has stopped kissing passionately or has never used tongue, teeth, or enjoyed full-mouth kissing, it is difficult to explain with words how to *really* kiss. It has been fun and rewarding for us to help a couple find a whole new area of sexual stimulation—their mouths.

If one or both of you have difficulty with passionate kissing, talk with each other about what you would like to discover and then start experimenting. At first it may feel rather awkward, but stick with it. Start by teasing with your tongue against your spouse's lips, then tongue against teeth, and finally tongue to tongue. Eventually the whole mouth can get into the act. Once the passion and arousal are experienced, allow further mouth involvement to flow spontaneously.

EXAGGERATING VS. WITHHOLDING
NATURAL BODY RESPONSES

When we sense that our bodies are becoming sexually stimulated, we can react in two ways: We can let ourselves take in the stimulation and respond, or we can tighten up and prevent the stimulation from naturally accelerating.

For the person who has had some difficulty embracing his or her body's responses, there is a need to exaggerate positive sensations. This is done to counteract years of conditioning that taught the person to withhold natural sexual responses.

Start by listening to your body. This is not an evaluation of your body—not standing outside yourself and checking your responses. Rather, listening to your body means getting with your inner self—going with your good feelings, focusing on the good sensations of touch. Sometimes this includes moving in a rhythmic pattern. The rhythmic pattern might be a response to vaginal or penile throbbing. It may be a response to your clitoris wanting rhythmic pressure or your penis wanting rhythmic stroking. If you are aware of your inner desire for such a rhythmic experience, become active in setting the rhythm in motion. Exaggerate the natural desire of your body by acting intensely in response to it.

The same thing can be true with breathing. A number of women who have had difficulty responding orgasmically have discovered that they stop their natural exaggerated breathing when they get highly aroused. Deeper and more rapid breathing is a natural bodily response to sexual stimulation (Chapter 8, pages 86–89). When we cut off our bodily responses, we inhibit the potential for release. So if you find your breathing intensifying, breathe even harder.

Noise can also be exaggerated or withheld. Sometimes external conditions hinder your freedom to let out all the sounds you feel like expressing. The most common inhibitor is the presence of children in a nearby room. This is a realistic interference. If it causes conflict for you, try to find some times away from children when you can both really let loose.

Another natural response to stimulation is to move our bodies toward stimulating contact. Often this means pushing one's pelvis toward some point of stimulation. Listen to yourself on this, too. If you notice yourself pulling away from points of contact, consciously attempt to reverse that withholding pattern by actively moving your genitals toward positive sexual stimulation.

The more we can open up and allow ourselves to take in and respond to stimulation, the more responsive we will become. It is important to get with our bodies, to enjoy God's creation in us, and to freely celebrate our sexuality within our marriage.

16 BY INVITATION ONLY

I don't understand why my wife gets so upset. I always check to make sure she's wet, yet she says I enter her whether she's ready or not. I'm confused.

WHEN?

Somewhere in the process of sexual stimulation, entry is likely to occur. The act of entry is what changes a sexual experience from sexual play to sexual intercourse. However, entry is not necessary for sexual enjoyment and release. For many couples, entry is not an automatic part of every sexual experience. When entry is not possible—in cases of prolonged impotence for the man or vaginismus for the woman—couples can learn to have totally satisfying sexual play without a full intercourse event. (Vaginismus is a painful contraction or spasm of the vagina.) There are some advantages to sexual play without intercourse. All of us would benefit from learning to totally enjoy the pleasure of each other's bodies.

When entry is possible, it should occur when both partners feel ready and desirous of having the penis in the vagina. Entry is likely to be desired when there is intense sexual stimulation for the man and the woman.

There is no one correct time for entry. The only physical criteria are vaginal lubrication for the woman and an erect penis for the man. Even these are not entirely necessary in that a man and woman can learn to stuff a slightly erect penis into the vagina. A lubricant can be used to substitute for or add to vaginal lubrication. So the right time is your time.

The physical signs of readiness do not always ensure emotional readiness. The man might desire love play for quite some time after he has a full erection. Women often do not feel ready even though they have plenty of lubrication. If a woman is feeling tense, she will not be desiring entry. This may be demonstrated by stiff legs or a withdrawing from sexual stimulation rather than reaching for it.

The woman needs the man to back off when her body is ready but her feelings are not. She needs room to allow her feelings to catch up with her body's response. This can happen only if she is free of the demand to be ready.

When the feeling of readiness is there, the woman knows it! It might be described as the opening up of the vagina, as well as a relaxed spreading of her legs. There are actual physical changes occurring during the plateau phase (Chapter 8, page 87) that correspond to this opening sensation. The labia majora (outer lips) have thinned and are folded back out of the way of the vaginal opening. The swollen inner lips gap widely to create a funnel into the vagina. A woman is only minutes away from an orgasmic release when she is experiencing the sensations of these changes in her genitalia. She may or may not pursue entry at this time. It is her decision. The woman is the only one who can decide when she is ready.

WHY ENTRY BY INVITATION?

We all have a sense of territory. All of us feel somewhat protective and possessive of our space. Children go through a time starting somewhere around age ten when they feel extremely violated if a brother, sister, or even their father or mother enters their room uninvited. When we are in our bedroom or bathroom with the door closed, we request that our children knock and wait for a response before entering. We give them the same courtesy. This is what it means to respect each other's territory.

Entry is an act of the man entering the woman's body. If he is going to feel welcome there, she has to let him know when she is ready. All of us feel much more comfortable when we *invite* someone into our space. This is true of our homes, our rooms, our feelings, and our bodies.

The invitation need not be formal. It might be a nonverbal message that communicates positively for both of you. That might be the woman reaching for the penis with her pelvis or inserting the penis in the vagina. It might be a pet word the two of you enjoy. There are many possible ways the woman can let the man know she is ready.

WHY THE WOMAN?

It is the woman's body that is being entered. Since she can easily experience a sense of invasion, both the husband and the wife will be more relaxed about entry when the woman assumes the responsibility to guide the timing of entry. A man will feel best about being in the woman when he senses her warm and desirous wish for entry.

WHAT ABOUT BIBLICAL SYMBOLISM?

In the early church, Christ's relation to the church was compared to the sexual relationship between a husband and wife. In Ephesians 5, Paul instructs the husband to love his wife as he does his own body, even as Christ loved the church.

Christ offers himself to us. He is ready to enter our lives and guide us to the extent that we, his people, will ask him to be there with us and for us. Christ does not invade. He gives, loves, cares, and waits to be invited. What a beautiful model of entry by invitation.

AFTER ENTRY?

Is entry the beginning of the end? No, entry is not a final event. Much love play can occur after the penis has entered the vagina. The penis can be withdrawn for more total-body play. Then reentry can occur. When the couple are having fun together, the focus can be on total enjoyment. The mentality does not have to focus on entry and thrusting to the point of ejaculation and orgasm.

During an extended lovemaking experience with focus on the enjoyment of the process, a person's level of arousal may vary in intensity. The level of arousal will tend to be experienced in waves. As long as the person isn't standing back watching and evaluating arousal, it is fun to ride the waves. However, if a person is in an evaluative role, a dip may cause anxiety that interferes with the possibility of another intense surge. It is the *anxiety* about the dips, not the dips themselves, that gets in the way of continued responsiveness.

The freedom to enter, withdraw, and reenter will also help a man last longer. This allows him to have dips in excitement level so he doesn't ejaculate before he is ready.

Flexibility and freedom add fun to sexual encounter. Let entry also be a fun part of the total sexual event. This can best happen when you communicate your own feelings of readiness, respect each other's feelings and territory, and focus on the process rather than on a specific intercourse goal.

17 LETTING GO

I think I have orgasms, but I'm not sure. What does an orgasm feel like? My husband doesn't think I've ever had one.

So maybe you've never had an orgasm, you're not sure if you've been orgasmic, you haven't been able to have an orgasm in some way that you wish you could, or you used to be orgasmic but now you aren't. Or maybe, as a man, your orgasm comes too quickly. You are confused about what is really going on in your body.

WHAT HAPPENS FOR WOMEN

Because what happens for a woman during an orgasm is so internal, there has been much confusion about the woman's orgasm. Women have more difficulty allowing release than men. This, too, has caused more focus on the woman's orgasm than on the man's.

You know if you have had an orgasm by understanding what happens during an orgasm. An orgasm is a reflex response that is triggered when there is enough buildup of sexual tension from effective stimulation and the freedom to pursue it without inhibition or fear of being out of control. Arousal builds to a certain intensity, causing engorgement or a building of sexual tension in the genitals, specifically, but generally throughout the entire body. This engorgement triggers the reflex of the orgasm.

An example of a reflex response is the jerk of your foot when the doctor taps your knee with a rubber hammer. The tap (the sensory input) occurs at one point of the body, the knee. The jerk (the muscular response) occurs at another point of the body, the lower leg. Similarly, the clitoris, breasts, inner thighs, vaginal wall, or other parts of the body may be stimulated (the sensory input), and the vaginal muscles and uterus contract (the muscular response).

Our sexual arousal and release (orgasm) are controlled by our involuntary or autonomic nervous system. *Arousal*, getting turned-on or sexually excited, is controlled by the passive branch of our involuntary nervous system. Arousal happens early in sexual play, in our sleep, and even throughout the day. Nipple erections and vaginal lubrications are indications of arousal. To get aroused, we have to be relaxed and soaking in pleasure, because the passive or relaxed branch of our involuntary nervous system has to be dominant. However, orgasm is controlled by the *active* branch of the involuntary nervous system. As arousal builds to the point where we are just about to go over the hill, our body shifts from parasympathetic (relaxed) nervous system dominance to sympathetic (active) nervous system dominance. So to have an orgasm, we have to get active and go for it. Many women who struggle to be orgasmic tend to remain passive during their sexual experiences, so they don't help their bodies make the shift from the passive to the active nervous system control.

Even though we cannot will an orgasm, it is possible to encourage it or resist it. We can condition our responses.

Involuntary sexual responses are similar to falling asleep. For example, I had difficulty sleeping as an infant, so my parents would take me for a ride in the car to get me to sleep. Even today, I tend to fall asleep when riding in a car. Likewise, if as a child or young adolescent you learned to block intense sexual feelings that would have moved you toward orgasm, you will as an adult continue to unknowingly stop your arousal before it leads to orgasm. Or if you innocently ran across pornography or had your first orgasm in response to a negative stimulus, you may now have to picture that same stimulus in order to have an orgasm. You are left in a lose-lose dilemma: to have an orgasm and feel guilty about the pictures in your mind or not to have an orgasm and feel sexually unsatisfied. Or you may have learned to be orgasmic by rocking on your pillow to help you fall asleep as a child and now you have no clue how to transfer that form of stimulation into sex with your husband. Fortunately, even if we have learned to respond or not to respond in a certain way, we can retrain our bodies to respond differently.

The woman's orgasm begins with an initial spasm (the muscle response) in the orgasmic platform (the lower third of the vagina) accompanied by an intense, genitally centered sensual awareness that occurs two to four seconds before the actual orgasm. This sensation is comparable to the man's warning that he is about to have an orgasm. This is the point at which many women stop their orgasmic response or feel that they're stuck and can't get over the hill.

The intense, genitally centered pelvic awareness associated with the initial spasms of the woman's orgasm is followed by a flow of warmth spreading from the pelvis to the rest of her body. This sequence is just the opposite of what men describe as happening to them. We might picture the difference with a diagram:

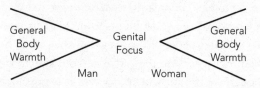

The flow of warmth for the man starts with the general pleasure and flows to the genitals. The woman's release might look like the following diagram:

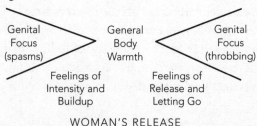

WOMAN'S RELEASE

One woman describes her feelings of letting go: "It is beautiful! It's as though my being withdraws from my extremities and is compacted in the clitoris. Everything recedes—there is nothing but this intense buildup of pleasure—nothing else exists. Then there is this tremendous explosive release that radiates outward in waves. I breathe in rhythm with the waves and my muscles contract . . ."

When our oldest daughter was twelve years old, we attended a sex education program with her. Following the class for parents and their junior highers, we talked with her about what she had learned. She explained what she had learned from the evening and then asked a question: "When the doctor was answering our questions, he used regular language except for answering the questions about masturbation and 'organism'—or whatever you call that. Then he changed to using big words I couldn't understand." She wanted to know what those words *really* meant. We went on to explain and then had her feed back to us what she understood. Her description of an orgasm was delightful and may help you.

"You get all good feelings down here (holding her hands on her pelvis). Then you get all jazzed (panting). Then you let it all out (sigh), and then you just sit there feeling good all over."

What better way could there be to describe it!

WHAT HAPPENS FOR MEN

For most men the orgasmic response is rather obvious because of the ejaculation of seminal fluid. The orgasm is an external happening. There are also internal feelings that accompany the obvious external release.

When we took you through the physiological responses of the sexual experience, we talked about the male orgasm having two stages. The first stage occurs between the time of warning that the man is approaching the point of no return and the point of ejaculatory inevitability (see Sexual Response Pattern graph, Chapter 8). The second phase starts with the point of ejaculatory inevitability or the actual point of no return. Each stage for the man has distinctive physical sensations. There are anticipatory tingling sensations that warn the man he is approaching the point of no return. These might be described as pleasurable burning sensations. There is the sense of wanting those feelings to last forever, and yet the urge to rush on with intense thrusting. Along with this, there is a feeling that warmth from the total body is being drawn into the genitals; the sensation becomes primarily genitally centered. As the man moves from this first stage to the second stage, he experiences a momentary sensation of being held in suspension. This is followed by the letting go—the rush of the ejaculation and a warm, flowing feeling inside the penis.

WHEN DOES IT HAPPEN?

Letting go can be allowed during love play before entry, after entry with the penis in the vagina, or after withdrawal of the penis from the vagina. Let us talk about each of these possibilities.

People's responses to release before entry vary. Sometimes both spouses desire it. Perhaps intercourse has become a demand. Entry is associated with many negative feelings. One means of relieving those pressures is for the couple to become comfortable with letting go without entry.

Some women find they are freer to respond before entry. Once entry occurs, they feel more demand. Or they might start to worry that their husbands will ejaculate before they have a chance to let go. These feelings interfere with their natural sexual responses. They soon develop a style of being unable to let go when the penis is in the vagina, so release before entry can be a valuable alternative.

On the other hand, when a man accidentally experiences release before entry, he usually feels like a failure and leaves his partner frustrated. Neither one of them planned for him to "come" that quickly. This is called premature ejaculation. We will deal thoroughly with this dilemma in Chapter 28.

The source of stimulation (the sensory input or knee tap) for the release that occurs before entry can vary. It may be manual stimulation around the clitoris for the woman and on the shaft of the penis for the man. There could be oral-genital contact—the woman sucking or licking the man's penis or the man using his mouth and tongue around the woman's clitoris and into the vagina. There might be a release during general body and/or breast caressing. Or there may be no direct physical stimulation. Some women experience orgasms while reading romance novels. Some men ejaculate in response to visual input. Sometimes men ejaculate and women have orgasms during their sleep. Therefore, letting go before entry has many possible sources of origin.

Letting go after entry with the penis in the vagina has traditionally been accepted as the ideal time. Indeed, many couples prefer this. The woman may enjoy the feeling of the man's penis in her vagina during the contractions of her orgasm. However, when a man insists that both his and his wife's release happen during intercourse, this demand is usually associated with false expectations and concerns about his masculinity. He may believe that a "real man" brings his wife to orgasm during intercourse. But for the woman who has difficulty letting go when the penis is in the vagina, this belief puts incredible pressure on her. It lays on her the responsibility to have an orgasm at a certain time so he can feel good about himself. This is a sure way to prevent her from freely letting go when having intercourse. This is true whether the demand is, in fact, imposed on her from her husband or is felt from within herself.

A question often asked is, "Doesn't an orgasm during intercourse feel different from an orgasm as a result of external stimulation?" We talked about the fact that there is no physical difference between orgasms (see the Vaginal vs. Clitoral Orgasm section in Chapter 8). In terms of what happens to the body, an orgasm is an orgasm. Women do report differences in feeling, however.

Many women talk about an orgasm from external stimulation as being more intense but not as emotionally satisfying. There are possible explanations for each of these differences. As we understand it, the vaginal contractions during an orgasm are more intense when there is no penis in the vagina. The muscle has nothing to restrict its contractions. Therefore, its range of expansion and contraction is greater, yet the lack of emotional satisfaction may relate to the empty feeling connected with a woman's sensation of readiness for entry that we described in Chapter 16. When the outer lips are out of the way and the inner lips are engorged and have formed a funnel into the vagina, many women experience an intense desire to have their husbands inside them, rather than to move to orgasm. Having an orgasm before entry leaves the emotional urge for entry unfulfilled.

Even after intercourse, a woman may want more sexual stimulation, perhaps because her husband does not have control of ejaculation. He cannot remain in the vagina long enough without ejaculating for her to let go of her built-up sexual excitement. This may be true whether or not she has had a previous release. If she had an orgasm before entry and became rearoused during intercourse, she may need to let go again. Or maybe she did not have a release before entry, she could not have one during, and so this is the first time in the experience that she is ready to pursue an orgasm.

For the man who has already ejaculated, the woman's need for continued stimulation after intercourse may be experienced as a demand. He is so relaxed, it is difficult for him to summon the energy to pursue his wife's body. The tendency is for him to fall asleep. This is a natural reaction. If this is a regular conflict for the two of you, talk about it at some time when you are not engaged in sexual activity. Explore all possible ways for the woman to get satisfaction without that being a demand for the man. Maybe learning ejaculatory control is the answer. Maybe she can be fulfilled with her husband's body close to her, his arms around her, and his hand available for her to use to bring herself a release. You might decide that you will take turns having sex his way sometimes and her way other times. Discover your own options to resolve your differences.

It is important to mention that some men experience retarded or inhibited ejaculation. Sometimes this can occur after drinking alcoholic beverages. Or it can happen when a man is very tired. A small percentage of men need a long time to be able to let go. If there has been extended thrusting with the penis in the vagina, the woman may be getting tired and sore so she needs the man to withdraw. He may still want a release. Sometimes manual or oral stimulation may be used to bring about his release. If this is not possible and the pattern continues, professional help is necessary.

If withdrawing to ejaculate is being used as a means of birth control, we would say, forget it. As we mentioned in describing the four phases of the sexual response (Chapter 8), some seminal fluid with sperm will often be secreted before the total ejaculate is expelled. These sperm can impregnate the woman just as easily as the sperm in the remaining ejaculate.

HOW MANY?

What are the possibilities for letting go? Men are usually limited to one release per experience. This is due to their need to have a rest period of at least twenty to thirty minutes (probably more like several hours) before they can become rearoused.

Men who experience release without ejaculation are an exception to this pattern. They report being able to maintain their erections after release and continue lovemaking with repeated releases.

Women are different from most men in this regard. Physically, women have the potential for many orgasms within one event. These may occur in rapid sequence without any relaxation of sexual excitement. They may also occur after a brief letdown followed by more stimulation.

It is important to recognize that although repeated orgasms are a physical potential for women, this should not be the goal. When orgasms become a goal rather than a reflex response, they are less likely to happen.

This same principle applies to couples who desire simultaneous orgasms. By that we mean the husband and wife letting go at the same time. Even though it is a delightful experience if your sexual activity can flow that way, simultaneous orgasms are far from necessary for a fully satisfying sexual relationship. They must remain an exciting option and not become a demanding goal.

Letting go is an important feeling in the whole sexual process.

It is the most individual aspect and the part of sex when the partners are least aware of being together. A person becomes totally caught up in his or her own being. It reminds us of soaring. Letting go requires being able to take a risk—to let yourself be totally you in the presence of another person.

We started skiing in our mid-thirties. When we skied downhill for the first time, Joyce's experience was similar to the sensation of an orgasm. "There was one moment that particularly captured that 'letting go' experience for me. I was at the top of one big, rolling hill with a flat area below and then an incline beginning another hill. There was a feeling of building excitement as I got my skis parallel and flat, flexed my knees and pushed off with my poles, ready to let my skis take me as fast as the momentum could build on the decline. The ride down was a beautiful, risky feeling of flying through the air, totally letting out all the stops. The flat place felt like soaring across open territory. I had already taken the risk, but there was still more speed to enjoy. The incline felt like the satisfied sigh; I made it and it felt good."

What experiences have you had in life where you have risked, soared, and had the satisfaction of releasing yourself to that situation? Capture these. Enjoy them. And, hopefully, have many such experiences with each other during sex.

18 AFFIRMATION TIME

When he's done he rolls over and is gone. I lie there wanting more contact. I need him to touch me and talk to me. I need to know he loves me. When he falls asleep I feel like he got what he wanted, and I don't matter. First I'm hurt, then I get mad, finally I just cry.

The emotional affirmation phase compares to the physical resolution phase. Affirming one another meets emotional needs. Resolution describes what happens to the body as everything reverses itself to the prestimulated state. We dealt with the resolution phase in Chapter 8. Now let's see what is happening emotionally.

After physical and emotional sexual release, both men and women experience a peaceful, relaxed feeling. The more complete the tension release, the more sleepy a person will be and the less he or she will need continued physical touching.

Some people feel their letdown very rapidly. Men report this more commonly than women. There is an intense release and an almost immediate urge to fall asleep. A woman's tension release may occur just as intensely and rapidly as a man's or it may be more gradual. The more gradually the body returns to its prestimulated state (gets rid of its vaso-congestion), the more the woman needs touching and affirmation.

The affirmation time is a time of confirming one another's nakedness. To be naked, open and vulnerable, and not ashamed, is the essence of sexual trust. This was the quality of the man-woman relationship before the Fall. The intense intimacy involved in allowing oneself to totally let go with another person can trigger strong feelings of vulnerability. This elicits the need to know that the other person still cares and will not take advantage of the exposure that has occurred.

What meets one person's need for affirmation may be very different from what meets another's need. Talk about your desires with each other. What are your feelings? What would each of you like? How might you resolve your differences or meet the needs of both of you?

WHEN IS AFFIRMATION NEEDED?

The need for affirmation depends both on the degree of physical release and on the emotional need. This is true for both men and women.

Physical sexual release has often been compared to a sneeze. That is, there is the full, tingling feeling of blood rushing to the area. This is followed by the good releasing feeling of the "ah-choo." The more intensely a person lets out the sneeze, the more rapidly the relief of the congestion occurs. Similarly, the more intense the orgasm, the more rapid the release of the pelvic congestion. When you stifle a sneeze, you can feel an uncomfortable congestion for some time afterward. The same uncomfortable congestion occurs in the pelvis when you do not allow a complete release.

Since more women have difficulty letting go, and since women have the potential to be restimulated to need further release, women more than men commonly find themselves wakeful after a sexual experience. They either want more stimulation, as we mentioned in the previous chapter, or they want to be held and affirmed. When the pelvis is engorged with blood and fluid due to sexual arousal without total release, there is a feeling of tension and irritability. The person will not feel relaxed and ready to fall asleep.

Emotionally, the need for affirmation varies with the degree of trust in each other and security with one's own response. A man may be as emotionally in need of affirmation as a woman. The trust and security issues are usually brought with the person from childhood and past experiences.

The idea that all women need to be caressed after withdrawal of the penis from the vagina is not necessarily accurate. Women may need it more often than men. But when a woman is physically satisfied because she has had one intense release or the number of releases she has desired, she is likely to feel like falling asleep rather quickly herself. On the other hand, if a man is feeling rather unsure of himself and uncertain that he can trust his wife, he may be the one desiring a close, gradual unwinding.

This need can vary from time to time. Some experiences provide more intense release than others, and a person may be more or less vulnerable from time to time. These conditions will affect the person's desire for touch and closeness in each encounter. Thus, each couple needs ongoing communication.

WHAT PROBLEMS INTERFERE?

Tension within the relationship concerning the affirmation time usually has to do with failure to communicate and resolve individual differences.

The common dilemma is the man who falls asleep, leaving the woman needy. We talked about ways to work on that in the previous chapter. Both people's responses are entirely legitimate. Having fully let go of the tension, the man's body is ready to drift off into peaceful sleep. Needing more release, the woman's body is irritable, tense, and wide awake. This is a situation of opposite individual needs in a mutual relationship. Both will have to look at what they can do to resolve the difference.

Other individual needs or differences may arise. Some men have an urgent need to urinate after intercourse. They may jump up quickly after withdrawing from the vagina. If the man has never told his wife why he gets up immediately, she is left feeling vulnerable and hurt. She feels that she allowed herself to be vulnerable with him, and he does not even care enough to stay with her; all he wants is his release. Communicating the reason for his hasty departure and making a plan to come back will usually turn this from a painful happening to a building time. Some men experience pain in the penis after release. They need to share this and plan together for him to withdraw, but to stay physically close.

Because of the anatomy of some women's genitals, they have a high susceptibility to bladder infections if they do not get up to urinate and wash right after intercourse. Again, this may be perceived as desertion. Usually the man feels that the woman was dissatisfied with the sexual experience. He then sees himself as inadequate.

Tensions concerning the need for affirmation after release, or after sexual arousal with no release, can usually be resolved if there is open communication in a caring relationship.

The process of affirming can be the most valuable, beautiful part of the total sexual experience. It can be a time of tenderness, of closeness, of having shared something extremely intimate and personal, and of having been out of control with each other. Sexual release is probably the most total expression of one's emotional and spiritual being without mental control. Thus there is a feeling of vulnerability, yet with intense caring and intimacy.

19 CLEANING UP

IS THIS NORMAL?

We were teaching our first seminar on Christian Perspectives in Sexual Enjoyment to a younger, newly married group. At our first break a young woman led Joyce off to the side to talk privately. She said she and her husband had been married for three months. After they had intercourse there was always a mess to clean up. She was wondering if that was normal and what other couples did about it. Since that time, it has become a rather common question. We now routinely address the issue of normal excretions and how to handle the cleanup.

How much discharge should you expect? The man's seminal fluid will be about one teaspoonful. Women's vaginal lubrication varies considerably. We really cannot give even an approximate measure. Maybe we can picture it for you. When the man withdraws from the vagina, his penis will usually drip with the secretions. If the woman were to sit up on the sheet and let the discharge run out of her vagina, it would probably soak a spot one to five inches in diameter. This is a combination of her own vaginal lubrication and the seminal fluid that has been deposited if her husband ejaculated while in the vagina.

Is this a turnoff? Should you let your spouse see it? Most men get turned on by vaginal lubrication. It's a sign of the wife's responsiveness, which many men take as a compliment. Besides, most men get turned on by a turned-on woman. They love it!

An exception to this might be some men who have difficulty even touching the vaginal area. They think of it as messy and do not like messes. Some women have a similar response to the man's ejaculate. To them it is repulsive. They avoid it as if it will contaminate them. These are the exception rather than the norm.

For most women, the ejaculate has a positive, warm, intimate feeling. It is a symbol of the intimacy shared.

Since the usual response is positive, we encourage openness about the discharge. It is clean; it has no germs. There is nothing embarrassing or innately repulsive about it. The result of a beautiful act, it gives life. This is the way God made us and intended us to be.

If it is a turnoff to one of you, that person should talk about it and possibly even get some professional help. Removing that negative barrier from your sexual relationship could open up a whole new world of freedom for the two of you.

HOW TO HANDLE IT

There is really no prescribed, correct, or proper way to take care of the sexual juices. Usually you can start by talking about what, if anything, you would like to do about it. What is comfortable for each of you?

Some couples take a box of tissues to their lovemaking spot. Others like to have a washcloth or towel handy. Some have a special lovemaking sheet or blanket to put under them. Still others feel no need to take care of the discharge. If they make love in bed, the sheets absorb the discharge and that is comfortable for them.

The cleaning-up time can become a pleasant, familiar ritual. The item(s) brought to the experience could be included in the "Something Old" part of setting the atmosphere (see Chapter 14).

WHEN THE "NORM" VARIES

A small percentage of women experience an expulsion of fluid that is not vaginal lubrication. Dr. Robert C. Kolodny of Masters and

Johnson's Institute has researched this phenomenon. He reported on this at a workshop and in a personal telephone call to us. A large amount of fluid—approximately one-fourth to one-third of a cup— is expelled from the urinary bladder, but it is not urine. The woman can urinate immediately before a sexual experience. Every drop of urine could be removed from the bladder with a rubber tube called a catheter; nevertheless, if she has an orgasm within even a few minutes of the bladder's being totally empty, she will still expel a fluid from her urethra, the tube that carries urine from the bladder to the outside of the body. This evidently happens in intensely orgasmic women. It is now believed that this fluid may be produced by the Skene's glands, which are located under the urethra.

Even though this release of fluid is experienced by only a small percentage of women, it is definitely not a negative experience. You will probably want to use extra preparation to protect the surface on which you have sex and allow the release. The fluid is clean, warm, and can be positive for both. Some women who experience this fluid expulsion have withheld their orgasmic response because of their embarrassment. They feel as though they have lost bladder control. Getting accurate data and sharing it with each other can free the woman to allow herself to let go orgasmically. It has helped some women to think of letting themselves go with the flow of the fluid. This helps them gain a warm, positive association with their body's responses, rather than tightening up when they feel the urge to release the fluid. For them, this is the body's normal response. It is something to go with, not fight!

The sexual organs, orifices, and discharges are clean. They are free of disease-producing microorganisms. As you are able to integrate the sexual parts of yourself into your total being, you develop positive feelings toward all aspects of your sexual expression, rather than feeling hesitant about bodily secretions. Your positive associations contribute to natural comfort in handling the sexual dimensions of your life.

WHEN SEX

ISN'T

WORKING

20 WHY SEXUAL PROBLEMS?

Our bodies are designed for sexual pleasure, arousal, and response. As we learned early in the book, God's perfect plan for us is to be intense sexual persons and to fulfill our sexual desires with our spouse in marriage. Physically, our sexual functioning is so predictable that it can be measured down to tenths of a second and is the same from one person to another and in the same person from one time to another. Emotionally and relationally, there is a definable process of desire, initiation, meshing, pleasuring, letting go and then entry or entry and then letting go, affirmation, and cleanup.

Yet, the fact is, we keep a full practice as sexual therapists and keep our associates busy as well. The need for sexual therapists is indicative of the fact that, somehow, what was designed to be a delightful, fulfilling part of our marriages is not always experienced as such.

What gets in the way of a satisfying sex life in marriage? Sometimes we may just not get it all together quite right!

LACK OF KNOWLEDGE

You may not know what is normal sexual interaction, or perhaps sex doesn't flow that naturally for you. Because of the haphazard nature of most sex education, we cannot count on everyone growing up with the same information. If we take, for example, the area of mathematics, most of us go through school and learn first of all, to add and subtract, then to multiply and divide, to do fractions and percentages. Finally, we move on to algebra and geometry. By this time, we have most of the basic concepts of arithmetic we need in order to function in our daily lives. Sexual knowledge, however, is learned mainly in a hit-and-miss fashion. We learn through what we hear from brothers, sisters, and friends, from what we see on television, in the movies, or on the Internet, and from what we read. Some of the information may be accurate, but much of it is not.

Since the sexual experience is so emotionally charged and so often misrepresented in the media, many adults, even well-educated adults, reach the point of readiness for sexual involvement with a dismal lack of knowledge regarding what is normal and natural. Some may not be aware of how to enjoy their partner's body or go after arousal for themselves. Others may not be aware of the acceptability of bodily feelings. Still others shy away from certain natural bodily responses as if they are abnormal. Often, a newly married couple's expectations for sex in marriage will be unrealistic.

Knowledge about one's self and one's partner is often lacking. Many, particularly women, come to the marital situation quite unaware of their own sexual feelings, desires, or needs. Every woman is different. There is no way we can write in a book or declare in a lecture what every woman needs. Some women enjoy rather vigorous physical activity with a lot of clitoral stimulation; others prefer much more general body pleasuring with only light clitoral stimulation. There is no way for a man to come to the marriage bed with a prescription in his hand that will guarantee a pleasurable response from his wife. If she does not know her own body and what is most satisfying for her, then he may feel the demand to determine what brings her pleasure. They are both likely to find the sexual times less satisfying than they ideally could be.

It can be the same way for the man. He may have learned a way of stimulating himself to the point of ejaculation, but that may be the extent of his knowledge about himself. He may have no idea about how to enjoy and savor bodily pleasure, so it is crucial that the couple's first year or two of lovemaking be a discovery time. They need to learn as much about themselves and each other as they can.

Another area where many lack knowledge is in an understanding of the sexual process and response. If we do not understand what is happening in our bodies, we often bypass many possibilities for pleasure. For example, if a woman assumes that the woman's desire and response are the same as the man's, then she will wonder why she feels negative when he begins with a focus on her genitals. Yet it is a fact that the woman's sexual response tends to be slower than a man's. She normally needs more general touching, caressing, and conversation rather than just the emphasis on genital-clitoral stimulation. But unless both understand and accept their differences and her need for connection, both will end up frustrated.

Similarly, if a woman is hesitant to let her body respond in the way it was designed to, she will inhibit her natural sexual expression. Many women want to stop the intense breathing that occurs when they become aroused. They are embarrassed about allowing intense sexual expressions. The body movements, the facial grimaces, the groans that occur naturally, will be cut off because they seem unladylike, even though these responses are arousing for most men and necessary for the woman's release. For men, there is often the belief that the man should be able to continue to be restimulated after an ejaculation. This may be possible for 1 or 2 percent of men in their twenties or early thirties, but most men are physically designed to require at least twenty minutes to an hour of rest before they become restimulated.

It is crucial for a couple to understand normal physical responses and to let themselves fully experience these responses. We are often amazed at the transformation that occurs when a couple gain some basic technical knowledge about sexual response. They experience greater freedom, greater relaxation, and greater enjoyment.

UNCONSCIOUS AVOIDANCE

Guilt

Some people cannot allow themselves freedom to enjoy sexual activities, even though their heads say that sexual feelings are great! They find themselves cutting off or even sabotaging their sexual response. Sometimes the reason is guilt. Guilt may be genuine, real, and authentic; or it may be false and inauthentic. When we feel guilty about something, it does not necessarily mean we have violated any of God's or society's laws. If we have been taught, for example, that the sexual response is evil and is a part of our earthly, fleshly lusts, then, regardless of the fact that the Bible endorses sex within marriage, we may still *feel* guilty. This is a form of inauthentic guilt— that is, guilt over an activity that does not violate any standard.

Sometimes we avoid sexual activity because of *real* guilt. A person who accepts the biblical teaching that sex is to be fulfilled in marriage and then chooses to be active sexually before marriage may carry guilt about that past activity. Guilt also arises as a result of extramarital activity after marriage. Real guilt can inhibit the sexual response and sexual enjoyment in marriage.

Anger

Anger is also a source of unconscious avoidance. Anger has several sources that need to be clearly differentiated. Sometimes anger or bitterness is brought into the relationship through life experiences from the past. And anger or hostility may grow out of the current marriage relationship. The old anger or bitterness present in many relationships has its source in pain and deprivation that occurred in childhood. If, for example, a man was continually put down as a boy by his mother or father for supposed inadequacy or incompetence, was continually stymied in his growth as an individual, or was continually limited in the expression of his feelings, his bitterness or anger may show itself in the marriage relationship. The person might not be aware of this old anger or bitterness, but old scars from the early years can affect the present relationship.

Current anger, on the other hand, is often the result of stress between spouses. The woman may be trying to be a submissive wife. Instead of being mutually submissive, the husband takes on the dominant role in such a way that the woman continually ends up feeling like a doormat. When this is the case, it is likely that anger and resentment will build. The resentment may not be entirely conscious, but is likely to evidence itself in the most intimate areas of the relationship. The woman who experiences disregard and provocation is likely to become less and less desirous of sexual activity. The bedroom is one more setting in which she feels violated and disregarded. Since she is the submissive wife, she will not usually express her anger directly, but she will find ways to avoid sexual activity.

Lack of Self-Worth

Lack of self-worth, too, can bring about unconscious avoidance. When we do not feel good about ourselves, whether in terms of our physical appearance, parental responsibility, or our competency as a provider, we may want to avoid being sexually involved. We will not want to put ourselves in a situation where our lack of worth is pointed out one more time. At times, this may manifest itself by unconsciously making oneself unattractive, either by lack of care for the body, by overeating, or by uncleanliness. To be together and responsive sexually requires a significant degree of self-worth. When this is not present, consciously or unconsciously, we are likely to avoid sexual activity.

Since guilt, anger, or the lack of self-worth are *unconscious* ways of avoiding sex, we naturally will not be aware of them. The way to determine if these are in operation is to observe our behavior. From that behavior, we can determine whether we are *needing* to avoid sex. It is usually necessary to have some kind of professional help to get at an understanding of anything subconscious or unconscious, since most of us are not equipped to uncover those realities for ourselves.

Sexual Anxiety

Fear of failure is another major source of sexual difficulty. This usually develops after actual experiences of failure, such as the inability to become aroused when stimulated or failure to be orgasmic after arousal. These experiences tend to be most common for women. Men may experience failure to get an erection or to maintain it, or the fear of ejaculating prematurely, or the fear of not bringing pleasure to their spouse. Any time we enter a sexual experience with fear, our responsiveness will be inhibited. This is a physiological fact. Our nervous system is set up so that we cannot experience fear and enjoyable sexual arousal at the same time. Those responses are mutually exclusive. When we fear failure, that failure tends to be perpetuated by the fear itself. The more I fear, the more likely I am to fail; the more I fail, the more I fear, and I'm into a downward spiral. This fear/failure situation is not a major source of sexual problems, but is a major way in which sexual problems are perpetuated.

Sexual anxiety grows out of the demand for performance. This demand may come from within one's self or from one's spouse. If during the sexual experience we feel pressure to produce a response in our spouses or ourselves, that demand will cause anxiety. A man may tend to place a demand on himself to provide a sexual response for his wife. If that demand becomes predominant, it is likely to reduce the pleasure of the experience. The woman may also feel a demand on herself to respond, to become aroused, to lubricate, to have nipple erection, and to experience intense erotic feelings. As that demand is felt, it is likely to inhibit rather than help the feelings. The woman may also feel a demand to have an orgasm, to prove to her husband that he is a good lover as well as to affirm that her body is working. With this demand the anxiety increases, making any response unlikely.

The man may also feel a demand for his performance. He may feel he must immediately get an erection and keep it. When this anxiety is present, he certainly will not be relaxed. Yet relaxation is a necessary prerequisite for the erection. As with the fear of failure, demand for performance fosters anxiety. When we are anxious, we cannot respond.

THE NEED TO PLEASE

When we carry the belief that our main function in the sexual experience is to please our spouse, the need to please is likely to become a source of pressure. The man may believe that to please her he must get an erection quickly and hold it as long as possible. The woman may feel she has to hurry to get aroused or have an orgasm in order to please him. Her thoughts will be, *I can't take this much time.* If there is something she needs for her own satisfaction and arousal, she will think, *I can't ask him for that—he wouldn't like it* or, *I'd be asking too much.*

People with an excessive need to please usually grew up having to work diligently for parental approval. Even with hard work, they received little in the way of reward to build their self-worth. These people go through life looking for approval and reinforcement they never received as a child. It is difficult to make the transition from a focus on getting the approval of the spouse to taking responsibility for one's own feelings. Once people realize that assuming such responsibility is the most satisfying way to please their spouse, they can relax and enjoy their sexual feelings.

In sexual therapy we regularly find that it is most difficult for a couple to change their focus from pleasing one another to pursuing pleasure with each other. Often each of them will report that they want the other one to be enjoying himself or herself. This will turn them on. Yet to make the shift from pleasing the partner to enjoying oneself is most difficult. It is difficult because the conditioning has taken place over a long period. The need to please is hard to overcome.

BLOCKED EROTIC FEELINGS

When we block good sexual feelings, we are unable to respond fully. This can happen in two ways. We can stop our feelings by focusing on certain thoughts, or we can get into what is often called the "spectator role."

What do we mean by stopping our sexual feelings with our thoughts? We stop ourselves from feeling natural bodily responses by thinking thoughts that get in the way of those feelings. For example, if we have had past negative sexual experiences, we bring those to mind and stop the erotic feelings. We may distract from sexual feelings by thinking about an argument we had or a negative characteristic of our spouse. Others will use thoughts about God and his judgment on their sexual activity as a way of stopping themselves from experiencing erotic feelings. Another person may become preoccupied with some of the mundane things in his or her world, such as what to do tomorrow or what didn't get done today. By taking our focus away from bodily enjoyment, we can stop the feelings that occur naturally.

It is important to recognize that natural concerns and nonsexual thoughts may pass through the mind without getting in the way. It is not uncommon, for women, particularly, to think about what they need to put on the grocery list, or something they must remember for their children in nursery school the next day, or a matter they must take care of the next day at work. These thoughts can and do commonly occur without intruding on the sexual experience. They get in the way only if they become a preoccupation rather than a short-lived reflection.

The spectator role blocks sexual feelings and responses. Spectatoring puts us in the role of observer and evaluator rather than participant. Sex is not a spectator sport! Spectatoring will interrupt the sexual experience.

The mental interruption of the natural sexual response perhaps can best be understood by an analogy. If we are trying to fall asleep, one of the surest ways to stay awake is to think about falling asleep. All of us have had the experience of feeling sleepy and needing to get to sleep, and then becoming anxious about whether or not we will be able to sleep. We notice ourselves beginning to doze and think, *Oh, at last I'm getting sleepy, I'm about to fall asleep.* And by the time we've experienced those thoughts, we have moved into the spectator role. We will be wide awake, because the falling-asleep response is involuntary and requires relaxation, not conscious control. Sexual feelings are, likewise, automatic responses that must remain free of conscious control. As soon as we stand back and observe what is happening, whether it be arousal, maintaining an erection, maintaining control, or having an orgasm, these thoughts will get in the way of our sexual freedom.

PAST TRAUMATIC EXPERIENCES

Past traumatic experiences get in the way of sexual freedom. Most commonly, children who experienced molestation or rape while growing up are very confused about their sexuality. Any time an adult plays with a child's genitals or stirs up the child's sexual feelings, these sexual feelings, which are good feelings, become connected with fear and pain. Conflict and turmoil become associated with sex. Even more confusing is that the molestation or rape is usually performed by a person who is close to the child—father, brother, grandfather, cousin, uncle, neighbor, or family friend. In only a small percentage of cases is the perpetrator a stranger. Molestation creates in the victims a great deal of turmoil about themselves sexually. The conflict is carried over into their adult sexual experience.

The pattern typical of those who were traumatized by childhood sexual abuse begins with heightened awareness of sex as a child or a sense that they are different from other children. Often they feel an intense sense of guilt, as though they were responsible for what happened. As adolescents and young adults, they are very sexual, maybe even promiscuous, but as they approach marriage, or shortly after marriage, they shut down sexually.

To break through the barriers created by the past trauma, they must share their feelings and past experiences with someone who can care and understand. A spouse may be the best person. If you fear your spouse's response, you may first want to share with a pastor, an understanding friend, a counselor, or a physician. You may want to join a group of others who were sexually violated as children. Once you have talked about the experiences, their hold on you will begin to diminish. As long as the past is kept secret and the awful feelings of disgust, embarrassment, guilt, and anger are present, you will not have the freedom to respond in a total and enjoyable way to the sexual experience with your spouse. While you are doing the work of healing, it will be important to avoid sexual activities that trigger flashbacks or aversion for you. The sexual experience needs to be in your control, not something that is done to you.

Similar sexual turmoil occurs for men and women who witnessed promiscuous sexual activity while growing up. If their parents were sexually active in their presence, or if they lived in a neighborhood where they observed open sexual activity, their sexual feelings will have been awakened prematurely and inappropriately. These children may determine that they will never behave in this manner, since it is so repulsive to them. Then as they get older, they are repulsed by their own natural, God-given feelings, even when those feelings occur in a completely appropriate and acceptable setting. For example, it is not uncommon for a woman who had a rather flirtatious or promiscuous mother to be very inhibited sexually because she does not want to be like her mother.

Another example is the girl whose older sister becomes pregnant out of wedlock. The little sister may, at a young age, determine that *she* will never cause her parents that much stress, so she shuts down her ability to respond sexually. Years later, as an adult, she finds it difficult to be responsive to her husband.

Similarly, a boy whose mother behaves seductively with him or overexposes herself to him will likely resist being sexual with a woman, even his wife whom he loves. His negative set toward appropriate open and free sex in marriage is difficult to overcome.

These barriers can be very deep and not easily understood. But as a person works to bring them to the surface and deal with them, he or she can find release from the limitations the barriers have placed on sexual activity and enjoyment.

Early exploratory play with peers can also interfere with an adult's sexual life. Often it is not the experience per se that causes the trauma but rather the reaction of parents when they discover the children in their play. If, for example, two girls at age six are discovered poking around at each other's genitals, the mother has at least two choices. She can inform the girls that it is natural to be curious about their genitals, but God created their genitals with special feelings that are private, so it is important to keep panties on and not to touch each others' genitals. Or she can go into a screaming fit, by which she frightens the children as if they have done a dreadful deed, often traumatizing them regarding their own sexuality. If their natural sexual and bodily curiosity is labeled deviant and perverted, they will carry this view into adulthood. Teaching about sexual boundaries needs to be accompanied by positive messages about our sexuality, especially about the wonderfulness of sex in marriage.

Young people who go beyond their predetermined sexual boundaries during premarital activity may find that as they enter married life and attempt to develop their sexual relationship, thoughts of their early experiences begin flooding in on them. These will cause distraction, sometimes disgust, and often guilt. The person will need to talk through all of the feelings surrounding the premarital activities before he or she can overcome the difficulties caused by those memories. Frequently those men and women find it difficult to feel forgiven. They *believe* they are forgiven by God and by anyone else they offended in the process, but they do not *feel* that they are forgiven. It is this lack of feeling forgiven that gets in the way of a full, free sexual experience.

Any traumatic sexual experience for a child, adolescent, or adult will tend to cause turmoil that has long-lasting effects. The victims usually feel that they somehow brought it on themselves, that they bear some guilt. "If only I had" done this or that—then, they believe, the whole thing could have been avoided. These feelings are natural, even though they are usually inaccurate.

Any traumatic experience that involved sexual activity or a sexual response can be the source of a major barrier for an adult. In all instances, it is essential that the opportunity be provided for communication of these events and the feelings aroused by them. For the traumatized person to find relief, this communication must take place with another committed, caring individual. This is one of the ways in which we can minister to each other. For without healing, the consequences of these violations are transferred from one generation to another.

RELATIONSHIP PROBLEMS

Difficulties in a relationship are bound to show up in bed. Relationship barriers may take many forms. Probably the most obvious is *rejection*. When one of you detests the other, it is not likely that you are going to function effectively as sexual partners. Contempt, or total disregard for one's spouse, usually develops gradually and is the result of both partners' participation.

Rejection commonly leads to *discord*. The discord may arise from a wide variety of events, but it usually has to do with one or both individuals feeling they are not being cared for in a way they experience as loving. This will stimulate anger, hostility, and distance. When these feelings are present, the sexual experience will not be satisfying.

Discord often shows itself in the sabotaging behaviors that couples use to destroy the possibilities of a satisfying sexual experience together. Helen Singer Kaplan, a pioneer sex therapist and researcher, painted the picture well:

He likes her to swing her hips—she lies motionless.

He needs to be made to feel loved and desired—she is tired and "does him a favor."

She likes to move actively—he pins her down.

He is very stimulated by touching her breasts—she feels "ticklish" and cannot bear to have her breasts touched.

She is aroused by having her breasts caressed—he does not want to bother, or implies that her breasts are not attractive.

She likes to talk with him a bit first to relax her before sex—he plunges in wordlessly.

She hates TV—he always watches TV before making love.

She wants and needs clitoral stimulation—he implies his other lovers didn't need that sort of thing.

He likes to experiment—she thinks everything but "straight" missionary position is perverted.

She is very turned on by oral sex—he is disgusted by the odor of women's genitals. . . .

He has his best erection in the morning—she insists on sex at night only.[1]

These forms of frustrating one's partner are usually subconscious ways of getting back when direct communication of negative feelings has not seemed possible. Obviously, sabotaging expresses a great deal of hostility and communicates much ambivalence about the sexual experience. The hostility and ambivalence need to be dealt with openly. Sometimes couples can do this themselves, but most commonly they need some help in sorting through their feelings without hurting and distancing each other.

Lack of respect can also be a source of sexual problems. It is difficult to make love with someone you do not respect. Respect may be there at the beginning of the relationship, but then diminishes because your partner does not measure up to your expectations. Lack of respect toward the man will usually have to do with either his competence in his vocation or his integrity and honesty as an individual. Lack of respect to the woman will usually have to do with how she functions in the traditional women's roles of cleaning, cooking, and caring or how she cares for her body.

"A second-choice mate" is one who was chosen on the rebound. If an individual is actively dating someone and then loses that prospective partner through death, rejection, or other circumstances, he or she may quickly attach to and then marry someone else as a way of soothing the painful emotions. People who do this often find themselves in a state of continual dissatisfaction with their spouses. The person is still attached to the lost love object and has difficulty bonding with the new spouse.

Communication is necessary, both about general relationship issues and about the sexual dimension of the couple's experience. If partners do not share what they need or are lacking in the sexual experience, they will begin to withdraw from one another. As they withdraw, their frustration increases. If communication does not take place, they withdraw further, and the problem continues to perpetuate itself. As we have said so many times, the starting point for resolving any difficulty is always effective communication. The interaction must be gentle, loving, and free of negative messages about the other person. Blasting the other person with all your built-up anger will not build the bridge.

THE NEED FOR RISK AND GUILT

The messages of caution and restriction that we received about our sexuality while growing up can lead to an association of sex with risk and guilt. "Sex is good when I'm bad." A couple who became involved sexually before marriage found themselves to be quite responsive to each other. But after marriage, they were much less interested in sexual activity and could not seem to experience the freedom and joy they had felt beforehand. If husband or wife subsequently becomes involved in an affair, they will again find themselves to be very responsive. These people need to experience risk in a guilt-producing situation before they can become aroused and responsive. Often these are people who have been raised with the message that sex is bad. When sex occurs in the context of marriage, the person cannot respond. Yet in the guilt-producing situation, intense sexual feelings surface naturally. When the person is unaware of the internal struggle, the spouse may be blamed for the problem.

∽

When sex isn't working, the bedroom tends to become a sober place. Laughter has to be rediscovered or maybe unleashed for the first time. Understanding the source of the problem may provide some relief but may not correct the issues completely.

Discovering true passion and intimacy in your marriage likely will require specific behavioral changes within a loving, committed relationship. Our book *Restoring the Pleasure* offers complete step-by-step programs to help couples overcome the most common sexual barriers. In the next chapters we will discuss some typical concerns and offer suggestions for resolution and new discoveries.

21 DIFFERING SEXUAL NEEDS

No two people are born the same. No two are raised the same. No two people have had the identical life experience. These three major factors—what we inherit genetically, where and how we are raised, and what we experience—will cause us to come to marriage with different needs and desires in every aspect of life. For some couples, these differences show up immediately upon marriage. More often, though, differing needs take time to surface. The years go by, and the marriage moves along from the excitement of the first years to the distractions of child rearing, establishing a home, building a career, and forming a solid financial base. During these years differing needs—including varying sexual needs—emerge and make themselves known.

BASIC DIFFERENCES

To begin with, we must state that there are some very basic differences among normal, healthy people. There is nothing wrong with a person who has a greater or lesser need for sex than his or her spouse. Such a variation is not necessarily the result of life experiences or how one was raised. Our differences reflect that each of us

189

was uniquely and wonderfully made. Just as people vary in their need for food or activities or hobbies, people will have a greater or lesser drive for sexual activity. To understand a difference in need, you must consider the normality of such differences. The importance is working with your differences—make them work for you as a couple. Negotiate differences.

ENERGY DIFFERENCES

As a couple move through their years of marriage, the amount of energy they have available for sexual activity changes. Often, during the first years of marriage when they are excited about being together and the newness is still fresh, the energy available for sexual play is boundless, particularly if both spouses are experiencing sexual satisfaction. But then the couple decide to have children. The woman may still be working when she becomes pregnant, and so she is tired. Or she may have uncomfortable pregnancy symptoms. She backs off sexually because of fatigue or discomfort.

Then the child is born, and there is the usual four-to-six-week period of physical recovery before intercourse is advised. But even after this time, the parents are likely to be getting up at night to feed the baby. Mother is adjusting to the changes in her body, to her new role, and to all the extra work and stress, so even for a year or two after the child is born she may not have much energy for sexual activity. By then the second child may be on the way. When we review people's sexual history, they commonly report that the decrease in their sexual activity occurred around the birth of the first or second child.

A man or a woman who is building a business or a career, or even just struggling to make ends meet as the family grows, may have little energy left for sexual activities. Perhaps the man is starting a small business. He leaves early to go over the books, works long hours, comes home tired, and is preoccupied because of various business problems and struggles. He finds that he does not have the energy he once had for sex. The same thing could be true for a woman. If she is trying to build her career as an executive, teacher, shopkeeper, nurse, or whatever, energy is diverted toward her vocation and away from sex.

FULFILLMENT DIFFERENCES

Differences in sex drive are determined in part by the level of sexual fulfillment. A woman who never feels sexually fulfilled will have a diminishing awareness of her sexual need. From a logical point of view, this makes good sense. If she is not being satisfied, she will shut down her sexual feelings. Her basic, God-given sexual need is not absent, but the felt need is. Because her need is never satisfied, she is not likely to be able to stay in touch with that need.

Let's consider an analogy: All of us have a need for connection—to be known and loved for who we are. If I go to a church and am alone and isolated, I may go back another time. If, again, I make no connections, my interest may lessen a little bit. I may wonder what's wrong with me and why no one is interested in me. I may go back again in a couple of weeks and if, once again, I am alone, I may decide to try a small group. So I go to a class; and if I still don't get connected, it's likely that my interest in attending that particular church will diminish. This is not to say that my need for connection, my need for fellowship, my need for community has diminished in any way. Rather, I have simply not experienced anything fulfilling in that particular church. In the same way, if a wife never experiences fulfillment in the sexual relationship, regardless of how much she needs it, she will have less awareness of that need.

If a man feels inadequate in the sexual relationship, he is likely to avoid sex with his wife and fulfill his sexual need through self-stimulation. If a man is not being fulfilled, his sexual need is likely to increase. He is always wanting and yet rarely receiving sexual satisfaction. It may seem as though he experiences satisfaction one out of ten times; he is in a state of perpetual hunger, like a person who is rarely able to eat a full meal. He is always hungry, and even when he does have a meal with enough food, he is anxious about the period of hunger to follow.

We are not certain why women tend to shut down when they are unfulfilled sexually and men tend to feel more sexual hunger with lack of fulfillment. Similarly, the longer it is between sexual experiences, the more eager a man is for sex, the more quickly he gets aroused, and the faster he will come to ejaculation. On the contrary, the longer it is between sexual experiences, the less eager the woman is, the longer it takes her to get aroused, and the more difficulty she has building toward orgasm. We are convinced that the 1 Corinthians 7 passage that instructs husbands and wives to come together regularly is a counter to our tendency to go the opposite direction the less frequently we are together.

EMOTIONAL DIFFERENCES

There may be differences in sexual needs and desires due to varying emotional intensities. Some individuals are very low-key, relaxed and easygoing, experiencing little stress or tension. At the same time they feel little intensity. This is the type of person who is seldom angry or excited to any degree. Their experience in life will usually be relatively stress-free, but also relatively excitement-free. Other individuals experience life at a high level of intensity; they move from one intense moment to another. When they are active sexually, they are involved with all of their being and with great intensity. When they are playing a game or cooking a meal or studying the Bible, they do it at a level of involvement that includes their whole being. When you put a person of low intensity together with a person of high intensity, you are likely to experience different levels of sexual need. This obviously can produce tension in a relationship, particularly when the one with a higher need interprets the partner's lower-level need as a lack of love or attraction for him or her.

MALE-FEMALE DIFFERENCES

With every discussion of male-female differences, there are exceptions. Some women identify more closely with the generalizations about men, and some men find themselves connecting with emotional needs or traits more likely to be true of women. Yet, the understanding of typical male and female differences is helpful for most couples to minimize conflict and enhance mutual acceptance. That is why each couple must talk about their differences.

What are some commonly identified differences between men and women that affect their sexual relationship?

For women, sex tends to be a total-person experience. Men tend to focus more on the sexual parts.

Women usually need to connect and feel loved to open up sexually, whereas men get interested in sex in response to visual stimuli or being physically stimulated. So when a man comes to bed all ready and anticipating sex but hasn't connected with his wife, she will not respond positively to his approach, and he may feel hurt and rejected. For her, it is not about her love for him; it is about her feeling cherished by him.

Women are just more complex than men. Women function on two tracks, the emotional and the physical, and these have to be in sync in order for a woman to be responsive sexually. Men tend to be ready emotionally when they are ready physically. The physical arousal carries the emotional for most men. It is like men have an on-off switch that is easy to find and figure out. Women have many buttons that have to be finely tuned and adjusted to be able to function well sexually.

Men tend to be more goal-oriented, and women tend to be more into the process of lovemaking. Men focus on arousal and release. Is he able to make hers work? Women focus on pleasure and communication. Women love to be held and caressed; men love to be stimulated and brought to ejaculation. Not that women don't eventually desire arousal and release, but that is a by-product of the process, not the goal.

Women vary more from one woman to another, and the same woman varies more from one experience to another than men do. Men tend to be more predictable than women are. If you've lived together even a week, you will have discovered this difference. As John Gray, in his book *Men Are from Mars, Women Are from Venus,* states:

Men are like the sun. They rise every morning and set every evening. Women are more like the moon. They are different every day but will likely circle back around next month. Women's ever-changing quality can be frustrating to a man. Yet, we are convinced that it is the combination of male constancy and ever-changing, complex femininity that is the key to keeping sex alive in marriage over a lifetime.[1]

THE DIFFERENCES MAY SEEM LIKE

SHE

1. All he ever wants is sex.
2. He never takes the time to listen to me.
3. Why doesn't he remember what I tell him?
4. He likes the room cold.
5. He'd rather get to bed.
6. He likes to be on time.
7. He loves for me to dress sexy to come to bed. He gets turned on just looking at me.
8. I'd love to sit on the couch and have an evening of just kissing.
9. I'm a night person.
10. I need conflict resolved before having sex.
11. He gets aroused and wants sex if I fondle his genitals.

HE

1. Why wouldn't she want sex?
2. All she ever wants to do is talk.
3. Why is she always changing her mind? She's so fickle.
4. She likes it warm.
5. She takes an hour to prepare for bed.
6. She's willing to be late so she can take time to be gorgeous.
7. She likes me to love her as a person and not make her feel like an object. When I do, it turns her on.
8. Why would she want to kiss, get all turned on, then not have sex?
9. I'm a morning person.
10. Sex is my way of getting close after conflict.
11. She pushes my hand away when I reach for her breasts or genitals.

Men tend to measure sexual satisfaction by quantity, whereas women tend to measure it by quality. So when a man rates their sexual relationship, he will tend to think of how often they are together. When the woman discusses her evaluation of their sexual relationship, she will likely be thinking about the quality of their times together. This difference has led to many arguments related to the topic of, "How are we doing sexually?"

The differences between men and women are both the source of greatest conflicts and the basis of the most intense intrigue. Our goal is to help couples make their differences work for them. We teach them to negotiate their differences, embrace their uniqueness, and have fun noting how they differ.

ADJUSTING TO DIFFERENCES

If the couple are going to survive differing levels of sexual need, they must find ways to adjust to those differences. The starting point is communication. Until a couple have clearly defined their differences, there is no way to resolve them. Each spouse must take responsibility for himself and his own feelings. He must express his feelings clearly, rather than criticize his spouse. Openness is crucial. Anything that can be done to reduce defensiveness will help make this kind of discussion more productive. When people feel accused, they become defensive. If they feel that what they are saying is being received and understood and reflected, however, they are likely to be able to continue the exploration (see Chapter 12 on communication).

Once the couple have discussed their differences, they must identify the changes that will enable them to adjust to their differing levels of sexual need. For example, if a man is frustrated because his wife is always too tired, the two of them must work out ways to lessen the fatigue so she can get in touch with her own sexual need. (If the fatigue is just an excuse, a cover-up for the real reason for lack of interest, the plans that are made will be sabotaged. The cover-up will be discovered quickly.) If a woman is frustrated because the man is expending all his energy on weekend softball games or building his business or watching sports events on television, the change in lifestyle must be acceptable to both. Radical solutions usually don't work. Moving the television into the garage will produce only frustration and anger rather than greater sexual desire, unless *he* decides to do so.

In adapting to differing levels of needs, stay open to various sexual options. There are many ways to satisfy sexual needs, and there are many different types of sexual needs. For example, many women report that they do not necessarily need sexual intercourse, but rather are hungry for cuddling and touching. Many men would be willing and happy to be involved in such caring and touching experiences if they knew that this was as far as it needed to go. The same is true of women. Many times they would be willing to participate in an experience if they knew there would be no demand for arousal, response, or intercourse.

When a woman is not needing sex for herself, she may be happy to manually stimulate her husband to the point of release. She may enjoy that process. Many women report that they are willing to satisfy their husbands if they don't feel like pursuing sex for themselves. Similarly, if a man does not feel a sexual need, he may be willing to bring his wife to orgasm if that is her desire.

Finding ways to meet each other's needs without making a demand on the other is the crucial dimension in resolving differences. As with so many other issues, spouses need to discuss their differences, make plans, experiment, and be open to move toward finding fulfillment without demand. Even in the sexual experience, Philippians 2:4–5 can well be used as a guideline: "Do not merely look out for your own personal interests, but also for the interests of others. Have this attitude in yourselves which was also in Christ Jesus . . ." (NASB).

22 NEVER ENOUGH TIME

As we travel internationally and around the country, talking to various church and educational groups about sexual adjustment, we always have the attendees complete a survey. One of the questions on that survey allows the respondents to check various areas of concern they would like to work on and improve in their sexual relationship. One of those categories has to do with the matter of time. Roughly 75 percent of the thousands of people who have filled out these questionnaires have reported that time is one of the greatest areas of frustration for them in their sex lives. It is difficult to find significant amounts of time to be together. In addition, it is difficult to coordinate the times that are available. Finally, it is difficult to be consistent about time together. This chapter will focus on time—not on how the time is used, but rather on prioritizing time, finding time, and being intentional about spending time together.

DEFINING THE TIME CONFLICT

Overscheduling is the primary reason for time issues. Over-scheduling can be used as a way to avoid sex, and it may be an inadvertent response to life's demands. Because it is often difficult to deal directly with negative feelings about sex, people may avoid sex by designing their lives so there is seldom enough time. The wife may become a compulsive housekeeper. She may be pre-occupied with always having the dishes done immediately after dinner, getting the children's lunches ready for school the next day, setting out their clothes, and making sure that everything is ready for the next morning. By the time she completes her tasks, she is ready for sleep, not play. She may take pride in her reputation as a good homemaker, but when her task preoccupation takes precedence over the couple's time together, then it causes conflict in the relationship.

The man may be at the office until seven or eight o'clock in the evening. He comes home, spends a little time with the kids, has dinner, and is ready to drop off to sleep. Although his focus on his career is laudable, if his outside energies are designed to or inadvertently cause him and his wife to avoid each other sexually, then those distractions from intimacy must be addressed.

In some situations both partners unconsciously collaborate to avoid sex. They design their lives in such a way that they are both overly involved. They never get together sexually because they have found no satisfaction in their previous sexual encounters or they have difficulty with intimacy.

Most often, however, hectic schedules inadvertently crowd out time for sex. Children's activities, civic activities, church and school, sports, education, and entertainment gradually crowd in so that the couple's sexual time together is either nonexistent or has become a quick encounter between two exhausted people at the end of the day.

The matters that take up time are usually good and wholesome activities. Often they have to do with various forms of service. Sometimes they are for personal development. One man always goes to bed at eight because he likes to get up at four in the morning to have an hour of quiet time with God, to study and meditate and pray. This is obviously a worthy commitment, but it still has the effect of causing sexual problems in his marriage.

DIFFERING TIME NEEDS

Couples often have differing time demands. For one couple it was the man, who was in charge of a growing business. He was earning enough money so that his wife didn't have to work outside the home. At the same time that his business was expanding and demanding his time, his wife had more time and energy available for sex. The difference in time demands led to stress, particularly for the wife, who was eager for more sexual activity. The man was just as interested in sex as his wife was, but he was just not available to his wife.

It may be that the woman is loaded with time demands because when she gets off work, she has to come home and cook and clean and care for the family. When he comes home from work, he wants both of them to relax. He's willing to let go of the cooking and cleaning, and he's certainly not willing to spend all his evenings tidying up the house. She feels the responsibility and pressure to do so. Thus this wife's available time to be with her husband is limited, so sex usually occurs when she is most exhausted.

Differing time needs may revolve more around *when,* rather than *how much.* "I'm an evening person, and he's a morning person" is often the way this difference is expressed. He wakes up at the crack of dawn and is ready to roar into life. By eight he has been producing for three hours. It may be the woman who is the morning person. We'll never forget the woman who came in at 8:00 A.M. for her therapy appointment; she had already jogged her ten miles for the day. Others come in an hour later, still trying to get their eyes open, but will be going strong until midnight.

There is nothing right or wrong about being a morning or evening person. It only requires attention when who you are doesn't coincide with who your spouse is. Some people are night people. They get going by about seven in the evening, and are then ready to continue until two in the morning. Some men love to wake up in the morning and make love. If the wife happens to be a morning person, there is no problem. Many women complain about husbands who wake them up in the morning to start their day with a sexual experience. Often these same men are dozing off to sleep in front of the television by nine-thirty. Yet this is the time when the woman may be ready and interested in sex. What can a couple do about their differing time needs?

SEX: A TIME PRIORITY

If the time issue is going to be resolved for a couple, both spouses must be ready to make a commitment to each other that they are going to make their time together a priority. It is of utmost importance that this decision not be an edict that comes from either the man or the woman; rather, it should evolve from the two of them together. It is easy to make a commitment verbally, but it is another thing entirely to make it work in day-to-day life together. What does the man do at 5:50 P.M. when he has promised to be home by 6:00 P.M., but gets an important long-distance call that is going to take an hour? Does he tell the caller he is not available because he has a commitment? Or does he take the call? It is the same way for the wife. Is she willing to let the work at the office go? Or to let the ironing pile up? Or to have the house in less-than-perfect order? Are they willing to work together in handling the responsibilities of the household in order to have time for each other?

The couple will need to spell out exactly how they are going to make their sexual relationship a priority. Some couples choose to have brief sexual times at home, and then go away for a few days at a time every several weeks for more focused times together. Others find that this leaves them frustrated, or that they are unable to do so because of financial or family limitations. These couples find quality at home. Each couple has to work it out in their own special way.

You might be saying, "Why all this preoccupation with time? If sex is important to a couple, they will get together." That may be true, yet there are many distractions from sex, and there are no outside pressures that pull us toward sex. When we agree to work for a certain company, we're expected to be there so many hours a week or to complete a given project. When we give our time for community service or at the church, there are other people to whom we are responsible, and we have deadlines. If we are involved in some kind of sports activity, there are practices to attend and games to play. The only accountability in the sexual relationship is to each other. Decisions to make this a priority have to come out of desire and the recognition that this is a crucial area of life that needs fulfilling and is not happening without a plan.

With busy lifestyles, sex may be best "by appointment." First-time responses to this idea are often, "But that takes all the excitement and spontaneity out of it." This is usually said by people who have not tried scheduling. The quality of the sexual experience is not based on spontaneity. The quality depends on what happens between two people once they are together, whether they are together by impulse or as the result of scheduling. Normally when people begin to schedule their time together, both the quantity and the quality of their times together improve measurably. Scheduling does not rule out the possibility of spontaneous times together. Scheduling is done only to assure that there will be allotted, quality time for the two to be involved on a regular basis. Spontaneous times together tend to be relatively brief. They tend to satisfy primarily the physical needs rather than meeting all the intimacy, touch, and emotional needs that are addressed in longer scheduled times. Scheduling provides for sharing, extensive touching, enough time for arousal, for repeated arousal and release if that is what is desired, and a time of affirming afterward.

Scheduled time must be planned without a demand for arousal, intercourse, or release. The time allows for all possibilities, but those are not to be preset expectations. Anytime couples approach their time with expectations or demand, those will get in the way of their freedom in that experience. We recommend that couples allow time to talk, to touch, and to kiss. Having connection as the focus reduces much of the pressure they would feel if they came to the experience merely with the intent to have an sexual time together.

One other stipulation necessary to make the sexual relationship a time priority is that the times together must be free of interruptions.

It is amazing how many couples report that their sexual experiences are interrupted by the ring of the doorbell, a telephone call, the cry of a child, or disturbance by a pet. As much as possible, it is necessary to remove all possibilities for distractions. Take the phone off the hook. If you live in an apartment complex where people are forever dropping by, put a "Do not disturb" note over the doorbell. When children are old enough to be safe when unattended, teach your children that there are times when Mom and Dad have to be by themselves without interruption. It is important for children to learn this in terms of respect for parents' wishes. It is even more important that they learn about a husband and a wife and the priority that their time together should have. Rather than shutting them out of your world, you are providing them with a good model on which they might choose to base their married life in the years to come.

We recommend our Formula for Intimacy that follows:

FORMULA FOR INTIMACY

15 minutes per day:
- To connect emotionally—share your thoughts and feelings
- To connect spiritually—read and pray together
- To connect physically—kiss passionately

1 evening per week:
- Date time
- Prep for pleasuring
- Pleasuring

1 day per month:
- Have fun and play together
- Focus on each other
- Find out likes and dislikes

1 weekend per season:
- Time away
- Time at home
- Time together

The fifteen minutes works best if you include some time to talk about your day and how you are doing, read a Scripture verse or short devotional followed by a prayer, and then kiss passionately for thirty seconds or more. We are convinced that daily connecting and passionate kissing keep the pilot light on so that it is easier to turn up the flame. One evening per week might be a date night to take more time to pleasure each other without demand. It may be your scheduled quality time together. A half-day or day per month may be a getaway time or a time of loaning children to friends or family and enjoying each other at home.

The weekend per season isn't possible for all couples, but it is a great bonus if you can take that time. So much reserve can be built during extended times together that will carry us through the stressful times.

Making sure you have time together is the responsibility of both partners. It takes forethought, planning, effort, and recommitment. There is no way it will happen automatically. If there is to be time together—you will have to take charge!

23 YOU WANT TO DO WHAT?

WHAT IS APPROPRIATE? COMMON AREAS OF TENSION

Questions of where, when, why, how, with what, which part, how long, and with whom all involve conflicts regarding the appropriateness of sexual activity. In this chapter we are not addressing the issue of moral right or wrong but rather the question of what is comfortable between spouses in marriage. We are primarily talking about the emotional and personal acceptability of various kinds of sexual activities rather than about their being right or wrong from a moral or biblical perspective. However, when sexual activities do involve a moral decision, we will look at the biblical view. For those interested in further study of biblical sexual ethics, we suggest the book *Sex for Christians* by Dr. Lewis B. Smedes.

Traditional vs. Experimental

The question of appropriateness can be thought of in terms of the traditional versus the experimental. Sexual activities that have become accepted over the years as the natural positions, styles, or stimulations—traditional approaches—are often thought to be the "right

way" to make love. Many people are uncomfortable with any devia-
tions from the traditional approach to lovemaking between a husband
and wife. Yet an open, experimental attitude toward sexual activity in
marriage is an essential ingredient for keeping the spark alive.

Places

"There is only one right place to make love. That is in bed, under
the covers, with nightclothes on." Right? Not so. It may be the most
comfortable, and it may be the least vulnerable, but there is nothing
sacred or exciting about that setting. Keeping a sexual relationship
alive requires experimentation and variety. Yet, unless both people
are open to new approaches, such attempts may cause stress.

A newly married couple experienced difficulty with where they
might make love The woman was an experimenter, and the man was
a traditionalist. Whenever his new bride tried to initiate an activity
that allowed more freedom, the man resisted. One day she encouraged him to join her for a time of sex play on the bear rug in their
den. He sneered in response to her suggestion. She felt judged. And
so their tension continued.

Experimentation without stress grows out of communication.
Talking about possible places and new settings can bring positive
anticipation when both spouses feel heard, respected, and valued for
their ideas and feelings. Experimenting with locations will bring
adventure and excitement. Even a minor change of switching directions on the bed can bring a whole new perspective.

There are boundaries that need to be heeded when choosing a setting. The key criteria have to do with respecting the space and privacy of others and the privacy and comfortableness for both spouses.
Given these guidelines, there are really no limitations. Some couples
enjoy shifting to another bedroom and a different bed. Others prefer a couple of comforters on the bedroom floor or in front of the
fireplace. Outdoor possibilities include the swimming pool, the backyard, the beach, or the forest. When there is adequate privacy, these
locations bring an exciting quality that can be quite delightful. Anything
from being on top of a dining room table to being underneath it or

anywhere in between can be a possibility. One couple purchased a massage table and took turns pleasuring each other on the table as a significant part of their sexual experience.

Looking for new places will work only when both spouses are comfortable with the idea. Pushing another person will only produce tension. When you experience stress about experimentation, negotiate your differences. The experimenter must be willing to take the initiative but, at the same time, be considerate while the other spouse attempts to overcome his or her hesitancy. So whether it is your pickup camper or your attic, it will take some holding back by the experimenter and some stretching by the more conservative spouse.

Positions

Having grown up in constricted settings, the two of us were determined to keep our sex life new and exciting. During our five-day honeymoon, we attempted to make use of every position we had read about or could imagine. It was like a beginning piano student trying to play a Chopin concerto before he knows the C major scale. It didn't cause us any particular harm, but it certainly was not necessary, nor that beneficial, at that stage in our marriage.

We think of the sexual relationship as a time of flowing, moving, and enjoying each other's bodies. In that process, we are likely to change from one position to another. A focus on getting into position may be likened to a still photograph, stilted and lifeless. But when positions flow naturally out of the couple's enjoyment of being together, it is like a movie, filled with motion and life. Yet, couples are likely to find they establish a fairly consistent position for entry.

The most traditional position for entry is the missionary position. It apparently received this name from the Hawaiians, who observed this behavior in the missionaries and thought it strange. In this position, the man is on top of the woman, with the woman lying on her back. Many couples prefer this position. It permits more solid clitoral contact, especially when the man moves his body farther up on her body during intercourse.

What are the alternatives to the man-on-top position? A natural variation is to have the woman on top—just a reversal of the traditional missionary position. The advantage to this position is the freedom it allows the woman. Often the woman needs more specific stimulation than does the man. When the woman is in the top position, she can be more active in going after the specific stimulation she needs.

The focus is on her having control of her own pleasure. If that is uncomfortable for her, she will not feel as free as she might in some other position. Some women do not feel comfortable pursuing pleasure. They adopt a double standard: It is acceptable for a man to be active in the pursuit of sexual stimulation, but it isn't appropriate for the woman to do so. The man may have difficulty with the woman-on-top position as well. He may feel that his manhood and leadership are challenged when his wife is on top. This man probably would not feel dominated if he and his wife were hanging wallpaper together, and she was on a stepladder while he was standing on the floor. But somehow the symbolism of the woman being above the man in the sex act has more meaning. Misconceptions about submission and dominance have caused a great deal of stress and turmoil in people's lives. Couples need to get their views out in the open, study them together, and find ways of incorporating the concept of mutuality into their sexual relationship.

Other intercourse positions include the lateral position. Both partners lie on their sides, with one person straddling one of the other person's legs, rather than being between them. This position can bring greater pleasure for women who experience more stimulation when the penis directly strokes the side of the vagina. There are obviously four variations of the lateral position. The man may be on top straddling the woman's right or left leg, or the woman may be on top straddling the man's left or right leg.

Standing or sitting can provide interesting variations. A fully pregnant woman might lie on her back with her buttocks at the edge of the bed while the man either kneels or stands at the side of the bed, holding her legs, so that he does not rest on top of her. Sometimes couples find that the rear-entry position, in which the man enters the vagina from behind the woman's legs rather than from in front of her, is most arousing for the woman. There are some advantages to this position. It allows the man's hands easy access to the woman's breasts and clitoris for direct stimulation. However, there is the disadvantage of the lack of face-to-face contact, which can be essential for a feeling of intimacy. Some women find the rear-entry position intolerable because of air pressure that builds in the vaginal cavity.

There are valid reasons to experiment with new positions. Any activity, even an enjoyable one, can become boring. If you listened to only your favorite CD day after day, as much as you love it now, you would eventually be bored by it. If you went to church and always sang exactly the same songs and heard exactly the same excellent sermon, you would become bored. If you went to your favorite restaurant and ordered your favorite meal three times a week, week after week, that, too, would grow old. Sex is no different. If you behave in exactly the same way time after time, it will become ho-hum and humdrum. Many couples find that after becoming adjusted to one another and getting used to the idea of lovemaking, they want to explore new ways of enjoying each other.

A fun experience we recommend for couples is to find a book that has diagrams of various positions. Then plan a time, create a mutually enjoyable atmosphere, and have fun practicing getting your bodies into the different positions without attempting entry. You could be in the nude, fully clothed, in underwear, or wearing what you wear to sleep. After this experiment, you might categorize the positions into (1) those you'd love to use for intercourse, (2) those you'd like to try but are not sure will actually be positive for the two of you, and (3) those that will never work for you.

Develop an attitude of openness and freedom so that you can let the choice of position grow out of the feelings of the moment. Thus you will not be overly concerned with the question of which position to use. We like to think of letting positions evolve out of the experience, rather than getting into position, as if you were on the scrimmage line in a football game waiting for the whistle to blow.

Style

Another question of appropriateness has to do with lovemaking style. When a couple is getting bored with their sexual experience, they have usually developed a routine style of lovemaking. It may be that at five o'clock in the morning, the man wakes up and rolls over. Experiencing his morning erection, he does certain things to his wife, and she gets the message that he is interested. They go through a ritual, entry takes place, and they move to orgasm—or at least he does. Once they have ritualized this pattern, they seldom deviate from it unless they are out of town on vacation by themselves. But as soon as they return home, they fall into the same old pattern.

If this is your situation, whether you are the man or the woman, do some experimenting. If the ritual is offensive to you, plan a time to talk about it. If it is just boring, take the initiative to plan some new elements into your sexual times. Schedule to be together at a time different from the usual. Prepare the room with candlelight and your favorite music. Start by focusing on pleasuring each other's bodies. If you usually make love in the dark, turn on the lights. If you usually turn on the lights, make love in the dark. Anything that will bring some change and variety is likely also to add a new spark.

Accouterments

Accouterments are small items that are used to pleasure each other. We recommend a creative pleasuring experience. Each spouse chooses three to five items that are different in texture. Start pleasuring each other's backs with the chosen items. Have the other person guess what it is you are using. Then the person being pleasured is encouraged to choose his or her favorite item. For example, some people are especially responsive to touch from soft articles such as fur or wool. To pleasure your partner with a small piece of soft fur may be just the kind of experience to bring special joy and delight.

It is important to use an accouterment that will be pleasing rather than offensive. And we are certainly not suggesting a deviant use of external objects. But you can communicate your love in a new or different way through the appropriate use of something enjoyable.

When couples begin to experiment with accouterments, they are often surprised at the new delights they can experience together. They use everything from various kinds of fabric to fans, feathers, or rolling pins (for stroking, not for hitting!) as special sources of touch that brings bodily pleasure. Such items bring newness, variety, and humor into the sexual loving process.

Even as you will be most totally fulfilled when you allow yourself to enter the sexual experience with abandonment, you will also be most fulfilled when your time together can include complete bodily freedom with one another. Not many couples can begin life together with such total freedom, but over time they become more and more intimate. The couples who are most satisfied are those who are moving toward greater levels of bodily freedom with one another. Total freedom means that there are no boundaries, no limits, no areas that you call a "no-no." This is quite a contradiction to those who feel most comfortable making love in their bedclothes, under the blankets, with the lights out and the curtains drawn.

Stimulation

Stimulation and the form it takes flow out of style and ritual. A free-flowing style encourages variety, whereas a repeated routine leads to a formulaic approach to stimulation. The traditional, ritualistic approach to stimulation is often referred to as the "three-push-button" approach. Many of the older marriage manuals assumed that it was the duty of the man to turn on the woman, rather than a mutual pursuit of enjoying each other's bodies. The way to turn on a woman was to kiss her, stimulate her breasts, and massage her clitoris; then she should be warmed up and ready to go. This is a rather impersonal and ineffective view of stimulation.

The fact is, most women are not excited by a predictable pattern, nor by any particular pattern. One day a woman may enjoy kissing; the next day she may not. One moment she may enjoy direct breast stimulation, and the next moment she might prefer it be very indirect. One day she might enjoy having her breasts nibbled on or sucked, and the next day that might be painful. Sometimes clitoral stimulation will be most enjoyable when done directly; other times, very indirectly. Part of the delight of the lovemaking process is learning how to respond to the desires of the moment. This moment-by-moment discovery about oneself and each other adds spark and spirit to a sexual encounter.

The kind of stimulation enjoyed will vary from one person to another, from day to day, and even from moment to moment. At the beginning of the lovemaking time the person may feel like kissing, but by the end may need more freedom for total-body movement. Kissing may be too constricting. On the other hand, a person may not feel like kissing at the beginning of the lovemaking time but will feel like it later as arousal builds. When each person listens to and takes responsibility for going after his or her own hunger in the moment, getting with those varying desires will initiate variety and freedom to enjoy the pleasure of each other's bodies.

Once the couple learn the delights of variation, teasing, and moving from one kind of stimulation to another, the couple will prefer that kind of loving. They will find it to be the most expressive and caring. It is also more exciting and less boring.

For some people, the method of stimulation seems relatively insignificant. Others experience so much dismay and disappointment that they feel, *If I have to go through this same routine one more time, I'm going to scream or quit forever.* Instead of screaming, try some effective communication: an e-mail, a letter, a tape recording, or a direct verbal message. Communication is not as likely to shock your partner as is a scream. He or she is more likely to hear you. You will need to repeat your communication more than once. Do not expect that because you have changed the routine for a week, the two of you will not slip back into old habits. Just like any learning experience, sexual change will take place over a period of time rather than in an instant.

Major Conflict Areas Regarding Stimulation. There are patterns of stimulation that can cause a lot of stress between a husband and wife. One pattern more typically practiced by men causes frustration for women. This occurs when the man finds a place that is arousing to his wife, becomes attached to it, and never lets go. This is particularly frustrating for a woman when a man attaches himself to the clitoris and tries to stick with it until the woman has an orgasmic response. This is almost sure to bring irritation rather than orgasm. Most women find stimulation much more arousing when it is varied in terms of its location and its intensity. Whenever we speak in public, women ask us to tell their husbands three things: (1) not to be in such a big hurry, (2) not to stick with the "hot spots" until they're worn out, and (3) to be able to caress and stroke each other without any specific sexual expectations.

A pattern more likely to be true of women that causes frustration for men is the woman's hesitancy to enjoy her husband's penis. The woman may feel shy, may be unable to because of past sexual abuse, or may be concerned that she will hurt him or will not do it correctly. The Nondemand Touching Exercise on page 134 would be a great tool for exploring and teaching ways that are comfortable for both the husband and wife to enjoy penile pleasure.

Couples often squabble about what forms of sexual stimulation are right or wrong within marriage. A typical question we are asked is, "Biblically speaking, is there any sexual technique that is not acceptable within marriage?"

Oral Sex

Everywhere we go to speak, whether it's to a mothers' group, a junior-high group, a high-school class, seminary students, college students, doctoral students, couples' groups, or an interview for a magazine, the one question we can count on is, "What about oral sex?" Oral sex or oral stimulation is the stimulation of the spouse's genitals with the mouth, lips, and tongue. The man may stimulate the woman's clitoris and the opening of the vagina with his tongue, or the woman may pleasure the man's penis with her mouth.

Solomon in the Song of Songs refers continually to enjoying the delights of his lover's body. He speaks of browsing among the lilies (4:5). His wife says, "Awake, north wind, and come, south wind! Blow on my garden, that its fragrance may spread abroad. Let my lover come into his garden and taste its choice fruits" (4:16). In the following verse King Solomon says, "I have come into my garden. . . . I have gathered my myrrh with my spice. I have eaten my honeycomb and my honey; I have drunk my wine and my milk" (5:1). His lover responds, "Eat, O friends, and drink; drink your fill, O lovers." There are many references to the oral delights of one's lover and the enjoyment of her full body. Every part is talked about: hair, lips, neck, breasts, stomach, legs, feet. The lovers usually refer to the genitals as "the garden of spices." The book speaks of total-body involvement. For some of us this freedom seems strange, unusual, and not part of the natural order, but the biblical model in the Song of Songs seems to embrace such freedom.

In thinking about using our mouths to find enjoyment and bring pleasure to our lover, there are usually three questions that people ask. First: Is it natural? Second: Is it right? Third: Is it clean?

When we ask whether or not something is natural, we are trying to discover the internal purpose for our creation. We are striving to avoid the violation of that perfect plan of creation. Some people find it easy to describe what is natural for themselves. However, their idea of what is natural is usually based on their own experience and does not necessarily represent what others might describe as natural. So how do we objectively determine what is natural? The Bible is specific in providing guidelines to restrict sexual activity to marriage, but within the marriage relationship there are no guidelines. Nothing is said directly about what is acceptable in our lovemaking activity. Hence what comes naturally must be the product of what we feel inside us, how we have been informed by the Scripture as a whole, and the sense of God's Spirit directing us in relationship to our spouse.

From our perspective, oral activity becomes clearly unnatural if one of the partners is violated by it. It does not violate anyone to avoid oral sex, but it certainly may violate someone to be pushed into it. Therefore, we recommend going with the most conservative partner. The decision to respect a hesitant spouse might be compared with Paul's concern not to offend a brother by eating meat that has been offered to idols—even though from a strictly technical point of view Paul does not find this eating of meat to be a sinful act. The sin would lie in the offense to the other person, not in the act itself. Therefore, naturalness will ultimately be defined between a husband and his wife.

The Roman Catholic Church has taken the stance that oral pleasuring of genitals is condoned as long as it does not lead to ejaculation outside the body. Ejaculation is intended for procreation and is always to occur inside the wife's vagina. That is the natural order.

Is it right? We refer to the Bible as our authority for rightness. As we said earlier, the Bible does not speak specifically about lovemaking activity within the marriage relationship, and thus does not at any point teach about the acceptability of oral-genital stimulation. So if we are going to say it is right or wrong, we must look for some indirect scriptural teaching rather than look for a quote about oral sexual activity.

Some have thought that oral sex was included in Paul's statements regarding men and women leaving their God-given ways and engaging in unusual acts. However, careful reading of these passages will usually show that these are references to homosexuality, not to oral activity.

The Scriptures are not clear on the matter of oral sex, and so it is one of those gray areas where various biblical teachings will come into play. The principle of what is loving and caring for the other person must be addressed. On the other hand, the teaching that our bodies are each other's to enjoy must also be incorporated.

One thing we would caution against: Many people use Christian or moral arguments to defend against an activity that is personally uncomfortable for them. Often their moral arguments, though relatively weak, keep them from dealing with the *real issues* of personal emotional conflict or discomfort. By finding some obscure passage or unique interpretation, they avoid working through their own reason for the resistance. While it is sometimes easier to call on an outside authority, this can cause a person to avoid facing the genuine issues that are present and need to be discussed with one's spouse.

The final question has to do with cleanliness. Is it clean? In an earlier chapter on the body we referred to the fact that there are three systems that open into the genital area: one sterile, one clean, and one contaminated. The urinary system is sterile when there is no infection present; that is, it has no microorganisms. The urinary system includes the penis for men and the urethra for women. The reproductive system, which includes the vagina, is clean. It is free of any disease-producing microorganisms. Finally, the rectal area and the mouth are contaminated with disease-producing microorganisms. Therefore, if the genitals are clean and washed and there are no infections present, there will be no contamination of the mouth from the genitals. If contamination takes place, it will usually be communicated from the mouth to the genitals rather than from the genitals to the mouth. The mouth carries many disease-producing microorganisms.

It is important to keep in mind that just because something is not clearly wrong or dirty or unnatural, does not necessarily make it right, natural, or necessary for you. Rather, the review of the information we have just given is intended to clear away myths and distortions concerning oral sex.

Our hope is that with the facts, you will be free to discuss your personal beliefs and feelings about oral-genital stimulation. This is a personal issue and can ultimately be resolved only between you and your spouse. Communication continues to be the essential way to arrive at a congenial conclusion. To the one who desires oral activity but is inhibited by the hesitancy of your spouse, we offer encouragement. Many couples change over time, and what was uncomfortable for one becomes more natural as that one is cared for and loved without judgment and without demand.

What About Anal Sex?

Anal sex, the penis entering the woman's anus, is dangerous. The anus is highly contaminated, whereas the reproductive tract is sterile in men and clean in women. When the penis enters the anus, there is high risk of infections and prostate problems. If the penis enters the vagina after having been in the anus, the woman's reproductive tract can easily become infected. In addition, the rectum is not designed for entry and thrusting. The small blood vessels along the walls of the anus and rectum break. We do not recommend anal sex.

Masturbation

> One night as I was sleeping, my heart awakened in a dream.
> . . . My hands dripped with perfume, my fingers with lovely myrrh . . . (Song of Songs 5:2, 5 TLB)

What part does masturbation play in marriage, if any? Is it a sign of not being fulfilled, or can it be used by either or both husband and wife during a separation period? Whenever the subject of self-stimulation is raised, it inevitably brings anxiety, tension, sometimes fear, and occasionally disgust. It is one of those topics that virtually everyone has thought about, yet many have never talked about. Unless you have lived an extremely sheltered life, you have found it necessary to make some kind of decision about it. The data that you received while growing up is usually what has most clearly shaped your view of masturbation; and yet that input may be difficult to remember. The reason it is so hard to remember is that the messages were often communicated to you before you reached your first birthday.

It is inevitable that babies and children will reach for their genitals in the process of discovering their own bodies. When they do this, regardless of their age, they will discover that touching themselves genitally brings pleasure. God designed our bodies to respond with those great feelings. It is natural, therefore, that they will want to do it again. This is often the moment when the first messages about sexuality are communicated. If the child reaching down and touching the penis or the clitoris causes the mother to move the child's hand away, this is a unique experience. There is nowhere else that child is not allowed to touch himself. He can poke his fingers in his ears, his bellybutton, or his nose without a negative reaction. However, there are areas around the household that he is not supposed to touch because they are "bad" (dangerous). Pulling the hand away from the genitals, therefore, may also be connected with "bad" or "dangerous." The next message may be "No." It may be because a little boy is playing with his penis while he's getting his bath; or the no may come as a result of the little girl lying on some towel or object on the floor and rubbing herself against that object in a way that stimulates the clitoris.

These activities can make the parent uncomfortable. So the negative messages begin early. Throughout childhood, children are appropriately taught, "Don't play with yourself in public," but they are also taught that it's wrong to enjoy touching themselves in private.

Parents may give warnings about what will happen if the child does engage in any kind of genital self-pleasuring. In times past, these warnings were extremely severe. Self-stimulation was said to cause warts, insanity, or the loss of one's hair. It was suggested as the source of impotence and of congenital defects in children. We now know that there are no physical effects from self-stimulation. However, the emotional effects may cause distress. When you have been conditioned throughout your lifetime to think of an activity or feeling as wrong or dirty, evil or uncivilized, it is natural that similar behaviors or feelings will set off some immediate primitive guilt. By primitive, we mean deep or old, having a long history. This usually has its roots in your childhood.

Although our focus in this book is on the impact of self-stimulation on marriage, we do want to reference Dr. James Dobson's teaching on adolescents and self-stimulation from his book *Solid Answers*.

We were teaching a class to a pastors' forum at Focus on the Family the week *Solid Answers* was released. The pastors were questioning our view on self-stimulation. The coordinator of the program, Dr. Ken Ogden, asked us to come back to this issue in a moment. He returned with a copy of Dobson's then newly released book and read the answer to question 276 on pages 286–88, which was almost identical to what we had just been teaching and confirms our findings:

> Between 95 and 98 percent of all boys engage in this practice— and the rest have been known to lie. It is as close to being a universal behavior as is likely to occur. A lesser but still significant percentage of girls also engage in what was once called

"self-gratification." As for the emotional consequences of masturbation, only four circumstances should give us cause for
concern.[1]

The first of these is oppressive guilt associated with self-stimulation, which we find is likely to be present when the child has been
given a punitive message to stop. It is rare that the behavior will stop,
but the child's God-given sexual feelings become associated with risk
and guilt. The consequence is that sex is "good" only when it is "bad,"
which leads to a high vulnerability to premarital and extramarital sex.

The second negative emotional consequence of self-stimulation
occurs when it becomes obsessive. Dr. Dobson believes "the best way
to prevent that kind of obsessive response is for adults not to emphasize or condemn it." This is similar to our finding regarding oppressive
guilt. We are convinced that oppressive guilt leads to obsessive practice.

The third negative consequence results when the young person
becomes addicted to pornography. We find that when the child or
young adolescent first masturbates in response to an external stimulus, like pornography, rather than the first self-stimulation being a
response to the God-given sexual feelings in his or her body, that
young person is likely to become addicted to, or need, that external
stimulus to become aroused and reach orgasm.

The fourth concern leads us to our focus in this chapter. That is,
when the practice of self-stimulation follows the person into marriage and becomes a "substitute for healthy sexual relations between
a husband and wife."

The Bible and Masturbation. In times past, various Scripture
passages were used to condemn masturbation. Virtually all current biblical expositors, however, believe that these passages have nothing to do
with masturbation. Still, it may be of help to take a brief look at them.

The first two passages are Leviticus 15:16 and Deuteronomy
23:9–11. Moses is writing about behavior that is acceptable "within
the camp." Leviticus says, "Now if a man has a seminal emission, he
shall bathe all his body in water and be unclean until evening"
(NASB). The Deuteronomy passage reads, "When you go out as an

army against your enemies, then you shall keep yourself from every evil thing. If there is among you any man who is unclean because of a nocturnal emission, then he must go outside the camp; he may not reenter the camp. But it shall be when evening approaches, he shall bathe himself with water, and at sundown he may reenter the camp" (NASB).

In the past, these references to a man's wet dream were thought of as references to masturbation. We now know that wet dreams occur without being brought on by masturbation. They are the body's way of taking care of the buildup of seminal fluid that occurs, particularly in young men, and may or may not be connected with erotic dreams. They are an automatic response that cannot be controlled by the individual. It is important to let adolescent boys know this.

If we look at the whole context of the passages, it is clear that the writer was thinking of nocturnal emissions as a natural bodily function, because he deals with other emissions from the body that occur for both men and women, including the women's menstrual cycle. If we want to say that this is a passage condemning masturbation, then we would also have to say that the same passage condemns the monthly menstrual flow.

The primary passage used to condemn masturbation is Genesis 38:8–10. This is the story of Onan. "Then Judah said to Onan, 'Go in to your brother's wife, and perform your duty as a brother-in-law to her, and raise up offspring for your brother.' And Onan knew that the offspring would not be his; so it came about that when he went in to his brother's wife, he wasted his seed on the ground, in order not to give offspring to his brother. But what he did was displeasing in the sight of the LORD; so He took his life also" (NASB).

Let us put this in context. The custom of the day was that if a man died without an heir, it was the duty of his living brother to provide an heir for him by means of a sexual union with the widow. When the son was born he would be considered the son of the deceased brother, rather than the son of the biological father. Apparently Onan did not like this idea. He wanted to operate in his own way, so in the middle of the sexual experience with his brother's widow, he withdrew and "wasted" the semen or ejaculated outside the vagina.

This has most frequently been used to condemn self-stimulation, even though this was not an act of self-stimulation, but rather intercourse and withdrawal. It has also been said that the Lord was so angry with Onan for masturbating that he slew him. This was used to indicate how severely the Lord disapproved of his behavior. Yet the exegetes agree that this was a reference to the Lord's displeasure with him for refusing to do the duty of a brother-in-law, rather than for the supposed masturbation. In times past, masturbation has sometimes been referred to as "onanism," in allusion to this particular passage.

The Scriptures we have examined are the three main Old Testament passages used to condemn masturbation; but, as we can see, they provide no basis for that condemnation.

In the New Testament, 1 Thessalonians 4:3–4, Romans 1:24, and 1 Corinthians 6:9 have at times been used to condemn masturbation. All three passages are now understood to be references to homosexuality or immorality, not to self-stimulation. Hence, we must conclude that the Bible does not deal directly with the subject of self-stimulation in either the Old or the New Testament. Any biblical guidelines we could bring to this subject would have to come about as an understanding of some other principle taught in Scripture. Here we think particularly of the principles of love, of self-abuse, and of lust.

Is It Loving? Since love and respect in relationships are the guiding principle of all our behavior, it is obviously a question we must ask. To determine whether self-stimulation is loving, we must first clarify who is going to be the evaluator or the judge of that behavior. Now obviously the Lord is the judge; the Spirit within us is the judge; and we can usually determine what is loving in a practical sense toward one another. If our adult self-stimulation takes something away from our spouse, then the behavior is not loving. On the other hand, if one partner desires sexual activity far more frequently than the other, the couple might decide that masturbation is the most loving act the highly interested person can do, so as not to put the spouse under pressure. There may be periods when abstinence from intercourse is necessary. At such times, it may be most loving and adaptive to enjoy a sexual release brought about either by self-stimulation or by mutual manual or oral stimulation. Some of these occasions might be during extensive periods of separate travel or illness. When there is extreme outside pressure for one individual either relationally or vocationally, that person may prefer that the other take care of his or her own sexual needs. Or there may be times when one partner needs to be free from the pressures of sex for emotional reasons. So, while it is possible that self-stimulation could be an unloving act, there is also the possibility that using it to relieve pressure would be the more loving act, not only for the self-stimulator but also for the spouse.

Even though self-stimulation may be a loving option, many couples find that the most satisfying approach is to stimulate each other (without entry), rather than one person having a sexual experience alone.

Is It Self-Abuse? On occasion, masturbation has been spoken of as self-abuse; and yet, from a technical, physical point of view, we know that there is no difference in the physical response that occurs, whether the arousal is the result of self-stimulation, mutual stimulation, fantasy, or sexual intercourse. The physical, bodily responses are the same. Now if someone is masturbating ten times a day, this obsession would suggest emotional deprivation and a need for help both psychologically and spiritually—whether the person is married or unmarried, Christian or unbelieving. If masturbation is used as a way of avoiding contact with one's spouse, this, too, is a deviation from the norm and a violation of 1 Corinthians 7:3–5, where we are instructed to give ourselves to each other in marriage and not to withhold except for a mutually agreed-upon time for prayer and fasting.

But if self-stimulation occurs on occasion, not as a replacement for contact with one's spouse, but rather to provide some physical release, then it would not seem to fall into the category of self-abuse. It is not likely that healthy married adults, male or female, are going to enjoy self-stimulation more than intercourse with their spouse. If they do, then something is amiss and help is suggested.

Self-stimulation may be a way for the woman to discover what brings her the greatest bodily pleasures. If she can learn by touching her own body what brings her satisfaction, then she can communicate this to her husband. This learning could hardly be seen as either self-abuse or an unloving act, since it is designed to bring greater pleasure to their experience together.

Is It Lustful? The Scriptures say that if one so much as looks on a woman to lust after her, he has committed adultery (Matt. 5:28). The question is often asked, "Is not all masturbational activity a lustful act?" We have talked with many people and have found that this is not necessarily so. Many people report that during self-stimulation, they don't think of anyone as a sexual partner. Others report that their thoughts are focused on their husband or wife. Still others may imagine some unidentifiable person, but only in a peripheral, still-life way, not with the intention of acting on the thought. Of course, there are many who *are* actively involved in lust in their masturbational activity. So we must be careful not to categorize all self-stimulation as lustful, but rather we need to determine from each person what is in fact happening mentally during the event.

Freedom Without Enslavement. In Romans 14:14–23, Paul teaches a principle that is also repeated in 1 Corinthians 10:23–31. The simplest way to sum up this principle is to say that many things in and of themselves are not evil or unclean, but rather become sin in their context. Romans 14:14 says, "I know and am convinced in the Lord Jesus that nothing is unclean in itself; but to him who thinks anything to be unclean, to him it is unclean" (NASB). He then goes on to talk about consideration for the other person—how we are to follow the principles of love in determining our behavior. He continues, "Do not tear down the work of God for the sake of food. All things indeed are clean, but they are evil for the man who eats and gives offense. It is good not to eat meat or to drink wine, or to do anything by which your brother stumbles" (vv. 20–21 NASB). We include self-stimulation under "do anything" here. It can be offensive and cause a great deal of stress in a relationship.

In 1 Corinthians 10:23, Paul says, "All things are lawful, but not all things edify" (NASB). Earlier in 1 Corinthians, Paul gives almost the same teaching: "All things are lawful for me, but I will not be mastered by anything" (6:12 NASB). Other translations talk about not being *enslaved* by anything. The principle enunciated here is that we must be sensitive to the needs of the other person. We are to be cautious in doing anything that causes someone else personal turmoil. If we are loving in how we behave, we will be understanding of our spouses. We should not be possessed, mastered, or enslaved by our sex drive, but rather should keep it in its proper subordinated place in our life. The sex drive in us is a natural, God-given drive. But it is not a drive that must be fulfilled regardless of how it makes others feel, particularly within the marriage. The principles in these passages provide us with a way to think about handling masturbation in our marriage relationship.

In summary, it is important to note that masturbation relieves the physical need and may be helpful in self-discovery for some women. However, a person's sexual need includes far more than just the physical release. It is true that all of us need physical release. But if that is the only need being met, then we are not living up to all we were created to be. Thus masturbation can never be seen as a total fulfillment of what we were made to be, but rather as a temporary, incomplete, but sometimes necessary pleasurable physical release, or a step toward reaching greater satisfaction within our relationship. Whenever we speak of masturbation, whether we are discussing it as a couple, teaching our children, or attempting to struggle with the issues surrounding it, we must see it in its proper perspective. We might think of it as a snack that will tide us over until the real need can be met.

■ EXERCISE 13

Resolving Conflicts

It is vital for us to continue to struggle with the biblical principles regarding relationships. The number one principle is to do what is loving. That is, we are not to violate the other person. This principle speaks to the person who is wanting more or wanting something different from what the other wants. For the hesitant partner, the best focus is on the principle presented in 1 Corinthians 7:5. It says that our bodies belong totally to our spouses. If the more experimental, exploratory, creative partner focuses on loving and not violating, and the hesitant partner focuses on learning to give his or her body more and more fully, then growth is sure to take place.

In addition to the two underlying principles just mentioned, we suggest using four steps to resolve conflict about what is acceptable or appropriate. These are described below.

Step 1: Communicate

To resolve a problem, you need to define clearly what the problem is. This process includes communicating how each person views the difficulty. Whether you are the hesitant one or the interested one, communicate your feelings about the activity that concerns you. This communication may include your history with this practice—the experiences you have had in the past, the teaching you received, the discomfort you feel regarding it, and anything else that may have a current effect on how you feel. If you are the one who wants to move ahead and experiment, and you are bored with the current limitations, share those feelings. Talk about your feelings concerning your present sexual relationship. Suggest where you would like to gain increased freedom in the future.

In the communication step, it is important to deal with your moral and Christian perspectives. If you view something that your partner wants as sinful, explore your ideas together. Determine where the ideas came from. Find out if the behavior actually is evil or if your reluctance comes from a part of you that is hesitant to be free and open. As you both are able, make this area of conflict a matter of study and prayer.

Step 2: Go with the Conservative Member

Whenever one person introduces a new idea the other finds negative, we recommend the decision be made in the direction of the more hesitant one. In this way, no one is violated. This is not to say that the one interested in new experimentation must be resigned to being stuck with the status quo. Rather, the conservative one is less likely to build up resistance if the negative feelings are respected.

People do change, and the hesitant partner will be more likely to loosen up if he or she is not nagged, bullied, or shamed.

Step 3: "Pusher" Retreat

When we have a desire, it is natural to want to pursue it until we get our way. It is natural to want to keep going after it by mentioning it frequently, thus riding the other person about it almost to the point of harassment. Pursuit does not help resolve the problem. It only builds resentment on both sides. If the person who is interested in expanding can back off for a time, this will usually relieve pressure and allow the possibility for change to take place.

Step 4: "Hesitant One" Stretch

If you are the one who is resistant to new ideas, try to discover why. Is it because of some old conditioning that took place while you were growing up? If your father was very demanding of you, for example, requiring you to clean up every speck of food from your plate, and was slow to praise, you may be hesitant to experiment in life. Is it because of some past experience you had before you were with your current partner? Does it have to do with previous experiences with him or her? What is the hesitancy about? Experiment on your own without his or her encouragement. Stretch beyond your current limit and see how that feels. Perhaps you will discover that what you fear will not happen. Throughout all of this stretching activity, it is of vital importance to keep talking, struggling, reading, writing to yourself, and praying in order to grow. If you reach a point that causes severe stress, sometimes brief conversations with a good friend or trusted professional can bring a new perspective in those areas of tension.

Whether your concern about appropriateness has to do with positions, places, style, self-stimulation, oral sex, or anything else, share about it and make plans on how to handle it in the days ahead. These four steps may help.

24 I DON'T LOVE HIM ANYMORE

WHEN THE "FEELING OF LOVE" IS GONE

After several years of marriage, when a couple has had children and survived a few traumas of parenting, and when the couple is solidly established in a business, profession, or vocation, the initial passion of a new relationship may have dissipated. If the couple is together only because they are married, have children, and own a home, but without the feeling of *love,* they may need to rediscover the love and passion that was a part of their relationship.

Pain-Filled Relationships

Whenever a couple experiences pain as a result of their marriage, it is likely that the feeling of love will drift away. Pain may come about because one spouse is inattentive to the other's needs for emotional care, physical help, spiritual guidance, or sexual fulfillment.

Pain may also result from a more destructive pattern such as anger. One spouse may have come to the marriage with accumulated anger. That anger may be due to a lack of affection as a child. The anger from childhood neglect got transferred to the spouse. Even though the angry outbursts are not really about the spouse, the mate will feel hurt and pushed away.

We remember the law student whose wife was helping him through college. He was raised by a punitive father who never showed care for his son. Even though the mother was very expressive of her love, his father's behavior left the son feeling unaffirmed. Now in marriage, whenever the wife did anything that could possibly be construed as having some negative reflection on him, his childhood anger came out toward her. The feelings of pain overshadowed the sense of love.

Drifting Apart

Sometimes a husband and wife drift apart because of external pressures. Probably the single most common external stress that pulls spouses apart is the conflict and pressure associated with raising children. The likelihood of spousal stress increases with long-term child behavioral problems or caring for a child with a chronic illness.

The stress caused by children may begin as early as during pregnancy. Some morning sickness during the first three months is likely to make the woman less interested in sex. During the second three-month period, her figure begins to expand. Her concerns about body image may trigger hesitancy sexually. In the last three months, the size of her abdomen may interfere with her comfort in lovemaking. During the last month, she may avoid sexual activity almost totally. It is important to point out that unless the physician has indicated a concern, there are no physical reasons a healthy pregnant woman should not make love. The reasons for avoidance are emotional responses or physical discomforts rather than physiological issues.

The husband may have difficulties with the idea of making love to his pregnant wife for fear of hurting her. He may not understand how well protected the baby is inside the uterus. And he may not be able to come to terms with the idea of being sexually involved with a pregnant woman, the woman who is carrying his child.

After the baby is born, it will usually be four to six weeks before the couple will be given doctor's approval to resume having sexual intercourse. Even then, the wife may still be very tired; her body will not yet have fully recovered, and she may experience some vaginal pain. In addition, she now has the responsibility of the child, who is totally dependent on her. This mother-child relationship will often bring about major changes in terms of how the woman sees herself and how free she feels to respond sexually. Some women experience dissonance between their roles as mother and lover. Some couples find this to be more true if she is breast-feeding. It is as if sex is a desecration of the beautiful mother-child-nursing-caring relationship. Even if there are no attitude difficulties with mothering, fathering, pregnancy, or nursing, the major commitment of time and energy necessary to get a child through the first few months is a disruption in any relationship. As beautiful and delightful as children are, and as much joy as they bring into our lives, there is no doubt that readjustment is a major event for most couples. Many couples will not consciously deal with this readjustment together and hence will begin drifting apart.

About the time the couple is ready to renew their sexual relationship, they usually begin thinking about having the next child. Often the whole experience is repeated, and then the mother has not only a nursing child but also a jealous two- or three-year-old. If the couple stop with only two children, there will be a four- or five-year period in which the relationship cannot maintain the closeness that existed before the first pregnancy. If they have more children, the time period lengthens with each new pregnancy.

We are not saying that every child introduced into a family will bring distance and the loss of love in the marriage. In fact, the shared joy and nurturing often enhances the feelings of love. But there is a likely possibility that the sexual relationship will be interrupted and that the couple's feelings of love for each other will change.

School, Career, or Business

College, graduate school, a new business, or any other outside focus can so capture the couple's energy and interest that there is little time left over for the expression of the love the couple had for each other in the beginning. It is easy for a student to let deadlines for papers, reports, books, or research projects become the controlling force. The marriage relationship, including the sexual dimension, becomes less and less significant.

The same thing can happen in building a career. It takes time and energy to become efficient and successful. Generally, the career person will be gone for more than eight hours a day. Even if active involvement is limited to forty hours a week, the career will often take much mental and emotional energy, leaving little for the partner.

Building a business can have the same effect. A start-up company tends to consume the person in charge if it is going to be successful. The marriage relationship may suffer as a result of such a business push.

Whether the distracting factor is school, career, or business, the effect is the same. When two people do not have continued, intense, intimate sexual involvement, the lubricant or oil of the marriage lessens and the friction in the marriage increases, taking away from their sense of "being in love."

Unfaithfulness

When we get married, we don't lose the attraction to others, but what we do with that attraction is very important. We recommend that you affair-proof your marriage. Recognize your vulnerability, and always turn any distracting feelings toward your spouse. Quickly replace other images with positive memories of anticipatory thoughts of being with your husband or wife. But when attention to affair-proofing doesn't happen or isn't successful, serious damage from an extramarital affair may ensue. Affairs grab the involved partner in a most powerful and controlling way. The feelings of the new relationship, which tend to feel like love, overtake the love of the marriage. The hurt of the spouses of the involved partners builds distrust and destroys the feelings of love toward the spouse who caused such deep hurts.

Because of its newness and excitement, the outside sexual involvement will often seem so much more fulfilling and satisfying than the marriage. When the spouse engaged in the affair has been unhappy and unfulfilled in the marriage and then experiences fulfillment and satisfaction in the affair, it is natural to have the feeling of being in love with the new partner. Since it is difficult to maintain an intense passion for two people at the same time, the wandering spouse usually feels that he or she is no longer in love with his or her spouse.

Sexual involvement outside one's marriage often forces a choice. If the person chooses to return to the spouse, and the hurt spouse is willing and able to engage in a process of forgiveness and restoration, love may be nurtured again in the marriage.

But if the person chooses to divorce the spouse and marry the new partner, the same problems are likely to develop in the second relationship that were present in the first. The pleasure and excitement experienced in a new relationship are deceptive in that they lead the participants to believe that the feelings of love associated with attraction will last; however, the passion of attraction usually dissipates within six to thirty months. In order for passion to last a lifetime, the attachment of intimacy must be developed. The scriptural directives about faithfulness to one's mate are not there just to make life complicated, but because God loves us, he wants the best for us and knows that commitment and faithfulness work best to bring about long-term fulfillment and happiness for everyone involved.

Never Were "In Love"

It may come as a surprise to many, but some couples marry for reasons other than love. The reasons always seem logical at the time, but over a period of months and years, that "reasonableness" often diminishes. It is not uncommon to hear such explanations as, "I thought he was the best I could do," "It seemed he would be a good husband and father for our family and would be able to provide well," or "I never really felt I loved her, but I thought the love would grow." Some will believe their reasons should have worked because, "I was taught that love was an action, not a feeling, and it seemed as though we had many common interests and that this would work out well." Then there's, "My mother really liked him and he was the first one that she liked, so I thought that would be best for me," and "I knew she was God's choice for me."

Whatever the reason, many couples marry without attraction, passion, or love for each other. In our culture, this lack almost inevitably gets in the way of a couple's sexual relationship. A sense of passion or love, though hard to define, seems to be a necessary ingredient for total sexual experience. If love was never there, as times get tough, as love develops with someone else, or as one spouse is reminded of past loves, it becomes much more difficult to maintain the relationship or to work toward sexual satisfaction. In some cultures where divorce is less acceptable, the relationship may be able to survive. But in our society, with all its emphasis on fulfillment, satisfaction, and love, and with divorce being common even within the church, a relationship not based on love is bound to have difficulty. It is our opinion that couples can learn to love one another if they are willing to commit themselves with all of their being—spiritually, behaviorally, and emotionally. Achieving that commitment will take work.

HOW DO YOU "FALL IN LOVE" AGAIN?

How can you build or rebuild love? First, both spouses must want to pursue love between them. If only one is interested in restoring the relationship and focuses on making the other happy, it will never succeed. It takes commitment from both people. With that commitment, a loving relationship is a possibility. And once you have established that loving relationship, you can build your sexual intimacy and passion.

Let's say that you and your spouse have made the commitment to build or rebuild love. Where do you start? Counseling, from a pastor or a professional therapist, may be necessary to help you deal with and heal painful memories.

In other cases, the couple may be able to develop love on their own. They do it simply by talking together, sharing their feelings and thoughts, expressing where they have been, where they are now, and where they would like to go in the relationship. The step-by-step process of sexual retraining detailed in our book *Restoring the Pleasure* is usually necessary to discover sexual passion and intimacy.

Sometimes love grows again almost spontaneously when a change occurs in the couple's life. The children grow up and leave home, or the career becomes less demanding, and without those external pressures the couple can rediscover their affection for one another. The commitment was there all the time, but the corresponding attention that nurtured the feelings was lacking.

Specific planning to clear out involvements that interfere with the development of love, and to allow time for positive experiences together, should include mutually selected nonsexual and sexual events. In these times together, the couple focuses on communication, fun, or bodily pleasure. We recommend our Formula for Intimacy (on page 202) of fifteen minutes per day to connect emotionally, to share spiritually, and to kiss passionately.

The couple may need to examine and deal with old habits that have a way of hanging around when a couple have been operating apart for a number of years. Examine those habits and decide which ones must be consciously altered. Don't just assume that everything will work out fine—strive to make sure it does!

If one spouse has been unfaithful, there is no way that love in the marriage can be established unless that spouse will make a firm commitment to the marriage relationship and to building trust through accountability. When trust has been broken, actions of love do not necessarily bring healing. There may be real struggles with the whole nature of commitment and the development of an understanding of what the marriage contract means for each spouse.

If you are in a marriage in which all the effort for the marriage seems to be up to you, and your mate does not seem willing to communicate—you are in a tough spot. It is difficult to give general directions about how to proceed, but there are several things we recommend as a way of getting started. Spend some time assessing your contribution to the problem. Are you nagging, withdrawing, demanding, complaining to friends or neighbors, or being the "suffering spouse"? Determine if there are any ways of change offered that you haven't accepted. Be sure your needs and desires have been clearly expressed without blame of your spouse. Don't wait for your mate's action—you make the first move. If nothing works, seek some help from a professional who has an unbiased perspective.

Focusing on building intimacy in the sexual area is often an effective approach to discovering or renewing a love relationship. Although sex is not the basis of love, a lack of sexual passion and intimacy is a symptom of a lack of love.

There are people who have, by their own efforts, built a relationship of love when those feelings were not initially there. For most people, outside help is required to achieve this. That support system may be a small group, an empathetic friend, a helpful pastor, or a professionally trained counselor. Always remember that people have the capacity to change. God can work in your life as you let him. If you don't have the feelings of love, you can grow into them in the days ahead.

25 BIRTH CONTROL GETS IN THE WAY

There is one common complaint that seems to hinder full sexual pleasure. Though it is often not identified as a hindrance, it involves birth control—either the lack of it or the method used. Sometimes this problem is identified only in retrospect; that is, when birth control is no longer an issue the couple discover how much relief they feel. For example, if the woman gets a tubal ligation or if the man gets a vasectomy, they suddenly realize that they are not nearly as anxious as they used to be. The woman is much more free to respond, the man is more relaxed. Concern about pregnancy weighs heavily on the minds of many couples. Some are not protected in any way, while others may be unsure of their protection, or the mechanical device used interrupts the pleasure of the sexual experience. Still others are in constant conflict because of religious restrictions regarding birth control: They either experience guilt for going against their church's teaching by using protection, or the fear of pregnancy dominates their sex life. Any one of these may cause low-grade anxiety that inhibits the couple's freedom to enjoy a full sexual involvement.

METHODS OF BIRTH CONTROL

Withdrawal

Some couples attempt to prevent pregnancy by withdrawing the penis from the vagina before ejaculation. They believe that this will keep the sperm outside the vagina and hence the woman cannot be impregnated. This is inaccurate information. During intercourse, a man will release some seminal fluid containing sperm before he ejaculates. Also, emotionally, regular withdrawal before ejaculation causes frustration. The experience of becoming aroused and building toward a peak of sexual release leads a couple to a sense of wanting increased intensity and momentum. The natural response for both is to push and thrust harder. To withdraw or pull away at that time goes against all our natural inclinations. Withdrawal is neither effective in controlling pregnancy nor satisfying in terms of the sexual experience. There is obviously not much to be said in its favor.

Barrier Methods

Mechanical devices can end up getting in the way. The most commonly used are the diaphragm for the woman and the condom for the man. The diaphragm, a small, soft, rubber device shaped like a bowl, is inserted into the vagina to cover the opening to the uterus (the cervix), thus preventing the sperm from traveling into the uterus to fertilize the egg. Some women report that they regularly insert the diaphragm so they don't find it to be interruptive. Other women who don't want to put the diaphragm in until they know they are going to be having intercourse find that insertion interrupts the flow of lovemaking. Condoms ("rubbers"), latex or animal-membrane devices shaped like the finger of a glove that are placed over the erect penis, also interrupt. In addition, many men experience diminished sensations with condoms. Not only is the condom a bothersome interruption and a sensation diminisher, but it also causes anxiety because the couple must be sure that all the sperm-containing seminal fluid remains in the condom. Thus they are not really free to relax even after the ejaculation.

In addition to condoms and diaphragms, other barrier methods, devices that keep the sperm from meeting with the egg, are available. The cervical cap is similar to the diaphragm in function. It is made of soft rubber, is thimble-shaped, has a rim, and fits over the cervix. The advantage of the cap is that it can be left in place for forty-eight hours and is less likely to dislodge than the diaphragm. The sponge is a two-inch-wide, round, soft, pillow-shaped polyurethane sponge permeated with spermicide and can be left in place for twenty-four hours with equal effectiveness for repeated intercourse. The female condom is a plastic pouch or sheath that lines the inside of the vagina. A flexible ring on each end holds the condom in place. We haven't received reports from women who use the female condom. The IUD, intrauterine device, rates high in terms of convenience compared to other barrier methods but has not been embraced by women since it was taken off the market a number of years ago due to complications many women experienced. The new, improved IUDs have been shown to be effective and no longer likely to be associated with the complications that were reported in the past.

Hormonal Pregnancy Prevention

The convenience, effectiveness, and lack of interruption of pleasure associated with hormonal methods make this choice highly desirable. The ration and amount of chemical activity of progesterone, estrogen, and androgen vary with the various types of hormonal intervention. Each woman's body has to be evaluated to determine which hormonal combination and delivery system will be most effective with the fewest side effects for her. When a woman is well matched with a pill, patch, or other hormonal method, she may benefit in her total sense of well-being in addition to the freedom she enjoys sexually.

Natural Family Planning

More and more couples are avoiding sexual intercourse during the woman's fertile phase of her menstrual cycle as their means of birth control. *The Ovulation Method: Natural Family Planning* by John J. Billings details every dimension of planning pregnancies without using contraceptives or sterilization.

Training is necessary to use any method of natural family planning effectively. For disciplined, determined, well-trained couples, these methods have been successful and enjoyable. One of the benefits is increased awareness of your hormonal cycle. The disadvantages include the lack of freedom to enjoy intercourse throughout the month.

Surgical Sterilization

The permanent methods—tubal ligation for the woman or vasectomy for the man—are sure ways of avoiding pregnancy without interfering with sexual process or pleasure. But these are not advisable until the couple have decided not to have any more children. Even then, the decision is a difficult one for most couples. Our recommendation is that the spouse who is ready for permanent intervention be certain that no matter what might happen to his or her spouse or children, he or she would choose not to have more children.

ख़

Family planning methods are much discussed and constantly being improved. We wish we could give clear and simple answers as to the best way to achieve absolutely hassle-free birth control, but each couple has to struggle out loud with each other as they plan their future. Having planned and decided, they must behave realistically and in good conscience in line with those decisions.

If you are determined to control impregnation, a discussion with your physician can determine which methods would be best for you. It is most helpful to get those methods working for you, and you working for them, rather than to continue being at odds with them and letting them interfere with your enjoyment.

This chapter is not intended to be a comprehensive treatment on the whole issue of birth control. Rather, it is designed to focus on the birth-control issues that get in the way of satisfying sexual experience. For more information on choosing a family planning method based on safety, effectiveness, convenience, and personal preference, refer to Chapter 9, "Choosing and Using Family Planning Options" in our book *Getting Your Sex Life Off to a Great Start.*

26 I'M NOT INTERESTED

In order for a couple to get together sexually, they must make a choice to do so. People usually choose what they desire. If people do not particularly desire sex, they are less likely to choose to pursue sex.

God designed us to desire sex in marriage, yet many times a person does not experience the urge for sexual intimacy, arousal, or response. What gets in the way? Throughout Scripture, the sexual relationship between a husband and a wife is used to teach us about how God desires a relationship with us. Yet, many times people do not sense an urge to connect with God. Just as sin gets in the way of a person's realizing a need for God, even so, barriers can block our awareness of our desire for sex in marriage. In this chapter, we will look at various situations that lead to lack of interest, and discuss some ways to solve this most perplexing and elusive problem.

WHEN HE'S IN THE MOOD AND SHE'S NOT

A woman may lack desire because the sexual experience itself is not satisfying. Lack of sexual satisfaction leads to lack of interest. Let's look at some specific reasons why a woman might find sex unsatisfactory or undesirable.

A woman might lack desire because she does not feel emotionally connected with her husband. He may not express warmth and care about her needs for sexual pleasure. It is essential for a woman in any sexual experience to feel loved and cared for, to feel some tenderness, some concern for her thoughts and feelings and her current situation. Without this connection, she is not likely to allow herself to be intimate and emotionally vulnerable. If emotional intimacy is lacking, sexual desire will be stifled.

Similar to the lack of emotional satisfaction is a lack of interest due to the absence of physical satisfaction. If the woman does not go from the excitement phase to the plateau phase to orgasm, any interest she may have had in sex will wane. Even if she experiences arousal, consistent failure to reach a climax will eventually squelch her interest in sex. It's no fun to have your body and your feelings prepared for an orgasm over and over again, and never or rarely be able to get over the hill. The frustration of arousal without release leads to lack of desire.

The graph for the woman who often becomes aroused without release is shown below. At one point her experience would be charted by line 1; in time it resembles line 4.

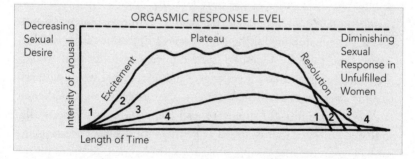

When a woman does not experience satisfaction even though there is arousal, over a period of time the arousal is likely to diminish, and eventually she will feel little or no desire. You will notice that the bottom line on the graph is almost a straight line. As a new bride, she may have been excited about being sexual with her husband and become very aroused. However, when she had no orgasmic response, and hence felt no satisfaction, she began to limit her arousal.

You will notice on the graph that it takes a little longer for her to get aroused, and she does not become quite as aroused. Then, as time goes on, arousal takes even longer and is even less intense. It also takes longer for her to return to a prestimulated state. Finally, she experiences almost no arousal and hence no desire.

This flattening out of the curve tends to occur between the fifth and tenth years of marriage. The timing is sometimes related to other events in life, such as having children and being occupied with heavy responsibilities. The pattern is certainly reversible, but the couple may need the help of a sexual therapist or a self-help book like our *Restoring the Pleasure*.

This lack of physical satisfaction may have been caused by the fact that the man ejaculated prematurely, not allowing enough time for the woman to respond with an orgasm. Or it may have come about because the woman could never allow herself to experience an orgasm, so she was left hanging in her preorgasmic state regardless of how long the man could maintain his erection without ejaculation. Whatever the original cause, the pattern must be reversed.

Another major cause of lack of satisfaction and decreasing sexual interest in the woman is the boredom that may set in because of mechanical or goal-oriented sexual activity. A woman's interest is not likely to be maintained if the couple repeats the same sexual routine every time they are together. Even our very favorite meal would become boring and no longer trigger our appetites if we duplicated it time after time. Sex is no different. Each time we are together is a new opportunity for discovery and connection. Likewise, goal-oriented sex—sex that is aimed at getting aroused, staying aroused, or having an orgasm—will get old for most women. Sex is to be an expression of love, caring, and affection. Lack of interest is likely to develop after a couple has functioned with a mechanical or goal-oriented approach for some period of time.

We might ask, Why would a woman continue to have sex if it has so little positive benefit for her? A woman usually has some understandable reasons for putting up with sex even though it is not satisfying for her. The main reason is to carry out her duty as a wife; she feels she must meet her husband's sexual needs to keep him at home and happy. However, duty sex does not work long-term. We are to give ourselves to each other. This is a mutual expectation, not a response to neediness. When a woman has sex to meet her husband's needs, rather than to give herself and enjoy the pleasure of her husband's body, eventually he will be frustrated with her lack of interest. Neither will end up happy.

Other women who don't enjoy sex avoid rather than perform their duty. But they are not usually very direct. Few women will just say, "Hey, I hate sex, so forget it, buddy." Rather, they will find more subtle ways to get around it. Fatigue or a physical complaint is often used to avoid sex. A busy schedule or getting up later or earlier than her husband may be ways of avoiding being around when he might be sexually interested. She may initiate a hassle when sex would be expected.

When a woman's lack of desire is secondary to not feeling cared for by her husband, an inability to let go and release sexual arousal, or because sex is mechanical and goal-oriented, the primary reason that led to her lack of desire needs to be addressed and corrected so that her sexual desire can surface. Marital and/or sexual therapy may be necessary. Other couples may find the help they need by reading and working through a book like our *Restoring the Pleasure*.

WHEN HE HAS THE HEADACHE

It may come as a surprise to some that we would even include the category of the uninterested male, since all men are supposed to be vitally interested in and even preoccupied with sex. How can it be that there are men who are not interested? There are those who are what we would call sexually naive or uninformed; there are the entrepreneurial or goal-oriented men whose interest in sexual activity diminished with acquiring a wife; and there are those who come to marriage with homosexual orientation. Let's look at each of these in some detail.

Sexually Naive

The sexually naive or uninformed man is usually one who has grown up in a very protected, almost overprotected environment. He was usually either a mama's boy or a somewhat frightened child. Such a boy had relatively little exposure to the normal sexual stimuli that most children receive in growing up, whether they receive it in the home, classroom, church, or on the streets. He may have been warned against the evils of sexual activity and never been taught about the joys and pleasures of life. Probably little physical affection was shown in his home, either between parents and children or between mother and father. He may have heard several warnings about the dangers of masturbation; any type of sexual interest or exploration was dealt with briefly but conclusively.

A man who was very successful in his professional career, had been married for fifteen years, and served as a leader in his church community had little interest in sex. As we explored the situation with him and his wife, we discovered that he lacked much of the basic information necessary for normal sexual experience. He found any kind of genital touching of himself or of his wife to be extremely distasteful; he tended to engage in sexual activity mainly to please his wife. He was reported by his wife to be someone who really didn't know how to do anything in bed. He didn't know how to kiss, and she could never seem to teach him; he did not touch her in a way that was comfortable either for her or for him. Evidently he had failed to learn about these activities at the appropriate time in his life. Now he found it extremely difficult to change.

The sexually naive man will often be perceived by his wife as a cumbersome and inadequate lover. It is gratifying to be able to help these couples, since the sexually naive man is very responsive to sexual retraining if his wife is willing to engage with him in a teaching-learning process.

Entrepreneurial Man

The second type of man whose wife reports that he is uninterested in sex is what we might call the entrepreneurial male. He has seen the process of acquiring a wife as a goal to be achieved; once he has done that, he moves on to other projects, even as he moves from one business venture to the next. These men are highly successful *ini-*

tiators of business projects who turn over the day-to-day operation of each venture to someone else while they move on to a new project.

It is not uncommon for these men to have selected extremely attractive, bright, and confident wives who will be good mothers for their children and who can function very adequately in the social scene. But such a woman soon finds herself emotionally starved because the man she married and had all her hope in, the man who romanced her in a most charming manner, now spends little or no time or energy to bring her the continued emotional sexual fulfillment for which she hungers. The energy that the man may once have had for sexual activity is now being put into other ventures.

Some men, on being confronted with their entrepreneurial approach, decide to change their priorities to a more personal, less business-oriented manner of life. They decide to go with the more loving side rather than the material side of their life. This obviously fits in with the biblical perspective of how men are to love their wives. Unfortunately, some men say, "No, if she chooses to live with me, she's going to have to recognize that this is how life is going to be." This places the woman in a dilemma and forces her to make a difficult choice. Such a man can change—if he *chooses* to change. His change may require professional help.

Gender Identity

The third category of men who lack sexual desire are those who struggle with gender identity—those who find themselves more attracted to men than women. The homosexually oriented man may have known of these feelings before he married but chose to ignore his inclinations, hoping he could make it work with a woman. If this man makes the decision to learn how to turn his attraction for men to pursuing and responding to his wife, we are able to help him do that. He is not likely to completely change his affinity for men to women, in general, but since he is married, all he needs to focus on is learning to enjoy his wife.

∽

How does a man's lack of interest in sex show up? Because the man in our society tends to be the initiator, what usually happens is that there is simply little initiation of sexual activity. Then the dissatisfied and unfulfilled wife expresses her concern about her husband's love for her and her concern about her own desirability. This may lead to some attempt to deal with the problem. Often the man will, in a brief flurry of activity, initiate sex a few times, which will bring temporary satisfaction to his wife. But then things will drift off to the same state in which they were before she complained.

Over a period of time, a pattern will often develop with the unsatisfied wife exploding every several months, followed by sexual activity, and then a period of little interest during which the woman again becomes increasingly disgruntled until she explodes again. The difference between the situations with an uninterested man and an uninterested woman is that if the woman is disinterested, the man may still be getting his satisfaction. But if the man is disinterested, the woman will usually be left frustrated.

LACK OF DESIRE EXPERIENCED BY BOTH MEN AND WOMEN

The apostle Paul, a follower of Jesus Christ, in one of his letters answered questions regarding sex for the people of the New Testament church at Corinth. Paul's answers, as they are expressed in the paraphrase of the New Testament called *The Message,* read as follows: "Is it a good thing to have sexual relations? Certainly—but only within a certain context. It's good for a man to have a wife, and for a woman to have a husband. Sexual drives are strong, but marriage is strong enough to contain them and provide for a balanced and fulfilling sexual life in a world of sexual disorder" (1 Cor. 7:1–2). Yet, as we are learning, it is not unusual for both men and women not to experience a strong sex drive. What are some of the reasons common to both genders?

Internal Conflict About Being Sexual

One cause of lack of interest in sex due to internal conflict is sexual ambivalence. The sexually ambivalent person was usually raised in an alcoholic, dysfunctional, or emotionally chaotic home. Because the home was out of control, the person tends to struggle with control issues. To be sexually responsive is to be out of control, a feeling that is very frightening and to be avoided at all cost. The person's resistance to engage in sex is not just a passive lack of desire; it is a tenacious fighting of sexual feelings or activities. This resistance is usually confusing to the spouse, since the person tends to be able to be very responsive once he or she allows stimulation and the body's arousal takes over. The person learned from the example in the home to be out of control, so he or she does respond intensely but strongly dislikes being out of control because of the negative association from childhood. This person's sexual response pattern looks like this:

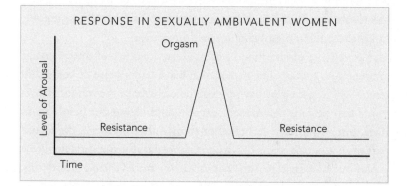

To counteract this syndrome, the first step is to recognize the pattern. Then the person must *decide to be sexual*. It is almost like a conversion experience. The person has been using his or her need for control to resist sex. Now the decision is made to use the need for control to take over his or her sex life positively. So the next step is to *take charge*. Be in control actively rather than with passive resistance. Plan and schedule sex not because of desire, but by decision. Recognize that sexual desire will not surface naturally, so sex will happen only because the resistant spouse takes active control and schedules sex once or twice a week. It has to be his or her agenda, not the spouse keeping track or checking. The final ingredient for success is that the spouse must back off. If this pattern is ever going to change, the spouse has to allow the one with the need for control to be totally in charge. The couple, with the resistant spouse leading, need to make a plan of accountability. For example, they might decide that if the one who had been resistant has not initiated in two weeks, the other spouse can ask for a talk time. In a loving, empathetic approach, check to see how it is going and how the person might need the other's care and support. Keep in mind that the person who is trying to change a pattern cannot wait for feelings of desire or discouragement to set in.

Another cause for lack of desire due to internal conflict is past sexual trauma. Sexual abuse or violation will usually have been kept a secret. There may be a fear of telling, or the person may have blocked the memories. If the abuse happened as a child, the person is likely to have felt responsibility, even though the child was a helpless victim. Guilt and shame are carried into adulthood, causing the internal conflict about being sexual in marriage.

The pattern of childhood sexual abuse involves advanced sexual awareness as a child. The person may have had a sense of being different—of knowing or having experienced what other children had not. Then there is heightened sexuality and acting out before marriage, but as marriage gets close or shortly after marriage, the sexual part of that person shuts down. It is almost as if sexuality were never a part of who that person was made to be. We have heard this expression hundreds of times: "If my spouse didn't want sex, it wouldn't matter 'cause I don't care if we ever have sex again. I think God forgot to put that software in me."

To allow desire to resurface, the person will need to deal with the past trauma. Talk about it. Share the details of what happened. Write about it. Keep a journal of any thoughts, dreams, or pictures, however incomplete or fleeting. Eventually, a complete picture may evolve. Remembering the abuse is not necessary to overcome the effects. If the symptoms are faced and dealt with and there is openness to listening to oneself, healing is possible. Professional help usually is needed to guide the process of healing. Joining a group of others who have been victims of abuse has additional benefits through engaging in others' past and healing process. Many churches offer these groups. Being able to enlist God's forgiveness and strength is vital. Sometimes people who have been abused feel compelled to confront their abusers. Confrontation is not always a part of healing. In fact, the person seeking healing through a confrontation may be reabused by being made to feel that this was all in the mind or his/her fault. Also, it is important to recognize that forgiveness only follows the freedom and ability to experience the pain, hurt, and anger toward the perpetrator. Forgiveness is an ongoing process of experiencing and then letting go of the pain. The person gets to the place where the perpetrator is no longer allowed to have control over his or her life. In the meantime, however, prearranged signals will need to be talked about and planned into the couple's sexual times so that when flashbacks or panic responses occur, the person can signal the spouse to change the sexual activity. The impact of sexual trauma can be undone, but it will take work and compassionate care from others.

Emotional-Sexual Blocks

Both men and women may have emotional blocks to sexual desire due to lack of bonding in infancy, rigid antisexual teaching during their developmental years, or a controlling, dominant opposite-sex parent who disempowered their same-sex parent as a sexual role model.

The woman having emotional blocks to her desire is not likely to be aware of sexual urges at all or have quickly fleeting desires. A man will tend to masturbate but not initiate sex with his wife, so he may describe his struggle as a failure rather than a lack of desire.

Nathan was a young, attractive businessman of strong character and values. He and his new bride were both committed followers of Jesus Christ. Even though there had seemed to be passion between them in their limited physical contact before marriage, the honeymoon was a rude awakening for her, and maybe even for him. He was sexually avoidant and aversive. She would try to initiate, and he would distract. We discovered that he had been raised in a home where the family was clearly divided. The children were aligned with the mother against his father. He had never felt good about his father as a sexual person or as a model for him as a husband. He was left with difficulty being sexual with his wife. Therapy and retraining was necessary and, at times, discouraging, but eventually they were able to work out a system of relating sexually that brought fulfillment for both. Bringing a father-image, male mentor to come alongside Nathan was a huge help in the therapy process.

External Stresses Interfere

Even though it takes sex to make children, they tend to be a major sexual distracter. Joyce recently taught a class to mothers of preschool children. She entitled her talk, "Are Real Moms Hot?" Many times being Mom and being sexual seem to be mutually exclusive. Dads are not exempt either.

If parents with children in the home are going to continue a fulfilling sex life, they will likely have to plan time for the two of them that will allow them to anticipate their time and enjoy each other physically without demands or expectations for specific behaviors or responses. They will also have to save energy for the two of them by setting priorities and managing their lives. It will help the parents to accept that they don't have to be turned on to initiate sex, but can decide to be sexual because it is a convenient time to have privacy. Knowing and taking responsibility to create the conditions that are best for them will enhance their times together. And above all, no matter how little or how much time they can carve out for their sex life, they need to keep their pilot light on by kissing passionately every day for at least thirty seconds.

Job stress, finances, and any other outside pressure will take away from sexual time and energy. If the couple keep connecting and talking about their outside distractions, they will be able to plan ways to counter those and focus on each other.

Physical Factors Hinder

Illness, alcohol, and drugs all will interrupt the natural flow of God-given urges. Eliminating those issues and staying connected will be the most helpful.

Hormonal imbalances are the most common physical reason for

lack of sexual desire. All the effort in the world won't work if the person's hormones are out of balance. When either a man or a woman comes to us reporting lack of sexual desire, the first step we take is to have the person's physician order a complete hormonal panel. For a woman, this means the estrogen, progesterone, total testosterone, and free or bioavailable testosterone levels are checked and compared with the normal range for the laboratory reporting the results. For men, both total and free (bioavailable) testosterone levels are necessary. Since testosterone is the drive hormone, if the free or bioavailable testosterone level is low normal or below normal, replacement will be necessary in order to have sexual desire. We usually suggest a 1 percent testosterone cream applied to the external genitals—the vulval area for the woman, and either a testosterone patch applied to the scrotum or a 1 percent androgen gel applied to the upper arms for the man. Daily application is usually recommended but can be adjusted according to the person's symptoms. The person's physician will manage both the dosage and frequency of usage.

Emotional Changes Hamper

Depression, anxiety, and sexual phobias will squelch desire for sex. When there is tension, the bedroom may become as somber as the funeral parlor. In that case there is going to be little interest in sex. Tensions, anxieties, depressive states, and phobias must be relieved in order to revive sexual energy. Psychotherapy or marital counseling may be necessary.

სა

If you are a person for whom desire does not surface easily or spontaneously, what steps can you take? How might you discover or be more aware of your sexual feelings?

In Chapter 9, we talked about building desire. We have emphasized that sexual desire is a natural, God-designed bodily feeling. It can surface most readily when you clear out distractions, identify what works for you, communicate openly about your needs to your spouse, and then take responsibility to get what you need to arouse your interest. The issues of feeling and expressing sexual desire within the relationship have to be clearly and openly discussed between husband and wife. That is the first step toward remedying problems with desire.

Let's assume for the moment that the man is the one who lacks interest. We would encourage a thorough and open discussion about how the man feels in this situation, what he thinks gets in the way of desire, and what he perceives to be his duties and obligations as a husband and lover. Then the wife can clearly communicate how his lack of interest affects her. Sometimes this process makes clear what is getting in the way and causing the lack of interest. In other situations it is much more difficult because at the conscious level a man believes he is interested yet rarely shows any interest. An unconscious barrier gets in the way and causes the lack of sexual pursuit.

When the barrier is unconscious, and the couple are not able to identify what is getting in the way of feeling or expressing sexual desire, they should seek professional counseling. Helen Singer Kaplan's work on problems with sexual desire shows that unconscious barriers to feeling the need for or interest in sexual involvement stem from early childhood environment. Because of the strong impact of early influencing factors, an individual is not likely to be able to resolve the problem without the help of a professional.

When the problem with desire is related to an obvious stress, it may be dealt with between the two of you. Talk about how the lack of desire feels to each of you. Then determine together how you are going to bring about changes that can allow the natural desire to surface.

Allowing for desire requires giving space to the person who lacks the feeling. Giving space means that the other spouse must avoid initiating sex or communicating expectations that will be felt as demands. The steps for reversing who initiates, as defined in Chapter 11, should be helpful.

Once the person with a desire block feels the sense of space, it is important for that person to find ways to encourage awareness of sexual feelings. You will need to find, or make, time for this. Maybe you need to reduce outside pressure. With this pressure-free time available, look for sensuousness in your world. Use some of the natural external stimuli mentioned in Chapter 10. Read the Song of Songs every day. Leave yourself reminder notes to turn on sensuous music while you're driving or working around the house or yard. If you are a woman, get acquainted with your own genitalia as described in Chapter 6. Ask God to free up your feelings for sex, and praise him every time you feel even a fleeting urge. Spend time looking in the mirror and thanking God for how he made you. Focus on listening to your body. Be aware of touch that has a tingle. What we're saying is: Give yourself a good tune-up.

Since each problem of lack of interest is unique, each couple will have to be creative in finding their own variations for working out the details. Levels of interest can change, and thus any couple who experiences lack of interest should begin working at it and seek help if necessary.

27 NOT ENOUGH WHEN YOU NEED IT: ERECTILE DYSFUNCTION

Everyone knows that all men are "supposed" to be ready for sex at any time of the day or night. This myth gets perpetuated from youth. The myth says that from adolescence on, a man is so charged sexually, he is always waiting and ready for a sexual experience. According to this theory, the woman is the one who is hesitant, unsure, and in need of extensive buildup. The symbol for this masculinity is the erect penis. It represents manhood and is expected to be ready to perform at a moment's notice.

We have been surprised at how early this concept is developed. One night when our son was five years old, we asked him to get into his pajamas during a TV commercial. His older sister was also in the room. During his changing process he covered his genitals with his hand. When we asked him about his new modesty, he replied, "Well, it pops up if it sees a girl." It responds on its own. It can see. And it is affected by what it sees.

For men, it comes as a major shock when suddenly the symbol of their masculinity does not respond on cue. It usually means much more to the man than the simple fact that he is not responding sexually at that moment. It causes him to question his status as an adequate male. Problems with erections hinder sexual satisfaction, diminish self-esteem, and cause tension in the marriage.

Erectile dysfunction, or impotence, refers to the man's inability to get or keep erections. E.D. does not refer to the inability to impregnate—this is sterility. Nor does E.D. refer to the inability to ejaculate—this is called inhibited ejaculation.

Erectile dysfunction can take on many forms. Some men achieve no erection at all. The usual kind of stimulation may occur, but the penis remains flaccid. For others, an erection may occur in the regular manner, but as the love play continues, anxiety sets in and the erection is lost. For still others, the erection may be maintained very adequately up to the point of entry. As soon as entry is either contemplated or attempted, the erection dissipates. For some, erection may be maintained beyond the point of entry and then wane after a period of activity inside the vagina. No matter when the erection goes away, its loss is always troublesome.

In any extended lovemaking time, it is normal for the intensity of the erection to wax and wane. For many men, an erection may disappear almost completely and then return again. This is a normal part of the process. The only time the loss of an erection is considered a problem is when the man is unable to relax enough or does not have the confidence to regain the erection.

How do you know whether your struggle with erections is the result of a physical problem or emotional distress? When we first wrote the original *The Gift of Sex,* professional experts on this topic believed that 85 percent of the time erectile dysfunction was due to emotional issues. Currently, the research is showing that 85 percent of the time erectile dysfunction is caused by physical problems. Today, E.D. is thought of as a symptom of an underlying physical condition or a side effect of medication. Because of these findings, whenever a man reports erectile difficulties, we advise a physical and urologic examination to rule out or identify and treat physical causes.

CAUSES OF ERECTILE DYSFUNCTION

The causes of erectile dysfunction are complex because the process of getting and keeping ejaculations is complex. The nerves, the muscles, the heart, the blood circulation, the mind, and the emotions all work together to make an erection happen. During sexual excitement, the penis must be continually pumped full of blood with a pressure greater than the blood flowing back from the penis.

Physical Factors

Because problems with erections may be due to either emotional or physical factors that interfere with the process of getting and keeping erections, a physical evaluation is very important. All medications the man is taking should be studied in relation to his struggle. E.D. may signal other diseases that are the cause, such as:

- Diabetes
- High blood pressure
- Cardiovascular disease
- Peripheral vascular disease
- Neurological disease

All these conditions and their treatments can affect the vascular system or the neurological input of the penis. Sometimes difficulty with erections may be a signal to get help for another medical problem that might have otherwise gone undiagnosed. One sixty-seven-year-old man left our office and went directly to his primary care physician, who referred him to a cardiologist. The cardiologist detected a cardiac problem that was corrected immediately and may have saved our client's life.

Aging

Erectile dysfunction is erroneously associated with aging. Even though the incidence of E.D. does increase from 20 to 52 percent with age, E.D. is neither a necessary consequence of nor an irreversible part of aging. The normal changes of aging may cause anxiety and spectatoring on the part of the man or the woman. In those cases, it is the lack of knowledge about the normal consequences of aging and the lack of adjustment to those changes that perpetuate the difficulty with erections.

How does aging affect the sexual response? As with all other physical responses, we begin to slow down as we grow older. Most sixty-five-year-old men cannot work as many days with long hours, travel as hard, play as hard, or put their bodies through the same kind of stress over a period of time as they could when they were twenty-one.

As we grow older, there are response changes that we may notice. The first effect of aging may be that we find ourselves somewhat slower to get an erection than we used to be, and direct stimulation may be needed to produce an erection. We may also find that the erections are less firm than they once were. Finally, it may be that we will not need to ejaculate with each experience of sexual arousal and may even need fewer sexual experiences. None of these changes, which usually happen gradually, need get in the way of our sexual experience unless we become anxious about them. In fact, many couples report that as the man begins to slow down, he is free to enjoy some of the more pleasurable dimensions of the sexual experience rather than being focused on just the excitement dimension. This brings more pleasure for the wife. For years she may have been feeling that he always moved through the experience too quickly, without giving her the chance to keep up with him. Women often consider the slowing-down effect of aging as a blessing rather than a loss. Yet the man may feel anxious about the natural impact of aging on his sexual experience. His anxiety is likely to exaggerate the effects of aging.

An eighty-four-year-old man sitting in our office sheepishly asked, "Do you work with people my age? My wife and I have been having great sex all these years, but lately it hasn't been going too well for me. Am I too old to expect anything different? Should I just give up?" His seventy-nine-year-old wife expressed how much she hoped they could work it out. Sex had been especially good for them since he retired nineteen years ago—she didn't want it to stop now.

The hesitancy reflected in the man's questioning depicts the commonly held attitude that sex and aging are mutually exclusive. Yet we know that we are designed as sexual persons from conception to death, and the capacity for sexual unity and pleasure continues long after the procreative function of sex ends. A bit of guidance and encouragement helped this couple continue to enjoy a fulfilling sex life.

Unconsummated Marriage Due to Vaginismus

Difficulty or inability to enter the woman's vagina will inevitably lead to loss of erection. The sequence often goes like this. Most couples go into their first sexual experience assuming they will consummate their marriage. They may be a bit anxious about how they will perform. Then, in the awkward and anxious attempts to make entry, the man will find himself pushing against what seems to be a solid wall that he cannot penetrate. This solid wall is the rigid tightening of the lower one third of the vagina (vaginismus). As he tries over and over, he finds himself beginning to lose his erection even as he thinks about entry. By this time, the pattern has been established. Now the couple has two problems: vaginismus and erectile dysfunction.

The discouragement can be overwhelming. Some couples are able to resolve the problem by themselves, but often it is necessary to seek competent help. Their embarrassment may keep them from doing so until they become eager to have children. The sooner they get the right help, the quicker they will find relief.

Premature Ejaculation

Erectile difficulties may come after years of struggling with lack of ejaculatory control. The man who ejaculates before he or his wife is ready for his release focuses more and more on his sexual response. As he concentrates mentally on trying to control his ejaculation, this concentration gets in the way of maintaining his erection and his freedom to enjoy himself with abandonment during sex with his wife. The focus on response and concern about it brings about the loss of erections.

Emotional Factors

E.D. may also be the result of psychological issues. Just because we now know that the physical causes are the most important to consider first does not mean that we ignore both the emotional causes and consequences of E.D. We have to be cautious that with the pendulum swing to the fixing of the hydraulics of E.D., we continue to consider the emotional factors that can affect erectile response.

Anxiety in the relationship (interpersonal) and within the person (performance pressure) can interfere with the man's ability to get aroused. For the sexual experience to be delightful, satisfying, and complete, you need emotional abandonment. By that we mean that you (man or woman) cannot be focusing your attention on how your body is responding, but rather you must focus on the joy and delight of the physical sensations, the emotional satisfaction, and the experience of loving and being loved. This usually happens quite naturally until for some reason your body does not respond the way you expect it to. When the natural bodily response of an erection does not occur or is not maintained, you may become preoccupied with the erection. As we discussed in Chapter 20, this preoccupation or self-consciousness usually moves the man into the spectator role. When either the husband or wife is the spectator of his physical response, the response stops working automatically and is affected by the attempt to take control of that response.

Any time you try to force your body to do something it cannot do on demand, you will most likely keep yourself from doing the very thing you are trying to do. The falling asleep example from Chapter 20 fits here as well. You can probably recall the times when you have needed to get a good night's sleep but you were keyed up or anxious. You went to bed and thought about falling asleep, or tried to get to sleep. You moved into the spectator role and observed how you were doing in your falling-asleep process. And so you kept yourself awake. Finally, you began to distract yourself from thinking about falling asleep. Distraction is also needed when you are attempting to overcome impotence.

The pattern thus begins with an experience in which an erection does not happen as it has in the past. The man becomes a spectator, attempting to bring about the desired response. During this time, anxiety is building about his competence to function sexually. There are several directions that it could go from this point. Some men try even harder by frequently initiating sexual activity in the attempt to get past the dilemma and to prove themselves as men. Others respond in just the opposite way. They begin to avoid sex.

Many men report that as the impotence perseveres, they are continually conscious of the state of their penis, watching to see whether it is responding at all. In some ways, this has the function of isolating the penis from the total body and the bodily responses. It may reach the point of feeling anesthetized, losing feeling, because of the anxiety that surrounds the problem. As the pattern progresses, it can bring about depression and discouragement because the man feels that he will never regain his ability to get or maintain an erection.

His wife, too, may be struggling. Her initial response is usually not one of great concern. She assumes this is a temporary situation that will pass. However, other times, the wife may be immediately concerned. Her anxiety may perpetuate his difficulty. If the difficulty persists, the wife may begin to feel rejected by the husband's lack of response, feeling that she is no longer attractive to him. Most women cannot help wondering if it is their fault that the husband is not able to respond as he used to.

Other women react with anger in response to the husband's impotence—anger that the man is not providing her with the kind of sexual experience that brings her satisfaction. This anger, whether expressed or only felt, will often increase the pressure on the man and further inhibit his sexual freedom, and thus increase his preoccupation with his sexual response. You can see how the downward spiral is perpetuated by the natural reactions of both the man and the woman.

Some women attempt to take on the responsibility of trying to reverse the problem. They become very provocative or seductive toward their husbands, either in the type of lovemaking scenes they set up or how they behave or talk. If the erectile dysfunction is relatively new, this may be just the distraction the man needs. But if the problem has been there for some time and has become an ingrained concern, this seductive behavior may be experienced as added pressure for the man to perform.

If a man is experiencing *clinical depression* that has nothing to do with his sexual functioning, it may begin to affect how he responds sexually. In this case, the erectile dysfunction is a secondary problem that will need to be dealt with after the clinical depression has been treated. Depression can come about as a result of long-term problems in one's life—loss, pain, or various other emotional traumas. Once the depression has been treated, sexual functioning will often return. If it does not, it should then be dealt with directly and behaviorally. Antidepressants that are used for the treatment of depression can interfere with sexual response. Work with a professional who is familiar with the potential sexual side effects of antidepressants. Continue to try different ones, if necessary, until you find the one best for you.

Other emotional issues can lead to erectile dysfunction as well. *Past physical, emotional, or sexual abuse* has not been as frequently identified in men and is difficult for men to admit and talk about, yet causes internal conflict with arousal feelings that interfere with erectile response. When a man struggles with *gender confusion,* he may be trying to function with a woman but wishing to be with a man. His internal conflict interferes with his response. *Relationship conflicts* cause stress and negative feelings toward the wife, which makes it difficult for the husband to enjoy being with his wife sexually. He may have difficulty pursuing the sensations that allow arousal.

WHAT KEEPS THE PATTERN OF ERECTILE DYSFUNCTION GOING?

Whatever the cause of the difficulty with erections, it is self-perpetuating. This is true even if the original source of the problem is removed. It is the anxiety caused by anticipating the difficulty that keeps it going—it is a cycle. First, there is the initial failure. As there are subsequent failures, the anxiety increases. As the anxiety increases, there is more preoccupation with the problem, which only makes the problem worse. Finally, it is a response so conditioned that it takes over as the dominating emotional force every time the couple tries to have sex.

GAINING CONFIDENCE WITH ERECTILE RESPONSE

Erectile difficulties are reversible!

A man said to us, "I have been plagued with this problem so long that all I can do is think about whether or not I am *going* to have an erection or whether I *am* having an erection." This vividly portrays the feelings of both the man and the woman. All the focus around the sexual experience gets centered on the state of a man's penis, rather than on the total experience of love. Hope is necessary.

The treatment of erectile dysfunction as we understand it today reflects the shift from psychological to physiological focus. Treatment options are available and are highly successful. Regardless of age or medical condition, most men are able to regain the enjoyment of a satisfying sexual relationship with confidence.

Given the highly successful options available, it is a shame that only an estimated 10 percent of men struggling with erectile difficulties actually seek treatment. Because men are reluctant or embarrassed to seek help *and* because impotence often signals an underlying physical problem, it is imperative that we encourage you to take the courageous step to contact either your physician, an expert listed in the yellow pages or on-line, or call us to guide your process of seeking help. You will probably need a referral to a urologist, a cardiovascular specialist, a neurologist who specializes in E.D., a sleep center, or a diagnostic center for men. Ask to identify vascular leaks, neurological impairment due to diabetes, early cardiovascular disease, other illnesses, or side effects of medications.

We want to acquaint you with the various therapy options available, recognizing that the physician will be the one to recommend the treatment plan that is best for you.

Androgen Therapy

As the world's population gets older, androgen or testosterone deficiency in men is becoming more widespread. And we are finding that androgen deficiency is not limited to elderly men. For most men and women who come to us with sexual dysfunction, we will work with the person's physician to obtain a free or bioavailable testosterone level.

As we have mentioned before, we recommend a patch, cream, or sublingual form of testosterone replacement as the most natural because the testosterone is absorbed continually and directly into the bloodstream. Injections of testosterone are too intense, too fast, and quickly lose their effect.

Nutritional Approach

To help the body produce and utilize testosterone more effectively, dietary and nutritional changes may be necessary. Try eliminating sugar and white flour. Decrease carbohydrate intake in general, making sure that you do get whole grains. Increase protein and vegetables in your diet. Drink lots of water and take a multivitamin/mineral supplement designed for men. One that we recommend is Formula 600+ Prostate Support by Nature's Life, but there are many others available.

We were working with a telephone client from another state. We referred him to one of the leading specialists in treating E.D. in the country. His testosterone level was found to be very low. Because of other symptoms, we asked about his diet. When we discovered that he was eating bread and cereal for breakfast, a sandwich for lunch, and pasta for dinner—all very high-carbohydrate foods—we suggested the above dietary changes. The physician had not yet started giving him testosterone. In six weeks, upon returning to the physician for reevaluation, his testosterone level had risen so significantly the physician was shocked and impressed. This man was able to regain confidence with erections by raising his testosterone level through a change in diet. In addition, we guided him and his wife through some of the sexual retraining process from our book,

Restoring the Pleasure. The purpose of the sexual retraining was to distract from the focus on his penis and refocus on enjoyment.

Pharmacologic Management

This is the most common form of treatment today. It may be used alone or with other therapies. You may go to your primary care doctor or look on-line and get a prescription for Viagra with little explanation or evaluation. We would discourage that quick a solution. Push your physician to find a specialist who will do a complete assessment before starting any medication. Pharmacologic treatment can be given through different modes.

Injections. Injections into the penis given to stimulate an erection were discovered incidentally in the 1980s. This discovery revolutionized the therapy and understanding of E.D. Although injections are an effective treatment, they are not always welcomed. Most men are not excited about the idea of injecting into the erectile tissue of the penis as a solution to their problem.

Transurethral Insertion. Medication that stimulates an erection can also be inserted into the urethra, the opening of the penis, with an applicator. The man urinates, inserts the 3.2 cm. (a little over 1¼") thin stem of the applicator into the urethra, and depresses the button to release the medicated pellet. Mild penile pain has been reported but not usually enough to discontinue usage.

Oral Administration. This is the exciting approach to treating E.D. At the October '98 world conference on the Pharmacological Management of Erectile Dysfunction, four types of oral agents with differing mechanisms of action were presented as being in the process of study by various pharmaceutical companies. Viagra was the one of the four to be released.

Viagra does not stimulate an erection like the injections or medicated pellets do; rather, it is a conditioner that allows the erection to occur in response to effective stimulation. Viagra works by relaxing the muscles to increase blood flow. This is important because effective love play and penile stimulation will be necessary to produce an erection, even after taking Viagra or any other erectile conditioner.

After complete evaluation and treatment of any other physical conditions that might be related to the struggle with erection, we recommend the use of Viagra whether the cause of impotence is physiological or psychogenic. It can be used at any age, when decreased androgen levels are present. It increases the effectiveness of other therapeutic approaches to E.D.

SEXUAL RETRAINING OR THERAPY

Sexual retraining is usually combined with androgen, pharmaceutical, and/or nutritional therapies. The focus of the therapy/retraining is to help the man struggling with erectile difficulties to

- gain confidence in his erectile response,
- develop his ability to enjoy face-to-face intimacy with his wife, and
- along with his wife, identify any patterns of relating that might be affecting his response.

In addition, to reverse E.D., the couple's focus during sex has to change. There are two basic ingredients necessary for that to occur. First, the man must experience some distraction and do some refocusing. Second, his wife must be able to positively enjoy his body.

The changes begin with some *new attitudes* that grow out of new understandings. The man obviously needs to regain his confidence. To do that, he must be convinced he does not have to try to do anything. You will recall that the erection is a natural physiological response that occurs when the man is relaxed enough to allow himself to be sexually aroused. Trying to change the pattern only gets in the way. The wife, too, has to stop trying to bring about an erection. Both must refocus. The refocus is on the man's sensual and bodily pleasure, without any demand for erectile response.

Part of the change necessary will be a new kind of *sharing*. As a way of cleansing the couple of all the hurts and disillusionment, a time of talking, confessing, crying, and forgiving will be a crucial start to a new beginning. This communication is crucial because by the time the erectile pattern has become ingrained, there has usually been so much self-doubt, blame, anger, resentment, frustration, and disillusionment that it is not possible to dive into a new format without communicating about all the past hurts.

There are four major problems to overcome, two for the man and two for the woman. The man has to rid himself of his fears of performance, that is, his *performance anxiety*. He also has to stop watching himself, or get out of the *spectator role*. The woman has to have her *fears or other negative feelings relieved* so that she can become a caring and loving participant. She also has to become comfortable *fondling the man's penis* for her pleasure, not for his response.

To get the focus off erection and on the enjoyment of pleasure, begin with some pleasuring experiences as outlined in our chapter on pleasuring (Chapter 13). These experiences should not include the possibility of intercourse. To have intercourse there has to be an erection, which immediately brings demand. Spend a number of sessions focused on caressing hands and feet and on facial and bodily pleasuring without any focus on the genitals. As there is response, gradually begin to move toward including the genitals in the pleasuring. If there is anxiety, back off. One man reported how he could enjoy all the body pleasuring until his wife touched his penis. Her hand on his penis felt like a demand for a response. Whenever he felt her touch, anxiety was the automatic response. If this is the case, the touching needs to be very gentle, brief, and indirect (not with the hands) until the man becomes comfortable having his penis touched for pleasure, not for response.

Even in the initial touching, there should be no expectation of an erection, only pleasure. As erections do occur, there should be no attempt to bring the man to the point of orgasm. This should extend over as many sessions as are needed. It is essential to proceed at a pace the man can enjoy without feeling demand.

As soon as there is any self-consciousness about how the erection is coming along, any getting into the spectator role, or any performance anxiety, it is absolutely vital for the man to inform his wife that he is having those kinds of thoughts. They should then move away from any direct attention on the penis to pleasuring other parts of the body. Gradually, as the demand subsides, she can move back to the penis, but if the self-consciousness returns, then he must again inform her.

This communication about the anxiety is one of the most difficult aspects to learn, and yet it is most crucial. Many men will say, "But why should I talk about it? If I just don't think about it, maybe it will go away." Others won't verbalize their anxiety because they don't want to ruin the wife's experience. Those are all understandable fears. However, if the anxiety is not expressed, it will become larger and interfere with response. This is the same as with any other fear. When you talk about it, it is often reduced. So wives, encourage your husbands in this, and husbands, be willing to experiment with the sharing of your anxiety. It is absolutely vital. As the pleasuring experiences continue and erections come and go, the man begins to build security about getting and keeping erections. This is the purpose of these experiences. The man has been concerned about erections, so now he needs to learn that he *will* experience erections. There may be a dip in the arousal and they will go away, but they can be regained. After a period of time like this, the woman can gradually move to where she stimulates him to the point of orgasm without entry. Before any attempts at entry, the penis and vagina need to become reacquainted. They need to be gently and gradually reintroduced to each other as friends, not feared objects. To help the penis become familiar with the vagina without performance anxiety, we encourage both the man and the woman to use the penis, whether flaccid or erect, as a paint brush across the clitoris and opening of the vagina. Through this activity, the man gains new confidence in the use of his penis to pleasure his wife without demand for an erection or for entry.

After a number of sexual experiences that include positive responses to paint-brushing, the woman can teasingly insert the tip of the penis into the opening of the vagina for a few moments. After several positive responses (no anxiety about the erection) to playful insertion of the tip of the penis in the vagina, she can insert it a little farther, maybe only half an inch more. This playfulness can continue until, eventually, the penis is fully in the vagina. The woman should take charge of this process without drawing attention to her plan. The more distraction the man has from the actual entry event, the less likely will be the occurrence of anxiety and loss of erection. She can be as creative as her own freedom and his response allow. Distractions during the playful process of moving toward entry might include verbalizing fantasies, pleasuring the rest of his body, or cooing love messages.

The next steps would be comparable to those of working on the problem of premature ejaculation. You move to the point of entry but without orgasm, just entering and being together, letting the erection diminish while inside the vagina. Then you begin to experience a small amount of movement, gradually increasing it. Finally, you withdraw and experience orgasm outside the vagina. When you have done this several times and feel quite secure, decide at some point while inside the vagina that this would be a comfortable time to go ahead to the point of ejaculation.

Along the way, it may be necessary to back up as anxiety grows. Keep in mind that it is crucial always to have the focus off the erection and on the pleasure. Any barriers that prevent this focus will perpetuate the erectile dysfunction. Any time during the sexual experience that you begin thinking about the erection, share the thoughts. At all times you should move slowly and gradually to the next step without any major jumps.

What about the woman in all of this? Every pleasuring experience for the man should be accompanied by one for the woman. If she is not having difficulty with orgasmic response, feel comfortable to stimulate her to orgasm manually if she wishes. If some barriers show up along the way for her in terms of freedom to touch or comfortableness with communication, these should be shared to maintain an openness between the two of you. It is asking a lot of the woman to go through the sexual retraining with the man, and yet it is important to bear in mind that the benefits for her are equal to those that will come for him. As he becomes relaxed enough to enjoy an erection and a release with her, she finds new fulfillment. This is one of those times when the deep love that two people share will be tested. Love is patient, bears all things, and hopes for all things, even when struggling with erection problems.

Professional Help

If you are a couple who has been experiencing years and years of difficulty and avoidance with all the ensuing frustrations, you may not be able to reverse the problem on your own. You may need some professional help. In a later chapter, we will talk about the various professionals who can help. There *is* hope, regardless of how long your problem has gone on.

After nineteen years of marriage, one woman finally reached the point of frustration and said, "We either need to do something about this, or I am getting out." With fear and trembling, she and her husband sought help. Their history was one of difficulty right from the start. It had been several months after their marriage before they even consummated it, and when they did, erections were an issue. Over the years they had made enough awkward lovemaking attempts to produce two children, but intercourse never brought them pleasure. As time went on, the man felt more and more inadequate and more frequently experienced impotence. By the time they came for help, he was not responsive at all. The woman was incredibly angry, and the man's self-worth was radically deflated. They did share a deep commitment to their marriage and family. By working diligently over a number of months, they moved past one barrier after another to the point where they now regularly enjoy total sexual fulfillment with each other. The hurt and defeat that used to be the inevitable part of every experience are no longer there. We tell this story only to encourage those of you whose lives fit this same pattern. You do not have to stay in the rut. You can move on to enjoy satisfying experiences.

28 TOO SOON, TOO FAST: PREMATURE EJACULATION

An engaged couple anticipating the joy and excitement of life together usually believes that their sexual life will be an unending stream of satisfaction and delight. They experience passion, desire, and arousal now, and look forward to total enjoyment within marriage. There is no thought that it might not work that way. They assume that the sexual response is a natural one, and that as long as they do what comes naturally, everything will be just fine. Fortunately, for some couples this expectation is fulfilled. However, for a large percentage this is not the case. At least one-half of those who attend our seminars have significant, serious problems that get in the way of their total sexual freedom and enjoyment.

The single most common problem reported is premature ejaculation (P.E.). The woman might describe it as, "Coming so fast that I am not able to get with the program, and then I am left hanging." The most interesting dilemma with P.E. is that, many times, the man and woman report the problem quite differently. It is not uncommon for a woman to report that the man ejaculates prematurely 80 to 100 percent of the time, whereas the man might report a 10 to 20 percent occurrence. This difference in experience points out the need for clarification of the problem within the relationship.

What do we mean by "premature ejaculation"? Various definitions have been given. We believe the problem is present when the man *does not have control* of his ejaculation. In other words, if the man ejaculates before he or his wife wants him to, he is experiencing premature ejaculation. There is great variation in terms of the seriousness of the problem. Some men may experience so little control that they will ejaculate before entry or upon anticipation of entry. Some will ejaculate as soon as their partner touches them. Others will ejaculate once entry is attempted or within a few seconds after entry. Probably the most common pattern of premature ejaculation is that which occurs after four or fewer thrusts.

It is important to realize that premature ejaculation affects both the man and the woman. For the man, lack of control of his body's functioning leaves him feeling unsure of himself. His pleasure is often decreased by the abrupt end to his sexual experience. Eventually, his preoccupation with trying to postpone ejaculation will hinder his ability to fully embrace sexual pleasure. In addition to P.E. interfering with the man's direct enjoyment, he also may feel like an inadequate lover to his wife.

When a man is anxious, feeling inadequate, and ejaculating unexpectedly, the woman will probably be left unsatisfied. Her frustration will only increase the negative pattern. However, P.E. does not have to be a negative experience for the woman. The confident man who really enjoys the pleasure of a woman's body may engage in so much sensuous body play that his wife is well satisfied before entry and/or ejaculation occurs. Unless the husband or wife has the need for the woman to be orgasmic with the penis in the vagina, this adaptation may be a successful way of handling P.E. For other women, P.E. is not a problem because they are quickly and easily orgasmic and don't experience as much need for extended time with the penis in the vagina. Whether or not the lack of ejaculatory control hinders the woman's sexual pleasure, gaining control inevitably enhances sexual enjoyment for both the man and the woman.

Premature ejaculation usually gets its start long before marriage. Most boys (95 to 97 percent) do masturbate. Because of the fear of being discovered, the boy may hurry through the experience as quickly as possible and thus learns to bring himself to the point of ejaculation very quickly. Similarly, adolescent sex play and premarital adult sex can be hurried, guilt-laden events. Often they do not take place in a setting where the couple feels safe. Whether it be manual stimulation or actual intercourse in a car or in the parents' living room, the man continues to learn to rush through the experience. The woman in these settings may not be oriented toward her own pleasure. She may be both highly excited and frightened, so she rushes also.

In addition to all the experiences that get the process of premature ejaculation going, the great all-American concept of reaching the goal quickly feeds the problem. In every other area of life, men are conditioned to believe that the faster they achieve their goal, the more quickly they are successful. In sex, however, success is just the opposite. A man will provide himself and his wife with the greatest pleasure when he is able to slow down, take his time, and control the experience. He has to learn to take the long, scenic route rather than the shortcut.

If men responded with their innate, natural inclinations, rather than learning to enjoy the process and extend their pleasure, their response graph would look like this one:

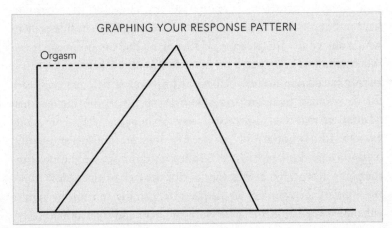

GRAPHING YOUR RESPONSE PATTERN

Orgasm

As men learn to savor the good sensations of arousal rather than rush to release, they can learn to play more and allow the intensity to build in waves. Soon their graph can look more like this:

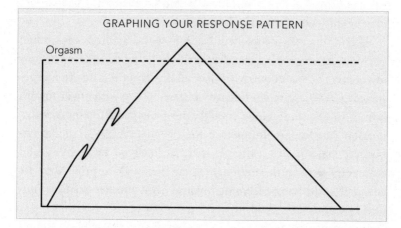

GRAPHING YOUR RESPONSE PATTERN

Orgasm

Couples assume that once they get married, the problem of timing will work itself out. Sometimes it does. Many times, however, the P.E. continues. The sequence usually goes something like this: After the initial sexual involvement the couple discovers his lack of control, but they are not too concerned about it. After a while, the wife begins to feel used and unfulfilled.

The husband may be concerned with only his own pleasure and therefore may not even notice the problem. If he is more sensitive, he may begin to be concerned about his wife's pleasure, but he may not know what to do about it. He may attempt to use some form of distraction to keep himself from ejaculating. He may try to think of something repulsive, start counting from one hundred backward, imagine himself in nonsexual situations, or seek any other mental distraction. These may have short-term benefit but soon are of no avail.

At about this time, he begins to suspect that maybe there is something his wife is or isn't doing that interferes—so blame enters the relationship. "If she just wouldn't touch me so much, or if she just wouldn't move so vigorously, or if . . ." The wife, too, begins blaming herself for sexual inadequacy and, at the same time, blames him. Many women feel that if he "just tried," or if he "really cared," he would be able to control ejaculation. As any premature ejaculator will confirm, it is not a voluntary action on his part, but that fact may be difficult to communicate to his wife.

After a time, the couple will begin to withdraw from each other, not wanting to enter an experience that is going to end up frustrating them. The man doubts his masculinity, and the wife often experiences a lessening of confidence in herself along with anger toward him. If this continues long enough, the anxiety and attempts at distraction can lead to impotence for the man. Even if the consequences are not that extreme, there is likely to be hostility and discouragement in the marriage. Some men seek to prove they are adequate sexually by becoming involved with another partner. Thus one disastrous event leads to another.

It is both encouraging and sad to report that the solution to premature ejaculation, when the couple are willing to cooperate, is really quite simple. That's the encouraging part. The sad part is that so many couples don't seek a solution. Premature ejaculation can be remedied in a relatively simple way. Some couples have done it without any outside help. Others, where the turmoil is long-standing or the pattern is a deeply ingrained habit, need to seek help from a competent professional.

Learning Ejaculatory Control

As with any sexual problem, regardless of who owns it, the resolution usually requires the active involvement of both husband and wife. It is a "couple" problem, not just an individual problem. Both people are affected by it, the experience of both is limited by it, and both desire the change. Hence, we recommend that both people be actively involved in the process. Besides, it's much more fun that way! Willing and loving cooperation from both is usually necessary if change is to occur. If the relationship is fraught with distress and discord, you need to work on the relationship before you can expect to bring about changes in ejaculatory control.

Attitude Changes. There are several attitudes essential to successful treatment. First, the man must desire control and believe that it can occur for him. Until that happens, there is no point in attempting the procedure. Second, he must be willing to allow his wife to participate with him in the process. As we will see, this requires his being able to relax and enjoy receiving pleasure from her. The attitude change for the woman is similar in that she must believe control can be achieved, and she must be willing to work toward it. She must also know that her participation in the process is vital. This requires that she see this as a "couple" problem, not just "his" problem. Even more essential is that she be comfortable with his genitals.

Communication Changes. The couple who experience premature ejaculation may have never talked about it. Until they can do that, no change is going to take place. The man needs to be able to understand what it feels like to the woman. He also needs to be able to explain what his own experience is like, some of the history as he understands it, and perhaps the inadequacy he feels. She needs to be able to talk about the thoughts she has had about herself, how the experience makes her feel about him, and how she feels about participating in the attempted solution. It is crucial that the couple share very openly all dimensions of their feelings and responses as they relate to this issue before they attempt to learn ejaculatory control.

Methods to Control. The goal is to be able to extend the sexual enjoyment by stopping all previous ways of stimulating to ejaculation while retraining the mind and body to

- learn to give and receive pleasure,
- increase bodily sensuous awareness,
- enjoy the passive soaking-in of the pleasurable sensations of touching and being touched,
- focus on penile sensations without stimulation to ejaculation,
- identify level of arousal on a scale of one to ten, and
- be aware of the warning signs of approaching ejaculation.

Although we will be teaching the squeeze technique as the method for learning ejaculatory control, there are two other effective approaches. The stop-start method, first described by Helen Singer Kaplan, is the same process as the squeeze technique, but without the squeeze. The scrotal tug is a method that makes most men rather nervous since the testes are so tender. The man has to have trust in his wife and know that she is not carrying anger toward him that might be expressed in the process of applying the scrotal tug. The effectiveness of the scrotal tug is clear: Early in the sexual response process, the right testicle rises and rotates a quarter of a turn. Just before a man ejaculates, the left testicle rises and rotates a quarter of a turn. If the wife keeps the testicles down, the husband cannot ejaculate.

Steps to Control. We want to take you through a series of steps. These will clearly define how you can become aware of the sensations in your body that warn you are going to ejaculate. We will be presenting the process of "the squeeze technique." Some of you will be able to learn this on your own; others will need help with it. As we talk about the various sessions and experiences, keep in mind that some of you will need to repeat each step several times before you move on to the next. The main task of these experiences is to *become aware* of when you are going to ejaculate and to be able to control your body and your activity because of that awareness.

One more guideline: When going through these learning sessions, it is important not to attempt intercourse until the procedure suggests it. If you do interrupt the procedure with intercourse and ejaculation, that will tend to get in the way of learning control. Should that happen, it would be best to begin the steps again.

This process is usually successful if the steps are followed correctly and both spouses are cooperative. Since the squeeze technique works by weakening a reflex response that has become a habit, the exact steps need to be followed to break the old habit pattern and establish a new one. When couples have not been successful in the use of the squeeze technique, it is because they wait too long after the man is aroused to apply the squeeze, they don't move away from genital touch and focus after the squeeze, or the man does not remain passive.

▪ EXERCISE 14

Procedure One: Body Pleasuring,
Excluding Breasts and Genitals

The goal of this experience is to learn to enjoy touching one another without the demand either from within yourself or from your partner to become aroused or have intercourse. Many of us have not learned the full satisfaction of pleasure that can be ours. This exercise is designed as a way to refocus on that dimension.

Underlying Principles:

1. *Receiver:* Your only task is to soak in pleasure and to redirect the pleasurer when the touch is not pleasing. Check out your concern if at any point you question whether the pleasurer is enjoying himself/herself.

2. *Pleasurer:* Touch your spouse in a way that brings you pleasure, trusting that he/she will redirect you when what you are doing is not pleasurable. Check out your concern if at any point you become anxious about your performance rather than enjoying the process.

3. When an experience is felt to be a demand—something you *should* do—stop, share, and either reschedule or shift to an experience desired by both. *No experience is preferable to an experience by demand.*

4. Make sure the room temperature and setting are comfortable for being without clothes or cover.

5. You may or may not use lotion or oil to pleasure each other. If using lotion, warm it in your hand first.

6. If sexual arousal should occur, this can be seen as an involuntary response but not the intention or purpose of the experience. The arousal can be enjoyed, but should not be pursued. *Do not become concerned if there is or is not arousal; the purpose of this experience is bodily pleasure.*

Steps:

Partner #1: Lie on your abdomen in a comfortable position.

Partner #2: Place your hands on your spouse's back. With your eyes closed, focus on the sensations of your spouse's body: warmth, pulsation, vibrations; begin to move over the entire back with a sensuous touch—then proceed to neck, arms, legs. Inform your spouse when you are ready for him/her to turn over.

Partner #1: Turn onto your back.

Partner #2: Sitting with your spouse facing up and his or her head in your lap, proceed with facial caress, then continue down neck, shoulders, arms, hands, and chest (avoid breasts). Move to sitting between the legs of your spouse (or to one side of your spouse) and enjoy the rest of your spouse's body, excluding genitals.

Reverse roles and repeat steps.

You may need to repeat Procedure One several times until you can fully experience the joy and delight of pleasuring. It is always important to have a pleasuring session for both of you. Both need to learn to focus on the pleasure of receiving and giving touch.

▓ EXERCISE 15

Procedure Two: Body Pleasuring, Including Breasts and Genitals
(Application of Squeeze)

Once you have become comfortable with the general body pleasuring, you may include the genitals. If penile stimulation brings an erection, the squeeze technique is applied.

When the man is in the receiving role during body pleasuring, it is extremely important that he be able to completely relax and focus on the sensations in his body. He must be able to let himself experience pleasure rather than feeling he has to do something for his wife. The procedure should be something like this:

Step 1: Shower or bathe together in a relaxed way so that you can begin the experience of being together in this gentle way and can come to it freshly washed.

Step 2: Pleasure the back of the man's body. Then get into the position as designated by Figure 8 in Chapter 13, where the man is lying on his back and the woman is sitting with her legs stretched out beside him, so that his genitals are within easy reach of her hands.

Step 3: The woman is completely in charge of this part of the experience. After pleasuring the upper part of his body, she begins to gently caress the penis and scrotum, with particular attention to those areas that he has let her know are most pleasurable. Some men report that touching the underside of the penis, called the frenulum, is most stimulating for them. Others enjoy general pleasuring of the shaft of the penis, with particular arousal coming at the ridge around the head—the coronal ridge. This is true whether or not a man is circumcised.

Step 4: As soon as the man experiences a full erection for a few moments, the woman should apply the squeeze. To do this, the woman should grasp the penis with her thumb on the underside of the ridge around the head of the penis and her forefinger and middle finger above and below the ridge of the head on the front side of the penis (see Figure 9). The squeeze should be firm but not hard and should last about ten seconds. Be careful not to use the fingernails in this procedure. When the squeeze has been applied, some men will partially lose their erections; others will not. The squeeze is effective whether the erection diminishes or not. The squeeze is not designed to cause loss of erection, but rather to lessen the intensity of the arousal. So whether or not there is loss of erection, the squeeze can still effectively do what it is intended to do.

Figure 9:
The Squeeze Technique

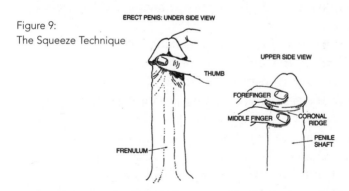

ERECT PENIS: UNDER SIDE VIEW

UPPER SIDE VIEW

THUMB

FOREFINGER

MIDDLE FINGER — CORONAL RIDGE

PENILE SHAFT

FRENULUM

Step 5: Whether the squeeze results in the loss of erection or not, the woman moves away from the focus on the genitals, pleasuring other parts of the body. The man also keeps his focus where the woman is touching him. After a few minutes or more, move back to caressing and stimulating the penis. Once the full erection returns or the feelings of arousal intensify, again apply the squeeze in the same manner as described above.

Step 6: Repeat the above procedure several days until the man feels confident that he will not move to ejaculation. Do not wait to apply the squeeze until the man feels he is about to ejaculate.

Step 7: Pleasure the woman's body by following Procedure One. Include breasts and genitals in a general sense.

Procedure Three: Total-Body Pleasuring, Including Ejaculation by Manual Stimulation

Repeat Procedure Two, but this time use a lubricant during the genital stimulation for both the man and the woman. The lubricant on the penis will more closely approximate the feeling that the man will have inside the vagina. In these sessions, after at least thirty minutes of total-body pleasuring, and after four or five squeezes and rest times after squeezes, decide together that you will not apply the squeeze again, but will allow the man to move to the point of ejaculation by manual stimulation. It is still important not to attempt entry. Again, be sure there is plenty of time for enjoying the total pleasure of each other's bodies and to savor the sensations of building arousal.

Procedure Four: Total-Body Pleasuring, Including Entry Without Ejaculation Inside the Vagina

Step 1: Repeat Procedure Three for two or three squeezes.

Step 2: After a squeeze, even if the penis is slightly flaccid (limp), with the woman in the top position, have her guide the man's penis into her vagina (see Figure 10). If it is somewhat flaccid, she may have to stuff it in.

Step 3: After the woman has inserted the penis, lie quietly together for two or three minutes without moving. This step is very important because it helps the man learn to be quiet inside the vagina. This may be very difficult for him because he has always tended to ejaculate quickly and hence move rapidly the moment entry has taken place. Be sure to incorporate times of "quiet vagina."

Step 4: After several minutes of lying quietly together and enjoy-

Figure 10:
Female Superior Position

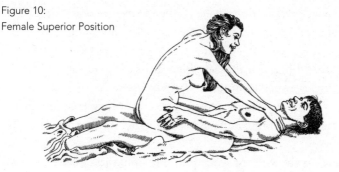

ing each other's bodies, the woman should begin to gently move her pelvis in a mild thrusting manner. If the man finds himself quickly erect, stop the thrusting, and the woman should move off the man and immediately apply the squeeze.

Step 5: After the squeeze has been applied and a rest time has been taken, move back on top of the man and reinsert the penis, even if it is slightly flaccid.

Step 6: Repeat the above procedure several times, allowing longer and longer times of arousal before withdrawal for the squeeze, unless the man indicates that he is experiencing the sensations that precede ejaculation, in which case the woman should apply the squeeze immediately. He should learn to identify his level of arousal on a scale of 1 to 10, always keeping it below 7.

Step 7: After repeating the above procedure several times, when the man is fully erect and there has been some thrusting by the woman, withdraw the penis and, using a lubricant, manually stimulate him to orgasm. This will often be a very difficult step to follow because the desire and inclination will be to ejaculate inside the vagina. For the man to be able to learn ejaculatory control, it is important that these steps be followed quite carefully.

At any point in these experiences, should the man ejaculate unintentionally (and we would expect this to happen for anyone learning this control), the couple are encouraged to enjoy the ejaculation, learn as much as possible from any sensations the man experiences, and move on to pleasuring the woman so that she, too, may have some joy and satisfaction. If she is able to respond orgasmically from external stimulation, that would certainly be appropriate.

Procedure Five: Total-Body Pleasuring, Including Ejaculation Inside the Vagina

Step 1: Begin by experiencing some total-body pleasuring, including some genital stimulation and applying the squeeze before entry at least once.

Step 2: Again with the woman in the top position, have her insert the penis, spend some time of quiet vagina, and then begin gentle thrusting. Let the thrusting become more intense as long as the man's arousal does not move above 7 on the scale of 1 to 10, and let the duration of time from the beginning of thrusting to the point of applying the squeeze become a little longer as the man can tolerate this.

Step 3: After a period of five or ten minutes of thrusting and resting, even if the man does not feel near the point of ejaculation, withdraw and apply the squeeze and then reenter.

Step 4: When you have repeated the above procedure for two to four squeezes, decide that you are not going to apply the squeeze on the next wave of arousal. This is intended to allow the woman some opportunity to get with her feelings so that she, too, can be at an emotional peak when the man ejaculates. Begin with very slow movements and a rhythmically built pace held for as long as possible, and then let yourself fully enjoy the ejaculation inside the vagina. It is important not to be in a hurry but rather to let yourself experience all the sensations so that you are aware of what it feels like as you reach the point of no return.

Step 5: If the woman has not experienced an orgasm as a result of the above processes and she desires one, focus on her needs so that she, too, can come away with full satisfaction.

Step 6: Repeat the above procedure on several different days until you feel very confident that you have it mastered.

Procedure Six: Adaptations of the Squeeze

Begin to learn new ways of incorporating the squeeze into your lovemaking activity, regardless of what your position is or where you are in terms of your arousal. Obviously, it is not our intention to suggest that lovemaking should always be a matter of numbered steps. This is a way of learning ejaculatory control. Once you attain control, go on to adapt the squeeze to your own style of free-flowing lovemaking. You will now want to begin to make love in positions other than the woman on top. After you have learned the squeeze in the regular manner, you can use the "bulbar squeeze." The bulbar squeeze is used at the base of the penis so that withdrawal from the vagina is not necessary (Figure 9, the diagram on the right).

Outline for Learning Ejaculatory Control
1. Total-body pleasuring (Procedure One)
2. Genital caressing until firm erection
3. Squeeze
4. Rest and general body caressing
5. Genital caressing until return of full erection or intensified arousal (but before point of no return)
6. Squeeze
7. Return to general pleasuring
8. Genital stimulation
9. Squeeze (Procedure Two includes steps 1–9, plus holding each other; Procedure Three includes steps 1–9, repeat 7 and 8, and bring to ejaculation manually)
10. Entry (stuff it, if there is loss of erection)
11. Quiet vagina
12. Gentle thrusting
13. Withdrawal of penis from vagina
14. Squeeze
15. Reenter
16. Gentle thrusting, gradually increasing intensity for a maximum of five minutes
17. Withdrawal of penis from vagina (Procedure Four includes steps 1–17, and bring to ejaculation manually)
18. Squeeze
19. Reenter

20. Gentle thrusting, gradually increasing to point of ejaculation (Procedure Five includes steps 1–20)
21. Adaptations (Procedure Six)

SOME HITCHES ALONG THE WAY

When you are attempting to learn control through this procedure, everything won't proceed according to the steps. There may be some individual idiosyncrasies that get in the way of things happening as they are supposed to. One of these might be what we would call "penis hesitancy." If you are a woman who was raised to believe that the touching of your own genitals was evil or dirty, then it would not be surprising that you might have some hesitancy about freely touching the man's genitals. If this is your situation, then before you can begin to learn the squeeze technique, you need to condition yourself to become comfortable with the penis in a general way.

Another dilemma that sometimes gets in the way has to do with the man's discomfort at being the total focus of the pleasuring. Some men find it extremely difficult to just lie back and enjoy. They feel they must be doing something for their wife, otherwise she will become disgruntled. Let us reassure you that if this process can bring you ejaculatory control, it is the best thing that can happen for your wife as well as for you. Count on it that she is enjoying herself. If she isn't, it is up to her to say so rather than for you to second-guess her.

Some men are totally unaware of when they are about to ejaculate, so they may find that the ejaculation will occur without apparent warning. Do not be discouraged by this, but rather proceed more slowly so as to allow yourself the time to become aware of what is happening to your body. Learn to attend to your level of arousal on the scale of 1 to 10.

The fourth possible roadblock may be the top-entry procedure for the woman. This may be new and somewhat uncomfortable emotionally; it may seem dominant since the upper position is traditionally the male's. Not being in the upper position also may bring the man emotional discomfort. We encourage you to push yourself beyond this barrier and use the woman-on-top position for these experiences because it has been found to be more effective than any other position. If there are any difficulties with entry in this position, be sure that you follow the position as pictured in Figure 10, and that the woman is in fact straddling across the man's genitals; second, be sure that you are using some lubricant to assist in the entry even if she thinks she is well lubricated. We recommend using lubricant during the time of learning as a way of facilitating the procedure.

Finally, some couples find themselves naturally resistant to the period of quiet vagina. While this period does go against what our bodies naturally want to do, it is important to learn this control. It allows the opportunity for the man to experience the sensation of the penis in the vagina without thrusting and without ejaculation. Since it is crucial for the man to experience these sensations, we encourage you to have those periods of being quiet throughout all your lovemaking.

NOW THAT THERE IS CONTROL

Once you have reached the point where you can choose when you will ejaculate, you may find it helpful to continue using the squeeze on various occasions to help lengthen the lovemaking period. This would be particularly true if it has been some time since the last ejaculation, because then you are more likely to ejaculate more quickly. The use of the squeeze should be incorporated into lovemaking and used at any point along the way for the rest of your life.

If the process of learning ejaculatory control does not work for you, you may be helped by taking Prozac or Zoloft four hours before sex. They are antidepressants that would be prescribed by your physician. Prozac inhibits orgasm so is very effective in learning ejaculatory control.

The process of learning can be a great time of building intimacy, trust, and closeness in your marriage, as well as increasing the pleasure of your times together.

29 LESS AROUSAL OR NO RELEASE: SOME WOMEN'S FRUSTRATIONS

"Sex is just too much work." This statement expresses the feelings of women who go through the sexual experience with little arousal and difficulty letting go.

Every woman is born with a capacity for sexual response. As we have mentioned, a boy has his first erection within moments after birth, and a girl lubricates vaginally within the first twenty-four hours. These automatic responses continue throughout life. Adult men have erections every eighty to ninety minutes while they sleep, and adult women lubricate vaginally every eighty to ninety minutes while they sleep. Unless there is some physical abnormality, all have the capacity for response.

Women who experience little arousal and have difficulty with release do not need to learn some new skill; rather, they need to uncover what is already inside them. The clitoris is that unique bit of human anatomy that is designed solely to receive and transmit sexual feelings. So for the unresponsive woman, the task is to strip away the layers of problems and past experiences that have obscured the sexual response potential that lies within her.

CAUSES FROM THE PAST

What are some of these layers that cover up and block the sexual response? The first input may have come from the home atmosphere. Women who were raised in homes where intense emotions were not expressed will tend to stifle the expression of their sexual intensity. Antisexual teachings, particularly if they have been connected with a rigid religious training, can also keep the response from happening.

For other women, the lack of response may be more directly related to their past experiences in their marriages. Many women are unable to experience release because their husbands ejaculate within seconds after entry. If these women have never learned to reach the point of orgasm by manual stimulation, they are left frustrated. Other women may be married to their second-choice mate. If a woman lost her anticipated partner either through death or through desertion, she may have quickly married someone else, thus finding herself married to a man whom she does not deeply love. Or there may be other reasons why a woman dislikes her husband. She may have difficulty trusting men. Sometimes the commitment of marriage raises a woman's anxiety and interferes with her ability to enjoy herself sexually with her husband.

Many such barriers may prevent a woman from experiencing the positive sexual responsiveness that is part of her nature by creation.

CURRENT SITUATIONS THAT LEAD TO DIFFICULTY

Uncertainty About the Right to Sexual Pleasure

Just as circumstances in a woman's past may inhibit her sexual response, some current thinking may also set up a lack of response. One of the most common problems is the feeling that she does not have a right to sexual pleasure. We cannot emphasize enough that women are created to enjoy sexual pleasure, even as men are. Their bodies need sexual release, even as men need release. They have an incredible capacity for sexual arousal and release. For the concerned woman, all of this sexual activity is heartily endorsed by the inspired

Scriptures of the Old and New Testaments. The clarity of this writing is most obvious in 1 Corinthians 7:3–5. Mutuality is spelled out in vivid terms: The man has sexual rights, and the woman has sexual rights. Accepting her sexual rights and pursuing sexual pleasure will be necessary for sexual response.

Fear of Orgasm

Related to the uncertainty about the right to pleasure is the fear of orgasm. For a woman to have an orgasm, she must allow her body to let go, to be out of control. She has to trust that nothing destructive or harmful will happen to her if she lets her body take over. Some women, as they approach the point of orgasm, get the same sensation that they might get if they were in a high place and were afraid of falling. Others have a sensation similar to the fear of dying. Still others report that they are afraid of "going out of their minds." Another fear connected with orgasm has to do with a hesitancy to allow themselves to experience and express all the things that happen to their bodies—the movements, the sounds, the changed appearance. They are embarrassed. Whatever the cause, if a woman fears orgasm, she is likely to inhibit any movement toward climax and will often even block the process of arousal.

The Duty to Please

A woman may come to the sexual experience with the idea that it is her duty to please her husband—and not expect anything for herself, in which case it is likely she will *not* receive anything for herself. Many girls have been told that the sexual dimension of marriage is something a woman has to put up with; it is her responsibility or her lot in life. It is a way to compensate a man for taking care of her. Anything that involves all of your being, your body, your emotions, your spirit, cannot be done out of duty or responsibility. You must desire the enjoyment and expect to enjoy the pleasure yourself. When a woman has been conditioned to believe that sex is something she must do for the man, the likelihood of a free and easy flow of sexual arousal and release is greatly diminished.

Physical or Medical Issues

Finally, a woman may have physical or medical issues that are interfering with her ability to become aroused and be orgasmic. Hormonal imbalance may need to be assessed, pelvic traumas identified, and the effect of medications evaluated.

A woman came to us with orgasmic difficulties. As we talked with her, we learned that she was struggling with other physical symptoms. She had difficulty falling asleep at night, became depressed before her menstrual period, and showed signs of early menopause. We referred her to an endocrinologist and a biochemist-nutritionist. The work-ups revealed that she was not producing adequate levels of hormones. Both her estrogen and testosterone levels were very low. There were also indications that her body was not absorbing nutrients properly. As her diet was revised, an exercise program was activated, and her sleep was regulated without drugs, she started to feel better. Along with her new energy came increased sexual responsiveness. We cannot prove that the increased responsiveness was caused by the changes in nutrition, exercise, and sleep. But knowledge of how our bodies work and years of seeing lifestyle changes benefit the sexual experience have led us to believe that attention to the body does add spark to the sex life.

Diet

Food affects our physical and emotional health. Dr. Diana Schwarzbein, an endocrinologist, has studied and reported her findings in a book, *The Schwarzbein Principle.*[1] Others have provided great information as well. Barry Sears, author of *The Zone,* shares some of his principles.[2] A diet of foods containing artificial dyes and additives has damaging effects long-term. Carbohydrates, especially white flour and sugars, affect insulin production, which in turn affects metabolism. This directly influences energy levels as well as hormonal production. When our bodies are not getting the nutrients they need because we are filling ourselves with empty carbohydrates and chemicals, our sex hormones will be the first to be affected.

Alcohol is another offender. Alcohol is an inhibitor. It slows down our bodily responses. Therefore, alcohol can inhibit sexual functioning and keep both men and women from responding.

We have often been asked, "Does being in good shape physically, that is, exercising regularly, increase one's sexual responsiveness?" Walking together rather than watching TV will benefit not only your relationship, but also your body and its responsiveness.

Regular exercise that increases cardiovascular functioning (heart rate, blood pressure, and so on) will enhance circulation, increase mental alertness, reduce stress, and improve muscular tone. Since one body system cannot change without in some way affecting the other body systems, those changes will impact sexual functioning. In addition, exercising will improve how you feel about your body. How you feel about your body will affect how freely you enjoy your body during sex. Exercising will also get you in touch with the sensations of your body. This inevitably increases awareness of sexual feelings and sexual enjoyment.

RELEASING RESPONSIVENESS

Even though our bodies have been designed for sexual arousal and release, one of several of the factors discussed above may be blocking those natural responses. Those blocks will need to be removed.

Physical Adjustments

Start with hormonal and medical evaluations. Estrogen or testosterone cream may be used to increase lubrication and enhance sensation. Estrogen cream is applied with an applicator inside the vagina. A 1 percent testosterone cream, prescribed by a physician and the prescription taken or faxed to a compounding pharmacy, is applied externally to the clitoris and inner labia. For a pharmacy in your area, contact the International Academy of Compounding Pharmacists at 800-927-4227 or at www.iacprx.org. We prefer the Women's International Pharmacy at 800-279-5708 or at www.womensinternational.com. The woman's hormones should be reevaluated every six months to a year.

Childbirth trauma or consequences of pelvic surgery may need special medical evaluation and treatment. Low blood flow to the woman's genitals due to smoking or cardiovascular problems or their treatments has been successfully treated with Viagra, Vasotem, and Prostaglandin E-I cream. These drugs, which require a medical prescription, enhance arousal and release.

Medications may need to be changed. Antidepressants typically suppress orgasm. If the woman is on Prozac or another antidepressant and is having difficulty with sexual response, the prescribing physician might instead prescribe Celexa, Serzone, Wellbutrin, or Lexapro. These antidepressants are less likely than others to inhibit sexual responsiveness.

Learning to Let It Happen

To learn to be sexual and allow spontaneous sexual feelings often seems like a contradiction. It seems that you ought to try to feel, and yet we are saying that you cannot try. Response will happen only if you do not try. This is a first principle to help you move to greater excitement and release through orgasm: *Stop trying!* The focus has to move away from striving for arousal. You must get away from seeing arousal as the goal and focus on the process of enjoying your body. Performance anxiety, as we discussed earlier, is an inhibiting force (see the section on Sexual Anxiety in Chapter 20). This anxiety interferes when a woman tries to get aroused.

The second principle promotes a positive *refocus*. The emphasis should shift from trying to focus on the pleasurable sensations and the communication of these sensations to your partner. If you are going to be free to respond sexually, your response will not begin by having a cataclysmic orgasm but rather by allowing yourself the privilege of enjoying any small bodily sensations that come your way. Each small twinge can be an encouragement. It is vital to share with your husband any enjoyable bodily sensations that you experience. If your lack of arousal and release has been a long-term struggle, he will need the boost of sharing in your sense of moving toward fuller bodily pleasure.

The performance anxiety must be reduced, there must be a refocus on and communication of the enjoyable sensations, and then there must be a reduction of self-consciousness. The natural noises and behaviors typical of the sexual response cause in some women an inhibiting embarrassment that must be corrected. If you recall from our earlier discussion, as we—men or women—get aroused, we respond. Our heart beat increases, we breathe faster and louder, we may experience slight muscular contractions, our bodies may feel like moving in thrusting or pushing motions, and we may have the urge to make gasping noises. Women who have difficulty allowing themselves to experience arousal or release are often unable to let themselves exhibit any or all of these behaviors. They are embarrassed and uncomfortable, and, as with any other discomfort, they tend to avoid that which causes these negative feelings. Thus they will hold back their natural sexual responses.

If you are going to change your response pattern, you must make a conscious attempt to become comfortable with your natural bodily responses. First notice what responses you are avoiding, then push yourself to experience and exhibit those responses. Throw in a little humor about them if that helps relieve the tension. For example, heavy breathing is a natural body response. If you notice that you back off from this response by stopping your breathing, reverse the trend by breathing even harder. Exaggerate the breathing to the point of absurdity. Pelvic thrusting is another natural body response. If you find yourself pulling your pelvis away from the thrusting, push it the other way all the more emphatically. *Decide* to *behave* and *sound* sexually aroused.

The last principle is that you must *take responsibility* for and control of what you need. Your husband cannot give you arousal or release. He can participate, but only *you* can allow it to happen as you free yourself to experience it. This may seem obvious, and yet it is one of the most difficult mental shifts to make, because for so long the subtle teaching has been that it is the man's responsibility to bring the woman sexual pleasure. On the contrary, sexual pleasure begins with taking responsibility for yourself and being ready to go after what you need.

Pinpointing Your Dilemma

If you are going to move past your point of blockage and release your responsiveness, it is crucial that you understand exactly where you are stuck. It is important for you to identify whether your problem is a lack of excitement and arousal or whether you experience a great deal of arousal but have difficulty letting that arousal reach the point of orgasm. For some this will be very clear. For others it may take some sorting out to define your situation. You will recall that as you enter the sexual experience, arousal begins with vaginal lubrication and nipple erection. Then other changes begin to take place, both physically and emotionally. From a physical standpoint, there is the formation of the orgasmic platform in the outer third of the vagina. The inner two-thirds of the vagina balloons out, the uterus tends to pull slightly up and away, there may be the sexual flush in the upper third of your body, and whole-body sensations of heightened arousal.

Many women report that they reach a certain peak and feel as if they are about to go over the hill, and then something dies or levels out. Often that something is exactly the same every time. We encourage you to identify what that point is. Perhaps you would even want to use the graph in Chapter 8 that pictures the four phases of the sexual response. You need to be able to identify where on this graph your feelings cut off and what is happening right at that precise moment. For most women, this is the point at which the control of your arousal shifts from passive or parasympathetic nervous system dominance to active or sympathetic nervous system control.

It may be that your feelings are cut off at the very moment you begin to wonder whether this will be the time you have an orgasm. The feelings are blocked as soon as you get out of your body and into your head. Or you may stop the feelings as soon as you begin the orgasmic triggers of breathing intensely or pushing harder against the clitoris. Perhaps some behavior in your spouse, such as vigorous movement, stops your response. Pinpoint this event as precisely as you can and share it. Your husband needs to know what is happening to you and may even be able to bring some added insight to your understanding. Keep in mind that any discussion about what will move you toward greater pleasure is likely also to heighten his interest and arousal. Normally, he will not be turned off by this kind of talk but rather will find it encouraging.

Getting Comfortable with Your Body

Before you can release your responsiveness, it may be necessary for you to learn to be comfortable with your body. Many women have been taught to think of their bodies as unpleasant or distasteful, particularly the genitals. They have learned that this is the doctor's area, the messy part of them, the bloody part, and certainly a complicated part. To overcome these teachings, begin with a time of self-discovery. Wash well, then take out a mirror and get to know your genitals in specific detail. Look at a diagram of the internal and external genitalia and identify the various parts, touching them as you explore. It may be necessary for you to do this several times before you feel comfortable enough to share such an experience with your husband. For a full discussion of this experience, follow the details as outlined in Exercise 2 in Chapter 6.

When you have reached the point where you are familiar and comfortable with yourself, then plan a time when you and your husband can share this discovery together. This should not be seen as a time for sexual arousal but rather as a time of education. You can best teach him about you and he can best teach you about himself. Go into complete detail, even if this feels a little awkward. Talk about your discomfort as you go along. It may take several experiences of this sort before you really feel comfortable sharing your genitals with each other, but this is vital in terms of moving on to experiencing greater pleasure (see Exercise 5 in Chapter 6).

Some people ask, Doesn't this take the mystery out of lovemaking? It is our experience that mystery based on ignorance causes only problems, not joy. After we know all we can about each other's bodies and have shared all we can about our feelings, mystery is still left. The mystery does not have to do with our various bodily parts but rather with all the sensations and feelings that come to us in the loving experience. Mystery about the body is better labeled "ignorance." Ignorance does not lead to fulfillment.

After you have discovered yourself genitally and shared this with your husband, spend some time in becoming aware of where you feel the most enjoyable sensations. The setting for this should be very secure and relaxed. It might be while you are in the bathtub, or it may be in your bedroom when everyone else is out of the house or the door is locked. Be sure the kids are napping or away and you have some time to yourself. You should be confident that you will not be interrupted and that you need not be rushed.

Every woman enjoys different kinds of genital touch. There is no right or wrong way. For you there is only your way. Some women like to have the head or glans of the clitoris stimulated directly, but for most that is too painful. That is why the majority of women enjoy the touch around the clitoris rather than directly on it. The main part of the clitoris—the clitoral shaft—is directly above the head of the clitoris. Thus, the skin that covers the shaft and extends to both sides may be the area that you most enjoy having touched. (Likewise, most men enjoy having the shaft of the penis stimulated rather than the head.) The opening to the vagina may also bring special pleasure. Discover for yourself not only where you like to be touched, but how—directly or generally, pointedly or broadly, with much pressure or light pressure. Keep in mind that there is no normal or right way, only your way, and even that way may change from day to day.

While you are in a relaxed state, test your pubococcygeus (PC) muscle to see whether you can feel it tightening. If you need to review how to do so, refer to Chapter 6, page 53. If you cannot feel the tightening against your fingers, then either you're not tightening the right muscle or the muscle is loose. For a vigorous sexual response, this muscle needs to be in good tone. Begin doing the exercises as outlined in Chapter 6.

This would also be a good time to identify any point in the outer third of the vagina that has positive sensations for you. Some women report that the lower right-hand and lower left-hand areas of the vagina bring them the most positive sensations. This may or may not be true for you. If it is, enjoy it and share it. If it is not, there is no need for concern.

With the finger still in the vagina, again tighten the PC muscle and push your finger toward the front of your body just beyond the upper inner edge of the PC muscle. That is the G-spot area. For some women, G-spot stimulation is necessary for intense arousal and release.

Whatever you learn from self-exploration, self-stimulation, tightening the PC muscle, and identifying the responsive parts of the vagina can be shared with your partner as a way of keeping him up-to-date on your own discoveries. Then he can incorporate this new information into his lovemaking pattern.

You need to be comfortable not only with the specifically sexual parts of your body but with your body as a whole. This would be a good time, therefore, for you and your husband to share with each other how you feel about your bodies from head to toe. This should include how your body looks, how it feels, how you think about it, and how you sense others respond to it. Take turns standing in front of the mirror without any clothes and describe what you see and feel (see Exercise 1, Chapter 5). All of these experiences are designed to help you be more comfortable together. They need not be experienced as arousing. Let yourself enjoy them without any kind of demand that there be sexual feelings. But if you find that in fact they are arousing, let yourselves enjoy the sensations without feeling you have to act on them.

Pleasure Without Demand

The previous experiences were designed mainly for educational purposes as a way of teaching you and your husband about your body, and also to learn the specific kind of genital touch you most enjoy. Learning to give and receive pleasure will be necessary to release your responsiveness. Know that in these experiences there is no expectation for intercourse. Rule intercourse out for the time being. Also know that there is no way you can fail in these experiences because there is nothing you have to achieve. The goal is to let yourself experience and enjoy as much of the pleasure as you can take in. Begin by getting clean and relaxed together. Bathe or take a shower, and if it is comfortable even wash each other's bodies. For some of you this will be a familiar experience, for others it may seem strange or awkward. Talk about those uncomfortable feelings, but push yourself to complete the bathing in spite of the discomfort.

After bathing together, get into a quiet comfortable place—perhaps on the bed—and take turns learning to pleasure each other through touch by the *foot and hand caress*. The idea is to receive pleasure through touch without feeling any demand for a response. As the receiver, your only task is to enjoy the sensations and to communicate anything to your spouse that is not enjoyable for you. He has to be able to count on this, otherwise he cannot relax in the giving. His task is to pleasure you in a way that brings him pleasure. We enjoy ourselves most when we can relax in the assurance that the other one will let us know if anything we do is not pleasurable. Limit your touching to the hands and the feet as outlined in Exercise 8 in Chapter 13. It may take several sessions of foot and hand caressing before you can really relax with it and enjoy yourselves.

In the next experience, move on to the *facial caress* (Chapter 13, Exercise 9). This is obviously more personal and involves more sensuous areas. The lips, the neck, and the ears can be sexually responsive and are certainly more personal than the hands and the feet. So, focus on receiving and giving facial pleasure. Take your time, sink into it, soak it up, and enjoy it. Couples are often amazed at what they learn about each other by slowly, carefully, and pleasurably touching each other's faces. Keep in mind that this is not a massage designed to get the kinks out, but rather a form of sensuous communication that brings familiarity and pleasure. After each experience, talk about what it felt like both to be the giver and the receiver. Alternate who pleasures first. Apply the same principles for both the pleasurer and the receiver.

Having learned to let yourself enjoy the pleasure of feet, hands, and face, do the same for the back. Then move on to the *pleasuring of the whole body, excluding breasts and genitals*. Take your time in this body caress. Let the pleasurer and the receiver enjoy the experience.

Again, keep in mind that there is no demand for a sexual response of arousal. Your only task is to let yourself receive the touching. If there is arousal, welcome it and enjoy it, but do not feel that you have to pursue it or extend it.

It is most common that with the total-body pleasuring, some demand or pressure may set in. This may be due to conditioning or to impatience. If you have always felt that as soon as your husband got near your genitals you needed to respond, this would be a good time to reverse that pattern. If you find yourself making demands on yourself to become aroused, share these thoughts with your husband as you notice them. Stick with this experience enough times to learn to receive, share, and enjoy total-body pleasure, realizing that many experiences can be fully satisfying without even touching the genitals. Both of you can come away knowing that you have given and received.

Once you are comfortable giving and receiving sensuous touch on the rest of the body, move on to *include the genitals in the total-body pleasuring*. Having finally come to this point, it is natural to become somewhat eager and to quickly focus in on the genitals. Usually this will bring immediate demand and hinder the relaxation and pleasure. Therefore, in these experiences it is particularly important to begin with hands, feet, face, and back, and then gradually move closer to the genitals. Let the first genital touches be light and whispery; move away to some other part of the body and then move to the breasts and then down the torso, down the stomach to the thighs and then to the opening of the vagina and the clitoris without a major focus on just the clitoral area.

Let the touches be light and of short duration, gradually increasing pressure and duration of touch. If any anxiety, spectatoring, or demand creeps in, share this with your husband, and have him move away from the genitals until that demand subsides and you are able to relax back into the total pleasure. Do not be concerned about the extent of the arousal. The focus here is on pleasure. If you desire more genital touch because it feels good, communicate this and let your body go after it, but let the desire come from deep inside you rather than from your head. Have a similar time of reversing roles while you pleasure your husband's total body, including genitals, in a playful way.

▓ EXERCISE 16

Simulating Arousal Responses

We assign couples an exercise to simulate the total-body responses. In this experience, the couple lies on a bed side by side, with clothes on or off, and practices breathing loudly, letting out gasps and moans, and making spasticlike faces and movements.

The purpose of this experience is to help reduce self-consciousness and inhibition of the automatic responses of sexual arousal. Fill in the blanks when you plan your daily or weekly sessions. Assign the lead to whoever is the least inhibited or the best actor. Read aloud together and follow the steps.

Step 1: _____, select a setting that is peaceful, free of distractions, and as soundproof as possible. You may need to set up a sound barrier, like a tape or radio playing at the wall or door that might carry your noises. This assignment should be done in daylight or with the lights on.

Step 2: Lie side by side on the bed or on a comfortable surface, fully clothed.

Step 3: Take yourselves through relaxation: First, together take in ten deep breaths slowly through your nostrils, hold, then breathe out through your mouths. _____, lead in the deep, relaxed breathing. Picture yourselves in a beautiful, sunny, private garden. As you let the air out through your mouths, feel the tension in your bodies relax.

Step 4: Keeping in the same relaxed mode, _____, lead in taking five to ten deep breaths slowly in through the nose, then hold them and breathe out through your mouth with a sighing sound. Go to the next step when you feel natural and comfortable.

Step 5: _____, lead in the next five to ten breaths. This time as you breathe in, imagine the breath warming the inside of your body, all the way to your genitals. As you let it out, imagine the breath coming from your genitals, through your body, up your windpipe, past your vocal cords. Let out a relaxed rattling noise while you say, "Ah." Vary the pitch of the "Ah" with each exhalation. When you feel natural and comfortable with the noises and breathing, stop.

Step 6: Talk about your experience. Write your reactions. Take a break, if you wish. Then, take off your clothes and proceed with the next steps.

Step 7: Lie side by side on your backs without any clothes on, with the lights on or in daylight. Imagine yourselves on a warm, sunny, private beach, totally secluded from anyone. _____, lead in taking three to five deep breaths, holding them, then relaxing into the "warm sand" as you breathe out.

Step 8: Now, imagine that you are doing your favorite sexual activity (each can picture something different). Breathe in and out slowly and loudly with the rattling "Ah" sound. _____, lead in five to ten of these.

Step 9: Let the sexual activity progress in your minds as you proceed with the noisy, loose breathing. This time speed the breathing slightly, making certain it continues to be deep and noisy. Tense the muscles in your body so that your foot extends outward, your facial muscles grimace, and you thrust with your pelvis. Imagine your body flushing as it does when you blush. If you have never experienced these natural arousal responses, simulate what your spouse is doing.

Step 10: Repeat Steps 7–9 in the nude with _____ lying on his back and _____ sitting on top of him in the typical woman-on-top position. Do not insert the penis into the vagina.

Step 11: Repeat Steps 7–9 in the nude with _____ lying on her back and _____ on top of her in the most comfortable male-on-top position. If this is uncomfortable, turn on your sides, face to face. Do not insert penis into vagina.

Step 12: Switch to the position that is most comfortable to both; continue to build the breathing, sounds, and movements to intensify the simulation of the release of the orgasm. If you have never experienced an orgasm, imitate your spouse's acting out of what he or she usually does during an orgasm.

Step 13: Rest together and hold each other closely.

Step 14: Write and talk about your reactions to the various steps of involvement.

▧ EXERCISE 17

Mutual Pleasuring

Now, incorporating all you have learned, move into experiences that bring both of you a kind of joy from touching that is most satisfying. Remember to begin slowly. Start on the outside edges of the body—face, feet, and hands—and gradually move in to breasts and genitals, then back out to the rest of the body. Never stick with any one part of the anatomy for too long. Enjoy the excitement together and learn ways to heighten the good feelings. Instructions for increasing aroused feelings are outlined in the chapter on stimulation (Chapter 15). By now, you should be able to count on each other to take responsibility to inform the other if anything occurs that is not positive. Don't rush into intercourse. Rather, continue to go after all the positive feelings.

In all your pleasuring experiences, follow these guidelines: Be sure not to fake a response even though you can intentionally simulate one; stop and rest any time you need to; communicate when you feel pressured; and remember that the goal is to increase the frequency, the intensity, and the duration of the positive feelings. If the woman should happen to become intensely aroused and wants to continue the stimulation, *she* (not *he*) may pursue her desires, even to the point of orgasm. It is critical that this be a possibility, not a goal! If the man desires further stimulation and that is comfortable for the woman, she may stimulate him to the point of orgasm, though this should be saved until they are near the end of the experience.

A word to the wives here may be important. Many a wife becomes anxious about what is happening to her husband during these periods of time when there is no intercourse. Manual stimulation to orgasm brings adequate physical release. A committed, loving husband understands that experiences without the possibility and demand of intercourse are necessary to allow you to realize your sexual potential. He will be willing to do without intercourse until you are ready.

Do not let your concerns about what he is needing or wanting get in the way.

As you feel comfortable, lie together with either one of you on top, having the erect penis in contact with the clitoral area. Many women enjoy using the penis, erect or flaccid, as a paint brush over the clitoris and vaginal opening. This brings extra stimulation. Use the penis in any way that brings you pleasure. Put the end of the penis at the opening of the vagina without entry. Be assured that finding ways to use his body to arouse you will bring pleasure for him.

Finally, as the previous experiences become free of demand, you may move ahead to entry when the woman wants and initiates it. Entry would be an option only after an extended time of total-body pleasuring with arousal. With the woman in the top position as pictured in Figure 10, guide the husband's penis slowly into the vagina, perhaps using a lubricant to make entry easier. After entry, rest together and focus on the good feelings of the penis in the vagina. While lying together, you may want to caress or stimulate other pleasurable areas, or you may choose just to lie quietly together. After a few minutes of rest, contract the pubococcygeus muscles around the penis both so that he can feel the tightening and so that you can be aware of the feelings in the vagina. When you feel ready, begin a slow thrusting motion up and down on the man's penis. The man's only task during this time is to let you know when he needs you to slow down or stop thrusting in order to avoid ejaculation. Other than that, you as the woman should take charge of the experience, going after those movements and sensations that bring you the greatest delight.

It is important to be free to experiment so that you can learn what is most satisfying. Take good feelings as high as they will go without pushing or demanding more of yourself, then back off, rest, and move into them again. As you are going after a "high" and realize you do not have energy left for much more, signal your husband that he may go after his ejaculation. It would be helpful to have a prearranged signal. Don't expect an orgasm for yourself during this first coital experience.

If at any point in this progression the experience becomes negative for you, *stop* everything, *rest,* and *affirm* each other. If relaxation and refocusing are not possible, back up a session or two and stay at that level until comfortable. Always keep in mind that your body was built for response. You will not get stuck at a halfway point as long as you can allow the security, the relaxation, and the pleasure to build.

As arousal becomes more common and natural for you, pursue the turned-on feelings by intentionally exaggerating the responses. This is not designed as a fake, but rather as a way to push past the barriers that block your response. If you feel like moving, move more vigorously. If you experience feelings of arousal, move toward them. Practice incorporating orgasmic triggers that help your body shift from the relaxed, passive side of its involuntary nervous system to its active, go-after-it branch. This is necessary in order to trigger the reflex of orgasm. Always bear in mind that the overall goal in this experience is to actively go after greater and greater arousal and pleasure. We are so made that when we allow this to happen, the orgasm will naturally follow. It is a reflex response that will be triggered as the intensity of arousal builds.

MOVING TOWARD POSTENTRY RELEASE

What if an orgasm can be achieved only by external stimulation before entering? All orgasms bring release, and one should not be held up as superior to the other. It is not uncommon, however, for a woman to want to be able to respond orgasmically during intercourse. What can be done? To learn to experience orgasm during intercourse, you may need direct clitoral stimulation while the penis is in the vagina. You can reach down and stimulate yourself, your husband can do it (particularly when using the rear-entry position), or a vibrator may be used. Some women might object, saying they want to be orgasmic without any extra manipulation of the clitoral area. Eventually this may be possible, but to learn the response you need to connect intercourse with more direct contact of the clitoris. When this pattern becomes ingrained, arousal and release may occur without extra manual manipulation. This pairing of clitoral manipulation with intercourse has been found to be quite effective for many couples.

Whatever the causes for your difficulty with arousal or release, we hope that you will be able to create an atmosphere that allows your sexual response to surface. As you feel affirmed, free of demands, comfortable with your own body, and able to soak in and go after bodily pleasure, sexual response will inevitably follow.

∾

As the woman, you must be in control and take responsibility for what you need. Keep moving toward the good feelings. Inform your husband as soon as the good feelings dissipate, then back away from that particular form of stimulation. Rest for a period of time until you are wanting more, and then go after it again. Stop at a point when the feelings are good, and rest together, holding each other. Ideally, these segments of pleasuring will grow in duration. Practice this pleasuring every day or every other day. After several sessions of comfort at each level, move on to the next step, but always at the woman's initiation. Be sure to attempt the insertion with the woman in the top position, guiding the penis. When you are aware of vaginal feelings, initiate the thrusting and the swiveling of the pelvis. With each thrust, attempt to tighten the PC muscle. Continue this activity with the concept that the penis is yours to play with in order to achieve your greatest pleasure. You can count on it that it will bring pleasure to your husband. This is sound thinking in every way—physically, emotionally, and biblically (1 Cor. 7:3–5).

30 PAIN REDUCES PLEASURE

After my children were born, which was an awful experience for me, I never again enjoyed sex. Sometimes I think it is all in my head, that if I could let myself enjoy it, I wouldn't feel the pain; yet I know there is something wrong down there. But my gynecologist hasn't been able to figure it out.

Pelvic pain is a significant problem. Both men and women sometimes experience pain associated with sex. However, in our practice, men rarely complain of pain. In contrast, women frequently report painful sex.

A Gallup poll found that 16% of women reported pelvic pain problems, 11% limited home activity because of it, 16% took medications for it, and 4% missed at least one day of work per month because of it. Chronic pelvic pain may lead to years of disability and suffering, with loss of employment, marital discord and divorce. . . . Often the woman suffering with chronic pelvic pain has been told that there is nothing wrong, the pain is in her head, and has been referred to a psychiatrist; or that there is nothing that can be done and she must learn to live with the pain.[1]

Pain interrupts pleasure. Sex is for pleasure, so painful sex cannot be allowed to continue. The type of pain and the details about the pain need to be defined in order to find help for relief of the pain. The following questions are the ones you will want to answer carefully.

What type? Is it stinging, burning pain; pressure pain; stabbing; stretching?

When in the process does the pain happen? Before entry, at entry, during intercourse and thrusting, or after sex?

Where? Is the pain on the outside of the genitals around the clitoris and the opening of the vagina? Is it in the vagina wall? If so, is it at the twelve-, three-, six-, or nine-o'clock position, and how far in? Is it in the abdomen?

What activity triggers it? Is it in response to any touching of the genitals, only with entry, most often during thrusting, after an orgasm?

There are entire books written on pelvic pain, so we will focus here on the most common types of pain that we have treated in our practice. Dyspareunia is the technical term for painful intercourse. Intercourse may have always been painful, it may have started to be painful only after years of being sexually active, it may be painful only in certain situations, or it may always be painful. The pain may occur only at entry or only with deep penetration or with both. Intercourse may be painful because of pain of the vaginal barrel or pain of the pelvic cavity and structures.

PAIN OF THE VAGINAL BARREL

Lack of Adequate Lubrication

Lack of adequate vaginal lubrication may be the cause of pain of the vaginal barrel, making intercourse very uncomfortable. The first step is to be sure that the two of you are engaging in adequate genital stimulation for the woman. Take plenty of time. We sometimes recommend a twenty-minute clitoral and vaginal stimulation exercise. The woman can stimulate her clitoris while her husband inserts his finger in the vagina for intravaginal stimulation. The next step is to be sure hormonal levels are adequate. Have a complete hormonal panel ordered by your physician. Particularly look at the results of your estrogen levels and your free testosterone level. If estrogen is low, an estrogen cream inserted in the vagina would be one recommended approach. Vagrifem, a natural estrogen tablet that is inserted in the vagina, may be a source of relief. If the free testosterone is low, a 1 percent testosterone cream applied externally to the vulval area once daily is recommended. These creams should *not* be applied immediately before intercourse because they may be absorbed by your husband's body as well. Also, plan to use a lubricant of your choice.

Vaginitis

The actual walls of the vagina may be irritated and inflamed, which is called vaginitis. Vaginitis may be due to an infection that can be treated by your physician with an antibiotic, but more often it is not. When it is not caused by infection, it is more difficult to label and treat. From our experience, we believe that vaginitis is usually due to an allergic response, a biochemical imbalance, or a hormonal imbalance. We recommend you have your allergies tested through having a blood sample sent to a laboratory to be tested with foods and external agents. This is called an ELISA Act test. Great Smokies Diagnostic Laboratory is the lab we use. You can contact them at www.gsdl.com or at 800-522-4762. To identify a biochemical imbalance, we suggest that you test the pH of your vaginal secretions. You can get pHydrion papers from a pharmacy. The pH of the vagina should be between 4 and 5. To restore your pH balance, eliminate all allergens, caffeine, sugar, white flour, citrus, preservatives, and take Kyo-Dophilus or another form of acidophilus. Take one capsule on an empty stomach in the morning and one at bedtime. Eat yogurt regularly throughout the day, and take a vitamin-mineral supplement that is designed for PMS—high in the B vitamins, calcium, and magnesium. High-progestin contraceptives like Demulen, Desogen, Ortho-Cept, or others that are great for correcting acne may cause vaginal irritation. A change in birth-control pills to one that has a higher proportion of androgenic activity to progestational activity often eliminates the irritation. Alesse works well for many women.

Tears and Fissures

Tears and fissures may be the cause of pain of the vaginal barrel. If you identify a specific spot within the vagina that is painful to touch, that is likely to be a tear or a fissure. Locate exactly the point of the pain and tell your physician where it is. During your pelvic exam, ask that it be looked at, and get information about what can be done to correct it.

Vaginismus

Vaginismus is often the cause of unconsummated marriages and is also a source of pain in the vaginal barrel. Vaginismus is an involuntary, spastic contracting of the pelvic muscles that control the opening and closing of the vagina. Penetration may be impossible or excruciatingly painful. The problem results from negative feelings associated with vaginal penetration or the anticipation of it. Ultimately, vaginismus must be diagnosed through physical examination by a gynecologist, hopefully a specialist in treating dyspareunia. Surgery is *not* the answer to vaginismus. A series of graduated dilators are used by the woman to help stretch her vaginal muscles. Obtain a set of graduated vaginal dilators through your physician, or they can be ordered through us at 626-449-2525. Physical therapy is very helpful and usually recommended. Vaginal muscle exercises to gain control of the vaginal muscles are necessary. For details regarding the treatment of vaginismus and help with unconsummated marriages, see the chapter "Overcoming Intercourse Barriers" in our book *Restoring the Pleasure.*

VAGINISMUS

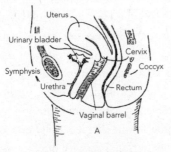

A. Normal female pelvis

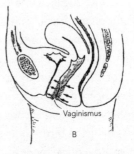

B. Involuntary constriction of outer third of vagina

PAIN OF THE PELVIC CAVITY

Childbirth or Endometriosis

Another type of dyspareunia, or painful intercourse, is pain of the pelvic cavity and structures. Many times this pain has been caused by childbirth trauma, but also may be the result of endometriosis—the growth of the uterus lining outside the uterus—or may be due to lack of sexual release. Injuries due to childbirth and endometriosis must be diagnosed and treated medically. Lack of release leaves the woman feeling a low-grade, dull pain in the abdomen and is best treated with sexual therapy. Finding release will bring both ecstasy and relief of pain.

Deep Thrusting

Pain during deep thrusting can also cause pelvic cavity pain. This pain is due to a tipped or retroflexed uterus that causes the cervix of the uterus to be thrust against. The cervix is sensitive to pain, so each thrust causes a sharp, stabbing sensation. Relief can be found immediately by a slight shift in position. The pain may be prevented by putting a small pillow or folded towel under your upper buttocks if you are in the underneath position. To correct the retroverted uterus, seek medical consultation. In addition, exercise the vaginal muscles and practice the knee-chest position twice a day for five minutes: Get on your knees and chest. While in that position, separate your labia to let air rush into your vagina. Stay in that position for five minutes. Do *not* do this exercise while you are pregnant.

PAIN OF THE EXTERNAL GENITALS: VULVODYNIA

Vulva Pain (Vulvodynia), as defined by the International Society for the Study of Vulvar Disease, is a "chronic vulvar discomfort, especially that characterized by the patient's complaint of burning, stinging, irritation, or rawness."

Vestibulitis or Urethritis

Vestibulitis is an irritation of the vestibular glands that run along the wall of the vagina at the four- and eight-o'clock positions.

Urethritis is an irritation of the urethra that carries urine from the urinary bladder to the outside of the body. To identify either of these conditions, carefully tap a Q-tip around the opening of the vagina while looking at your genitals in a hand mirror. If pain is triggered with any tap, note the location and explain this to your physician.

For the external irritation defined as vulvodynia, as well as for vestibulitis and urethritis, the same dietary changes as those recommended for internal irritation would be encouraged. A low-oxalate diet has been found to be helpful and is the recommended treatment of Dr. Clive Solomons of Denver, Colorado. In addition, the daily application of either an estrogen cream or a testosterone cream is often the choice of medical treatment.

GET HELP!

Work with a physician who treats dyspareunia—painful intercourse. Usually this is a medical doctor who has specialized in both gynecology and urology. To find a specialist in your area, contact either the Vulvar Pain Foundation at www.vulvarpainfoundation.org or at 336-226-0704, or the National Vulvadynia Association at www.nva.org. Both are excellent and helpful resources.

Whatever the type of pain, the husband needs to be included in the adjustments that will be needed. Continue only the sexual activities that do not elicit pain. The goal must be to pursue help until the source of pain is identified and relieved. Pain should not be tolerated. In fact, pain cannot be allowed to continue if you are going to enjoy sexual pleasure as God designed it.

PREVENTING PAIN FOR THE NEW BRIDE

Our book *Getting Your Sex Life Off to a Great Start* is the best resource to help in preparing for your first sexual experience and preventing unnecessary discomfort that first time. But we also want to give you some basic tools in this text.

For the new bride who is a virgin, it is not surprising if there is a small amount of pain. Most women experience at least a little. This can be due to the opening in the hymen being tight and small. In the great majority of situations, it is due to a combination of newness, excitement, and anxiety, which prevents the woman from relaxing. When the necessary physical changes do not take place (the opening up and laying flat of the majora lips, plus lubrication), entry will be more difficult and pain more intense. Entry under these conditions increases the pain and reduces the possibility of pleasure. Once the woman feels pain, tension is likely to set in. This tension will inhibit arousal and block any kind of release. While many couples begin this way, they usually get past the sequence quite quickly. But the sequence can be avoided to begin with.

If you are an engaged couple or if you counsel engaged couples, attending to a few small details will reduce much of the anxiety and potential for pain. First, six weeks to two months before the wedding date, the woman should be *examined by a gynecologist* or qualified family practitioner. In this experience, the doctor should be able to communicate to her whether her physical anatomy is normal and whether there are any particular barriers of which she should be aware. The couple and the physician should also discuss birth-control methods.

In the weeks before the marriage, every time the bride-to-be takes a bath, she should use her fingers to *stretch the hymen* until she can insert three fingers into the vagina and pull it apart slightly. This stretching procedure will prepare the vagina for entry and will also help the woman become familiar with some of the sensations of having the vagina stretched. As the wedding comes closer, this might be done several times a day.

The couple should be encouraged to *take along a lubricant* that is not sticky (not Vaseline). Probe or Astroglide is recommended for genital use. The couple should plan to use the lubricant for all entry experiences, whether they think they need it or not. The lubricant protects the woman in case she dries up during the excitement. It also provides a distraction from the focus on the entry. A small amount of lubricant should be applied to the head and ridge of the penis and to the opening of the vagina.

A final word of instruction to the new bride and groom is to move *slowly*. No matter how many times they tell themselves this, they will still most likely move ahead too quickly. If a couple can plan to move into their first experience with a great deal of gentleness, patience, ease, and relaxation, they are most likely to create a positive beginning to a life of loving. If you should encounter pain, call us at 626-449-2525.

31 PORNOGRAPHY AND THE INTERNET

God's intention for sex is for unity, pleasure, and procreation. We are to leave father and mother and become one flesh. We are to be totally open and unashamed with our spouse. We are to be fruitful and multiply. All these purposes of sex are to be fulfilled in marriage.

Our sexuality as boys and girls and as men and women is good and of God. And sexual fulfillment and pleasure in marriage are good and of God. It is the misuse of God's gift of sex that brings immorality into the home and church community.

Paul addresses the people in the church of Corinth with affection and firmness regarding an issue of immorality. This misuse of sex was brought into the home of one of the believers, and thus into their church. Sex is being misused in our homes today, and thus it is infiltrating our churches.

The most prevalent sexual immorality that we bring into our homes is sex on the Internet. This powerfully addictive force is invading the Christian family today. *The destructive impact is beyond our imagination!*

At last check, there were 137,000,000 (yes, that is millions) Internet sites to visit under the subject of sex. Surely some of those are healthy sites that offer medical and psychological information, including our own Web site, www.passionatecommitment.com. The great majority, however, are pornographic in nature.

If you started visiting those sites at a rate of one hundred per day, it would take thousands of years to visit them all, not to mention all the additional sites added each day. Sites are currently being added at the rate of one million per month. When we checked four weeks ago, there were only 136,000,000 sites. That is one million fewer than at the moment of this writing. By the time you are reading this information, it is difficult to imagine how many sites will be available. There is an endless supply of sexual material, most of it addictive garbage.

While sexual addictions may control many different sexual actions, the most common these days is the visiting of pornographic Web sites on the Internet. They are available on your home or office computer. You can access them in complete privacy. The sites do not screen for your age. They are available twenty-four hours a day. Thousands of sites are free. A person can visit for five minutes, five hours, or five days at a time. There is always new material. Every possible sexual variation or deviation is available. And "no one gets hurt." Right? Wrong!

Consider for a moment what has happened in the past twenty-five years. Back then, if a man wanted to get a pornographic "fix," he had to go to the sleazy part of town, park his car some distance away, pull his hat down over his eyes and lift up his collar, look about furtively, and slink into an adult bookstore or a massage parlor. The need to sneak began to change when pornographic videos became available for rent. Even though access to pornography was made easier, the process of getting it still held the risk of embarrassment or discovery. The risk was reduced almost completely with cable television, which brought the pornographic possibility right into the home. But there were still limits and risks. A subscription was required, so it could be discovered by others. If anyone flipped through the channels, it would become evident. Plus, the television was usually centrally located in the home. The Internet introduced the greatest possibilities for variety and privacy.

Most sexual addictions begin early in life, usually between the ages of eight and fifteen, but not so with the Internet. The Internet is not age-selective. We are finding that many people who have never struggled with a sexual addiction before get hooked even as adults. They develop this addiction in their thirties, forties, and fifties. Men and some women of every educational and socioeconomic level are potential Internet addicts.

HOW DO YOU KNOW IF YOU HAVE A PROBLEM WITH THE INTERNET?

What defines a problem? If you struggle with any of the following, you have a problem.

Do you:

- Visit sexual sites on the Internet?
- Visit sexually oriented chat rooms?
- Make these visits a secret from family, friends, and coworkers?
- Masturbate in response to the Internet content?
- Find that your viewing is affecting
  —your marital relationship?
  —your sex life?
  —your work production?
  —your sleep patterns?
  —your feelings about yourself?
  —your relationship with God?
- Design your life around the Internet times?
- Find that you lie more and more to cover your Internet activities?
- Need ever more titillating material to become aroused?
- Download material from sexual sites?
- List sites on your "favorites" list for easy access?
- Pay for certain sites and hide these charges?
- Clear out your Internet "history" regularly?
- Lose track of time while searching for the perfect image?
- Take safety and moral risks by meeting in person with chat connections?

If you relate to any of the above descriptions, you know down deep inside that the Internet is a problem for you. That struggle will not go away by itself. It will not go away as a result of your willpower. The habit will not be overcome because you feel terrible afterward, confess it, promise God never to do it again, or because you can white-knuckle it for a few days or a week. You need help!

WHAT IS A SEXUAL ADDICTION?

An Internet addiction is a sexual addiction. What is a sexual addiction? Simply stated, if you lack control over some sexual behavior, you are struggling with a sexual addiction. The sex addict feels controlled by the urge in the same way an overeater is controlled by the eating disorder or an alcoholic is controlled by the urge to drink. Even as we have come to think of alcoholism as an illness, so we also should think of sexual addiction as an illness. The sex addict has a sexual preoccupation. If the addict is married, his preoccupation interferes with his marriage; he is unable to be fully satisfied by an intimate sexual relationship with his spouse. Because the great majority of those struggling with sexual addiction are male, we will refer mainly to that gender, even though women, too, become hooked on sex, especially through the chat rooms on the Internet.

The sex addict may feel the urge to have sexual relations repeatedly in a short time with the same or different partners. When the sexual urge is pressing, the addict feels anxious; he is captured by the drive, but afterward he is guilty and ashamed. This pattern often takes an extensive amount of time away from the family or work as the addict pursues sexual activity or looks for the possibility of sexual activity. This secret drive escalates to become the major focus of his life. It is his way of hiding from the realities of his life that he does not want to face.

Sexual addiction is perpetuated by the mood-altering effect that comes from engaging in the behavior. It is an adrenaline addiction that is designed to give the momentary high the addict seeks. The compulsion and fulfilling of that compulsion become the predominant drive in his life and the main source of his self-nurture. This is no different from a drug addict who relies on a regular daily high from cocaine or relaxation from marijuana. The sex addict feels as though he no longer has the capacity to make choices about his activities, but he is compelled to engage in them regardless of the self-loathing that follows.

To define what a sexual addiction is, we need to clarify what is *not* a sexual addiction. For example, having sex every day might be normal for one couple. However, for certain individuals, it may be an expression of an addiction. So we cannot say that anyone who wants frequent sex is a sex addict. For one man, the violation of visiting a prostitute may be something he does every year or two when he is out of town, but he feels no great compulsion for it. As reprehensible as this behavior is, it would not be an addiction. Some men may masturbate occasionally as they experience the urge to do so, but this does not comprise an addiction. There are men and women who on occasion will view pornographic material in a magazine, movie, video, or will go to a topless bar, but they are not hooked on those activities and would not be considered sex addicts.

The emotional factors that distinguish various behaviors as sexual addictions are the obsessive and compulsive qualities that drive the person, almost against his or her own will, to do them. Most sex addicts struggle with other addictions as well. The sexual behaviors may be a symptom of underlying emotional and relational needs that have not been met; hence there is an addictive personality that needs help. The person with the addictive personality does not consciously *choose* to act on his sexual urges; rather he tends to zone out or split off from his real self and take on a life separate from his usual personality and convictions. These emotional and mental qualities are radically different from the motivations of a couple who go to a topless show in Las Vegas or Atlantic City, or a couple who rent a pornographic video once a year. We are not implying that these are advisable or morally acceptable activities; they are not! But we are differentiating between a sexual addiction and choices about sexual activity.

Dr. Patrick Carnes has been a pioneer in the study and treatment of sexual addictions. Dr. Carnes first brought the subject into public awareness with his best-selling book *Out of the Shadows.*[1] Since then, he has lectured extensively throughout the country, trained many professionals in both clinical and academic settings, and further defined sexual addiction in his book *Contrary to Love: Helping the Sexual Addict.* Most recently, he has written *Sexual Anorexia: Overcoming Sexual Self Hatred,* and *In the Shadow of the Net: Breaking Free of Compulsive Online Sexual Behavior.*[2] We have come to believe very deeply in Carnes's formulations because they fit so accurately with our clinical experience. We have also come to accept his treatment approach because it is the only one we have found to work. To avoid being pedantic, we will not specifically cite Carnes as the source of every important idea presented. But it is essential for you to understand that we are indebted to Carnes for virtually every concept that is presented here.

The Addictive Pattern

For some, the habit takes hold from the first accidental or intentional exposure to the Internet, a pornographic magazine, a strip club, or whatever. It quickly moves from a compulsion to an obsession and addiction. For others, the habits develop over a period of months or years. Since the Internet has not been an option for long, we do not have long-term data, but we are finding that many get hooked very quickly. Ten- or twelve-year-old boys, as well as grown men without a history of addiction, can quickly get hooked on the pornographic sites. Women in general, who tend to be more relational than men, are likely to get caught up in sexual chat sites. That can happen quickly for some. For others, there is a steadily increasing involvement that moves relentlessly toward addiction. It should be noted, however, that some women get hooked on the pornographic sites and some men get hooked on the chat rooms. If you find your preoccupation with sex on the Internet (or any other sexual habit) growing, and you are acting on that impulse with ever greater frequency, you have reason for concern. You may have made serious efforts at controlling your growing habit, yet always find yourself back and more involved than before.

The preoccupation can grow to the place where the planning for the next Web site visit and anticipation of the next experience are always on your mind. The addiction can become so dominating that life is organized around it. As the sexually addicted person retreats from life's normal relationships with wife, family, coworkers, and social friends, he moves into his own world. In that world, he carries on a secret life known only to him. The loneliness grows, propelling him ever farther into his private, addicted world. The addict's aloneness reinforces his belief about himself—the belief that he is basically an undesirable person whom no one can love. He becomes more convinced that his deep needs can truly be met only by himself. Sex seems to be the deepest need and promises to fill the void. Because relationships have usually brought hurt and pain, the addict avoids closeness. In fact, sexual addiction and the avoidance of intimacy almost always go together. Addictions are an intimacy problem. Neither the Internet nor magazines demand a relationship. The images cooperate completely with the needs and fantasies of the addict, who never has to give of himself and his own needs.

This self-centeredness is rationalized as justified and deserved. "I deserve it." "I work hard." "My sexual needs aren't being met." "It doesn't hurt anyone." If you are someone who uses these explanations to excuse your private sexual behavior, you are struggling with an addiction, whether you admit it or not.

WHAT TO DO?

Step 1: Change Starts in the Heart

If you are hooked, it is most important to acknowledge that the addiction will not go away by itself. You are powerless. Only God's power and the help of his people will help you break the chains of addiction. Until you admit that you are powerless and decide to turn your life, your will, and your actions over to God, nothing will change. We all know the parable of the prodigal son. After he had tried everything and wasted everything, he found himself in a pigpen. Then, as the King James version says so clearly in Luke 15:17–18, "And when he came to himself, he said . . . I will arise and go to my father." The starting point of change is the moment of repentance when you "come to yourself," face yourself in the mirror, accept the reality of your powerlessness, hit bottom, and put your life in God's hands. If you've been busted by your wife, husband, boss, or kids and are only acknowledging what they know, you have not truly repented. Twelve-step programs require a full moral inventory, admission of your sin before God and to those whom you have wronged. The first step is a change of heart.

Step 2: Change Your Life Patterns

If an alcoholic is going to stop drinking, we have to get the booze out of the kitchen. That, in and of itself, will not control the addiction but is a necessary step. Going to a bar to hang around with old drinking buddies will have to stop.

What needs to be changed for you? It depends on your addiction. If you always buy pornography at a certain shop, you can never go there again. If the massage parlor or strip joint is on your normal route home, choose a different route. If you act out only on the road during business travel, stay only in hotels that have no adult movies. If that is not possible, have the front desk shut off access to those movies, just as an alcoholic would not take the mini-bar key.

If the Internet is your area of struggle, there are a number of steps to take:

- Always have the computer screen face the door so anyone who walks by or into the room can see the screen—at home and in your office.
- Locate the computer in a central, high-traffic room in your home.
- Get filters that block out pornography sites. There are some that are 98 percent effective.
- Give *all* passwords to your spouse.
- Teach your spouse to check the history of your Internet usage on the computer, and encourage her to do this at random times.

- Never use the computer when you are the only one at home or the only one awake.
- Go to bed at the same time as your spouse.
- Identify the pattern associated with logging on to sexual sites. Stop the associated behaviors or habits.
- Stop masturbating to the Internet.
- Select a person or persons to whom you are accountable at home, at work, or wherever you struggle. Set a check-in time with that person.
- Seriously consider getting rid of the Internet and replacing it with an e-mail-only system.

Step 3: Focus on the Internal You

Yes, it helps to keep the alcoholic away from the alcohol and to stay out of the bars or wherever the drinking was done, but unless there is inner change that is then reflected in lifestyle changes, the behavioral changes will not last. When genuine repentance has taken place and you have changed direction, then change for the long haul begins. This is a war. You have to attack from the air, the sea, the ground, and from outer space. What does that mean in real life?

To change your *heart* and help control your *behavior,* join with others to "work the steps." There are accountability groups available that will take you through a twelve-step process. Commit yourself to that process. Don't concern yourself with the group labels. What's necessary is that you regularly face your powerlessness, your dependence on God, and your flawed moral character. Be willing to make amends and, perhaps for the first time, live an honest and open life. This involvement in a group is central. We rarely see long-term change without it!

To change your *mind,* learn new ways to think about your sexuality. Read some books. Get into Carnes's books, especially *Out of the Shadows* and *In the Shadows of the Net.* Mark Laaser, a good friend, has struggled his way out of a sexual addiction. His work has the benefit of personal experience, having been on Carnes's team of professionals, as well as his biblical and psychological perspective.

His book *Faithful and True* and his three-part video series The Geneva Series are not only practical and helpful, but also reflect a powerful message of hope for marital restoration.[3] Steve Arterburn, in his book *Every Man's Battle*,[4] does a wonderful job of teaching us how to put hedges around our mind. There are now many wonderful resources—books, tapes, videos, and programs—that can be of great help. Don't try to go it alone. It rarely works.

To bring healing to your *emotions*, you may need to get into therapy. A caring, insightful, biblically guided counselor can help you work through the wounds from the past, the injuries from your original family, the never dealt with losses in your life, and the low self-concept that not only led you to your addiction but also was brought lower by the addiction. You will be best served by a therapist who deeply understands and works with sexual addictions. Not every addict will have therapy available as a resource, but if you do, use it! It can be one more extension of God's grace to you in your struggle.

Step 4: Focus on Your Relationships

We've addressed changing your heart, your behavior, and your mind and emotions. Your *relationships* also need changing, especially your relationship with God and your spouse. Wherever you are in your pilgrimage with God, your sexual acting out will have put a strain on that relationship. If you are typical, you will have cycled through many rounds of acting out, despair, anguished confessions, sincere promises, and earnest devotion, only to find yourself acting in your addictive behavior again. You may have rationalized or justified your behavior, denying that it had any detrimental effects, all the while knowing that you were rebelling against God and violating yourself and your marriage. Get yourself into a group, a fellowship, or a class where you can connect with others as you grow spiritually. Recommit yourself to practicing the spiritual disciplines of Bible study, prayer, worship, and service. The internal work of God's Spirit in your life is essential to your healing.

Since sex addicts avoid intimacy, it is not only important to get control of your addiction, it is especially important to work on developing your capacity for intimacy with your spouse. We are not referring solely to sexual intimacy, but, first and foremost, to emotional and spiritual intimacy. Since you may have spent a lifetime avoiding intimacy, this could be the hardest dimension of the healing process. Remember, at first it will have to be intentional. You will need to spend time talking, reading, praying, connecting. It will not come naturally. After you focus on emotional and spiritual intimacy with your spouse, take some deliberate steps to build sexual intimacy. Sexual intimacy will fill the void you were trying to satisfy with your addictive behavior. When men come to us ready to let go of their sexual addiction, we bring the wife into the therapy soon after control is established. We take the couple through the sexual retraining process from our book, *Restoring the Pleasure*. The primary focus for this couple is on using the touching, talking, and teaching exercises to build their sexual intimacy.

Step 5: Be Accountable

Remember, you cannot do this alone! You need someone to be accountable to. In the twelve-step programs, this person is called a sponsor. The title does not matter. What matters is that you have someone with whom you are totally and bluntly honest. There can be no secrets with this person. If you are going to heal, you need complete openness. This means that you fully trust this person in terms of his or her confidentiality, good judgment, and having your good as his or her highest concern.

∽

So how do we gain control over an Internet addiction or any other sexual addiction? We get control by facing ourselves and our powerlessness. In that process, we must have a change of heart as we throw ourselves at God's feet, repentant and ready for his healing. That healing requires external monitors that help us get control of our acting-out behavior and internal changes that lead us to be the authentic person God created us to be.

ENHANCING

THE SEXUAL

EXPERIENCE

32 INVITING GOD INTO THE BEDROOM

A LITTLE HISTORY

God is often excluded from a person's sexual experience. One woman talked about this exclusion of God as something that happened very literally for her. As she explained to us, "When I walk into the bedroom to make love with my husband, I close the door and leave God outside." She could not imagine God associated with sexual pleasure. Even though God through the Scriptures sends a positive message about human sexuality, many of our fears and inhibitions about sex have been connected with God, which may make it difficult to invite God into our sexual experiences.

COUNTERING SEPARATION OF GOD AND SEX

There are many ways in which separation of God and sexuality can affect us. The most likely is that it will impede our freedom to enjoy sexual pleasure. If we understand God to be a punitive parental figure who towers over us menacingly when we enjoy ourselves, obviously we are going to be inhibited in our sexual expression. Or if our great sexual times occurred totally separate from knowing God, it will be difficult to connect God with our sexual expression. Some find that the only way they can let go is to put themselves in a sinful, "risking" setting. Sexual pleasure is not condoned by the teaching they have received, so they can experience arousal and excitement only in unacceptable places or with unacceptable partners. They have great difficulty responding in the condoned married situation.

If we are to destroy the pattern of separating God from our sexuality, we have to become active in that process. This attitude of inviting God into the bedroom starts with the individual person. It means including one's sexual life and feelings in one's prayers as a matter of concern. A woman came up to us in tears following a seminar because we had closed the session in prayer after speaking of some very explicit sexual issues. The connecting of those two events—prayer and overt sexuality—was so foreign to her that she found it a very jarring experience. Yet as she voiced her thankfulness to God for her own sexuality, she found that God was no longer excluded from her sexuality; she began to experience him as approving of her as a sexual person.

Another way to actively pursue inviting God into your sexuality is to study what the Bible teaches about sex. Rather than focusing on those passages that talk about limitations on sexual activity, study the other portions of Scripture that encourage the full enjoyment of sex in marriage.

You might consider studying the topic of sexuality in your small-group Bible study. Actively studying together, sharing, and praying together can have the effect of reducing your resistance to recognizing that God is the source of the sexual you. Our video series (The Magic and Mystery of Sex), seminars, tapes, and books also promote a healthy sexual message with a solid scriptural perspective.

INVITE GOD INTO YOUR SEXUAL TIMES

Begin by thanking God for any sexual feelings that you experience during the day. Then, as you prepare for sexual times with your spouse, ask God to bless your intimacy. As you begin to make love, do not draw back from your feelings, but offer a quiet inner prayer, thanking God for those pleasant, exciting, satisfying feelings. Recognize that God approves of these feelings. Pray together before or after pleasuring as a way of admitting to one another that the enjoyment of sex is good and of God.

Include God in your activity as you become more aroused; know and admit to yourself that the ability to experience excitement is something God has given you. Actively thank him for all these delightful feelings. You are a sexual person. He made you that way.

If you continue to have difficulty connecting your sexuality with God, select someone to help you. This person may be a mentor or a friend from your church or community. Choose someone who has demonstrated maturity and personal integrity in his or her walk with God and communicates an openness and ability to affirm the whole area of sex. As you talk with this person, share your need to allow God to be a part of the sexual dimension of your life. Listen willingly to his or her responses. As you and your friend discuss the matter, and as you hear this respected and trusted person's responses, he or she becomes God's ambassador to help you break through the barrier regarding your sexuality.

God is in the bedroom—whether you invite him there or not. God has made you the responsive person you are—whether you acknowledge it or not. Your body is designed for pleasure—whether you let it experience pleasure or not. You begin to reach the point of enjoying all the pleasure for which you are created if you recognize that God is with you—always.

33 BUILD SEXUAL PASSION AND INTIMACY

If you're looking for passion and intimacy, you may want to focus intentionally on building the qualities of a married sexual relationship that keeps going long after the initial spark of newness is gone. What we have to share in this chapter will not be new to you. These concepts, which summarize key points for any healthy, fulfilling, lifelong sexual relationship, have been developed throughout this book.

Go for Enjoying Rather than Scoring

Sex is *not* about conquering, achieving, or scoring. Sex is about relating. It is about enjoying the process and the moment. Sexual responses are not the measure of your sexual prowess or success. The measure of success is to come away from a time together with both partners feeling deeply loved, cherished, and respected.

Results-oriented sex leads to pressure and demand. When either or both of you focus on getting aroused or having a certain response, you move into the spectator role. Sex is not a spectator sport. Our bodies can't work when they are being watched. Instead, focus on mutual pleasure, which brings deeper ecstasy than you ever imagined.

Plan Rather than Wait for Spontaneity

For some couples, unplanned, spontaneous sex works great and both spouses are happy. But for most couples, the anticipation of being together builds quality, and allotting time to be together increases quantity. If we lived in a simple world without electricity and the many other conveniences technology has brought us, we might be able to depend on spontaneity. If we had no way to continue life's tasks once the sun went down, we would have a lot of time in bed with each other. However, in our complicated, full lives, everything is planned and scheduled. If we don't set aside time for ourselves as couples, we will get the leftovers or maybe even less. Again, we strongly urge you to adopt our Formula for Intimacy.

$$\text{Formula for Intimacy} =$$
$$15 \text{ minutes per day}$$
$$1 \text{ evening per week}$$
$$1 \text{ day per month}$$
$$1 \text{ weekend per season}$$

Leave Anger, Shame, Guilt, and the Need for Control Out of the Bedroom

When negative emotions and destructive ways of handling emotions are allowed in the bedroom, sex becomes encumbered with conflict and the bedroom becomes a sober place. It may feel more like a funeral parlor than like a love nest. Resolve issues outside the bedroom. If you want to make changes in your sexual pattern of relating, schedule a talk time away from the bedroom, which is associated with sexual arousal. Each define how you experience sex and how you would like it to be different. Take time to really hear and feel heard before the next spouse shares. If you can't resolve the conflicts on your own, get help.

Identify Problems and Get Help Early

Sexual problems don't heal with time. A downward spiral tends to develop and feed itself. The sooner you get help, the sooner you will build a positive feedback system, because positive experiences also feed themselves.

When couples come to us shortly after tension sets in or something isn't working, we can quickly find relief and build positive solutions. When the couple have experienced years of dissatisfaction, many other resentments will have developed and the marriage will be affected in more ways than just sexually. Since we see sex as the lubricant of the marriage, when the lubricant has run out, the machine of the marriage starts to experience friction and ultimately wears down.

Accept Mutual Responsibility to Keep Your Sex Life the Best It Can Possibly Be

Don't focus on what you want your spouse to do to make sex better; do what you can do! What *can* you do?

Stay Physically Fit. Our sexual response is a physical one. If our bodies are in good shape, they are going to experience sensations more intensely and respond more effectively. We will also feel better about ourselves and, therefore, enjoy each other more fully.

Stay Well-Groomed. When our bodies look good, smell pleasant, and are clean, we will be more inviting. Tending to issues like breath, smoothness of legs for women, no harsh whiskers for men, and many other personal-care details communicates value and importance.

Stay in Touch. Even as a gourmet cook is always looking for new recipes, the sexually attentive spouse is alert to discover new feelings, sensations, and ways to enjoy pleasure. Reading is one avenue to discovery. Reading together as a couple not only provides ideas for newness, the process brings a whole new depth of intimacy.

Keep Your Sexual Feelings Turned Toward Home. Affair-proof your marriage. Accept your vulnerability. No one is exempt! The feeling or attraction is the temptation. What we do with those feelings or attractions is what leads to trouble. The action is the sin.

To affair-proof your marriage:

- Invest time and energy in building and keeping your marriage strong. A strong marriage is a protective shield against affairs.
- Claim biblical promises. First Corinthians 10:13 assures us that no temptation is greater than what others have had to face. The verse

promises that "God is faithful, who will not allow you to be tempted beyond what you are able, but with the temptation will provide the way of escape also, that you may be able to endure it" (NASB).

- Keep your mind pure; stay free of input that encourages infidelity. What you put into your mind will eventually influence your choices. The Internet, daytime soaps, sitcoms, movies, and novels all infiltrate our minds with images not associated with a deep, fulfilling married life. To counter the distracting input in our world, be deliberate about filling your mind with marriage-enhancing information.
- When tempted, make a speedy exit; turn your heart toward home. When you see an image or a person who attracts your sexual thoughts, place your spouse in that picture and pursue the feelings and thoughts with your spouse in mind.

Make Your Differences Work for You

You have differences. Some couples have more differences to overcome than others. We came from such similar backgrounds that adjusting to our differences was fairly minor, but we did have some. Negotiate your differences rather than expect similarities. Our finding after thirty years of hearing couples' stories and studying about our differences is that our differences are a positive, not a negative.

It is those differences that keep sex alive throughout marriage if we make them work for us rather than against us.

Work to Keep Sex Fun

Sex is to be fun, but it's a lot more fun when you work at it:

- Anticipate time together.
- Plan for it.
- Talk about your likes and dislikes.
- Keep changing and discovering.

Create Erotic Adventures with Your Spouse

If you're looking for an erotic spark in your life, look at home. It doesn't matter how long you've been married, you can nurture a deeper and fulfilling passion that will last a lifetime by planning in creative newness. Make a commitment to take risks with each other and make plans. Plan special treats to prepare yourself for sex, and plan times for the two of you. Select a favorite CD to listen to. Consider lighting options for the room you are planning to be in. Use lotions, oils, or sensuous objects to pleasure each other.

Keep Talking and Learning

Learn about your own and each other's likes and dislikes. Read books on sex, like this one, out loud together. Take time as you read to talk about your thoughts and reactions to what you are reading. Experiment with various touching possibilities. We have been married forty years, and we are amazed that we still keep learning about each other. We still discover places to touch that bring a new level of pleasure.

We suggest that you each complete the Couple Talk exercise that follows. Use active listening skills of taking turns sharing your responses while the other one listens and reflects. Then reverse roles. You can alternate for each question or one person completes all responses first and then the other completes his/hers.

▓ EXERCISE 18

Couple Talk
What You Want Your Spouse to Know About You Sexually

Complete the following statements and discuss with your spouse:

1. Sexually I see myself as

_____

2. To make sex more fun, I'd like to

_____

3. What I like about you sexually is

_____

Women, check the response that most accurately reflects you:

Statement	Disagree	Agree	Strongly Agree
It is better to keep me hungry for more than to smother, bombard, or push me.	_____	_____	_____

Sometimes, I like kissing and cuddling
that don't lead to intercourse.

I need to feel emotionally connected
before I can connect sexually.

My monthly hormonal changes
affect my interest in sex.

I like to plan for our sexual times.

Men, check the response that most accurately reflects you:

Statement	Disagree	Agree	Strongly Agree
I often connect and feel loved through sex.			
Nothing turns me on more than when you are turned on.			
Since your needs are complex and ever changing, I need you to guide me.			
I feel rejected when you say no to sex.			
I like to plan for our sexual times.			

Keep Kissing Passionately

We saved the best for last. Daily, passionate kissing is the key to keeping the spark alive in married sex life because kissing is the barometer of the state of your sexual relationship. If kissing isn't good for you, say it just that way: "Kissing isn't good for me." Talk about it, but be very sensitive. Don't blame; only express what would make it better for you. Then ask your spouse if you can spend a set-aside time teaching each other how to kiss. Take turns leading and following. We usually have the woman lead first and then the man.

Good sex in marriage doesn't just happen, but you can make sex great by being deliberate about it. Enjoy a lifetime of growing acceptance of each other and pursue pleasure with a passion!

34 A PLAN FOR CHANGE

*After ten years of a woman's 'shelving' her sexual needs and enter-
ing the 'avoidance' stage, can a couple pull out of this pattern
without professional help (e.g., self-help books, etc.)? If so, can you
recommend literature and/or a basic, generalized plan of action
for revitalizing a sexual relationship? How do you make it fun
again? Perhaps this is too much to cover.*

So you want to do something about your sexual unhappiness, but
you don't know where to start. The unsatisfactory activity has been
going on for so long and is so natural, it seems to be the only way
the two of you can function together. Sometimes you think it would
be easier to start over with someone else than to try to resolve all the
bad habits and uncomfortable feelings that have grown up between
the two of you. But you can be encouraged. Many couples have
changed for the better after long, unrewarding years. This is true
whatever the source of the problem—but it takes work. This chapter gives you guidelines for doing that work.

DEFINING YOUR EXPERIENCE

How do you start? Begin with a period of individual reflection and
writing. This writing should be done separately, when you are not in

the middle of some intense stress. Describe as best you can your total sexual experience. If you are not a person who is likely to write, plan a time to talk about the sexual process with your spouse. Begin with the desire phase. Write about various ways you *feel desire* throughout the day. What sets off that desire, how long does it last, what do you do with it, and what is it that you are desiring? If you are one of those people who experience little desire, write about your understanding of what might be blocking that desire. What kind of feelings do you have about your sexuality? What do you do with the sexual stimulus or input that comes your way? If you are aware that other people get turned-on by music or exercise or reading or seeing certain images or thinking certain thoughts, and this does not happen to you, attempt as best you can to understand why. Be aware that this is not a composition to be published or a term paper to be handed in. You need not write in full sentences or paragraphs. Just get your thoughts down on paper while you are thinking them.

When you have written all you can about your understanding of your own sexual desire, move on and write about how *initiation* takes place between you. Write about who does the initiating, how it is done, how you feel about it. Is it a demand or a burden to always initiate? Describe in detail what you would think of as a typical scene when the two of you get together. Who does what and how does each respond? Finally, note any areas of change that you would like to see, both in yourself and in your spouse. If you are the one who always initiates, would you enjoy having your spouse assume that role on some occasions? Communicate this. Be as specific as you can about ways you would like to see things changed between you. This could include not only the "how" but also the "where" and "when" of your lovemaking.

Write about the *pleasuring* part of your experience. Begin with a description of your understanding of what takes place. Again, be very specific as to who does what. Write about that pleasuring in terms of how much demand it brings to you or any demand that you sense your partner feels. Describe the kind of touch that takes place and what you enjoy most. Describe the places that you enjoy being touched and where you would prefer not to be touched. Many couples are not aware of each other's sexual triggers. Describe any part of your body that is erogenous or highly susceptible to stimulation. If you happen to particularly enjoy being kissed and caressed around the neck and ears, your spouse needs to know that. On the other hand, if this turns you off, he or she also needs to know that. Point out not only the general areas where you feel responsive to touch, but also the most intense pleasure areas that bring you satisfaction. Finally, discuss the emotions that you experience during the pleasuring phase. Do you feel rushed, pressured, or bored? Is this really a meshing of your two worlds, or do you sense that you are disconnected? If so, talk about your concerns and your joys.

Stimulation focuses on those behaviors and activities that you find most arousing and that bring you to the point of orgasm. If there are certain things that happen which are negative for you, describe them. Share any changes you desire in stimulation, even if you have been uncomfortable sharing these in the past. Some women, for example, when they become aroused, feel smothered if the husband is too close to their face. Others want to be smothered with kisses. Some men enjoy vigorous activity from the woman as they near the point of orgasm; others do not. These individual preferences need to be shared.

Describe your *orgasmic release,* if you have one. Be very clear about what your favorite positions are for intercourse, what brings you the most sensation, and what kind of lovemaking usually precedes your most intense arousal. If you do not experience an orgasm, describe in detail what it feels like to you at the peak of your sexual experience. What is it that stops your arousal? What happens to you during your partner's release?

Finally, write and talk about the *affirming-relaxing time.* First, describe what normally happens. Compare this to what you desire. If the experience is good for you, say so. If there are some changes you would like to see, write about them. Note also what you experience from your spouse during this time. It is important to know that there are many different desires during the affirming phase. For some couples, this is the most pleasurable and "together" part of lovemaking. Others feel exhausted, and both partners quickly drift off to sleep. We met one couple who liked to get up and go jogging after making love. We were happy they had met each other. In times past, it was suggested that the woman needed more affirmation than the man. This is not necessarily so if the woman has had an orgasmic release. There is no right or wrong way to be during this time, only how you need to be for yourselves and each other.

In this last section, include any issues that did not seem to fit anywhere else. Note special positive conditions you are aware of or areas of change you desire. Conditions for sexual experience may have to do with room temperature, new kinds of stimulation, body odors, or experimentation. If you have faked responses, this is a natural time to let it be known. Some of you may rather talk this through—do whatever works for you.

SHARING AND CLARIFYING

Having set your thoughts down on paper, plan an hour or two in which you can sit down and discuss what you have written. It usually works best if you take one point at a time, one person sharing first and then the other. Begin, for example, with one of you reading to the other what you have written about your sexual desire. When you have finished reading, amplify anything that you did not write. The listening partner should then attempt to feed back what he or she has understood you to say about desire. Keep working at this until the communicating partner is convinced the listening partner really understands what has been shared. Then welcome any reactions or different viewpoints. Finally, the listening partner becomes the communicating partner and reads his or her statements about sexual desire. The other partner feeds back, then gives reactions and so on.

Proceed in this way throughout the whole experience, always being sure that what has been shared is completely clarified before the listener gives any reactions. It is amazing what a difference it makes when you feel understood. It is natural to become defensive toward criticism. Fight that impulse by trying to understand what is being said. So the pattern is: Share, listener reflect, and sharer clarify. Reflect not only the words and details that were said but also the emotional undertones. When the sharer feels understood, you are ready for the listener either to share his reaction or to share his own view from what he or she has written.

DEFINING YOUR DILEMMA

All of us have some area in our sexual lives that could be improved. For some, that desire is intense because the problem is severe. For others, the desired change would lead to enhancement. Whatever the case, spend some time clarifying what the two of you most desire to work on. Determine your greatest area of concern. Is it frequency of intercourse, variety within lovemaking, or the amount of pleasuring that takes place? Do you particularly lack desire or wish for a new style of initiation? Perhaps you need for your partner to respond more quickly or to slow down. You may need more active or verbal responsiveness, or want to attempt some new activity that you have been hesitant to experiment with before. For some there will be several problem areas. Do not take on the largest problem as the first step. Choose a small problem and work up. For example, you might begin by becoming comfortable pleasuring one another before you attempt oral stimulation.

Once you have specified a growth area that you want to focus on, be very clear about the changes you desire. Let's say that you want to change your initiation pattern. If the man has initiated 90 percent of the time and you would like to make it 50/50, then be very clear what you are moving toward: "I want to initiate about as often as you do." Or if the problem has been that the woman has been very immobile and unexpressive during lovemaking, identify exactly what it is that both of you would like to see changed. Plan to take small steps toward your goal.

Factors That Influence the Dilemma

Together, look at your individual histories and your history as a couple to see what has influenced your current situation. Some factors in your home background may have contributed to where you are now. Some early experiences during dating, or a traumatic experience either before or after marriage, may have pushed you in this direction. Or you may have certain beliefs, either social, moral, or religious, that influence you. Be as clear as you can in defining what you see from your past that affects your current situation. Then talk about what perpetuates the dilemma now. What keeps it going? Is it fear, anxiety, old habits? What behaviors happen between you that make it continue? Include as many factors as possible.

If there have been times in your history in which the current situation did not exist, pay special attention to those periods. Attempt to understand what made a difference then. If there were any periods of time that were notably low times for you in regard to your pattern, be clear about that. Some of you will find that your emotional or spiritual state is closely related to how you have been functioning sexually. Share as much of your understanding in this area as you have available to you.

GOALS TOWARD ENHANCEMENT

Once you have defined where you are, identify your desired changes and clarify the influencing factors. Develop some specific goals that you want to work toward. Often it is good to write these down almost like a contract. For example: "We have decided that we would like to improve our sexual relationship and enhance our marriage by focusing on the following area . . ." and then outline the specific conditions you have decided to work on. Keeping in mind what you have identified as the influential factors for your good times and for your not-so-good times, write out what you think needs to happen to improve this precise area of your sexual life. It may be helpful to determine together exactly what your ideal experience would be. Note any ideas from all your writings that may be of help in the task ahead.

A CLEAR PLAN

It is easy to talk about the kind of change you desire and how you wish your partner would bring it about. It is a different matter to sit down and determine together specifically how and when you are going to work toward a goal. We would encourage this to be part of the written contract also. Write out as many steps as are necessary to bring you to your goal. *Be careful to keep the steps small and manageable.* Both of you need to be in agreement about these steps. Plan to set aside adequate time for their accomplishment. The most common error when setting out a plan is to expect change too quickly. We think of letting the cement dry on one step before moving on to the next. Keep in mind that you have years of experiencing the old way. It will take some time for these patterns to be reversed. You have a whole lifetime to learn together, so give yourself a generous amount of time for the changes to take place. Some of you will naturally make this a matter of concern in your prayers. If you can comfortably pray together, this can be most constructive and encouraging. The Lord does want and expect you to have a fulfilled and happy sexual life, and he is there to help.

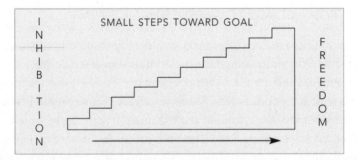

After you have begun to put the plan into practice, keep it fluid. Talk about it as you go along. Make adjustments as necessary, bearing in mind that the plan is there only to bring you toward your goal. If it is not doing that, it must be readjusted. To get yourselves together, you have to know yourselves, be ready to share, and agree on what needs to change. Understand what has caused the problem and how you are going to go about changing it. Finally, work together lovingly, with commitment and diligence, to bring about desired changes.

35 GOING FOR HELP

Couples can work out many of their sexual issues without professional help. Success requires commitment to each other plus diligence and perseverance to work on maximizing the positives in their sexual relationship. Certain situations, however, may demand assistance from a competent professional. This is particularly true if a man's premature ejaculation is severe, if he struggles with erectile dysfunction, or if he is controlled by sexual addiction. Professional help would also be necessary for a man who is unable to ejaculate at all (inhibited ejaculation). For the woman, professional help may be necessary if she has difficulty getting aroused, is unable to experience orgasm, or has pain during sex. If either of the spouses is unable to feel desire for sexual activity, this, too, would suggest the necessity for professional help. In some situations, the main barrier has to do with coordinating religious beliefs and sexual responses that a person finds incongruent. Here, a Christian helper would be needed.

WHO CAN HELP?

There is much confusion as to the difference in qualifications and competence of the various professional helpers. Let us briefly state

341

their backgrounds and qualifications. All of the professions listed here *could* be helpful with a sexual difficulty, but may not necessarily be trained to help with sexual issues. Let us begin by talking about physicians. There are several medical specialties that tend to be helpful in dealing with sexual difficulties.

Psychiatrists, who have received a medical degree and then specialized in psychiatry, would be one obvious source of help. Yet many psychiatrists have neither the specialized training nor the interest to work specifically in sexual therapy. Their focus may be more on a hospitalized population or on long-term, psychoanalytically oriented therapy. More and more gynecologists, urologists, and family practitioners are being trained in the treatment of sexual dysfunction. These are the main specialties among physicians who would be able to provide sexual treatment.

Psychologists are trained with many different areas of specialty. There are educational psychologists, social psychologists, industrial psychologists, and clinical psychologists. Those who provide sexual therapy are usually designated as clinical or counseling psychologists. All clinical psychologists are now required to receive a minimal amount of training in human sexuality, but this does not qualify them to work as sexual therapists. Further specific training would be necessary. Psychologists normally have a Ph.D. degree.

Psychiatric social workers (M.S.W.), *marriage and family counselors* (M.A.), and *nurse therapists* (R.N. plus M.N. or M.Sc.) may also be of assistance with a sexual dilemma if their background and training meet the qualifications.

Finally, *ministers* (B.D., M.Div., D.Min., Th.D., or Ph.D.) may all function as pastoral counselors. Some have been trained to work with sexual problems. One sign of a competent counselor is that he or she knows his or her area of expertise and refers patients to other helpers when needed.

All of the above-mentioned helpers would be competent only if they were specifically trained and experienced in doing sexual therapy. Some will work as a team, others will function individually. Both approaches have been found to be effective.

CHOOSING A HELPER

Any time you are going to open your inner world to someone, you want to be convinced that he or she is the right person for you. You want to be confident that the helper will not lead you in a wrong direction. Make your selection by asking questions. Any helper who is threatened by your questions or unwilling to answer them should be suspect. Look for someone else.

What kind of questions can you ask? Ask what qualifies them or what qualifications they have as a sex therapist. Inquire as to their training. Was it a one-day workshop, or was it more extensive? Did they have any supervision? What approach were they trained in? Find out also what approach they are currently using. All counselors who provide sexual therapy should be able to outline in brief their own particular approach. Determine what their previous experience has been. All professionals have to get started sometime, but if they are going to start on you, you need to know that and make the choice. Most successful therapists gain experience while being tutored by an experienced and competent sexual therapist. Ask questions about their success rate. Anyone who claims phenomenal success or uses terms like "always," "100 percent," or "the great majority," needs to be questioned further. There are always those situations that do not work out for many different reasons. If a therapist is unwilling to be honest with you about failure, you have reason for reservations.

In addition to asking questions about competence, it is absolutely necessary that you be personally comfortable with the helper you choose. If he or she gives you the creeps, seems disinterested or boring, or evidences any other personal trait that gets in the way, move on to someone else. You do not need to have communication problems with your therapist. A sense of ease with him or her is an absolute necessity. A good therapist will always be aware of this issue as the therapy proceeds.

Is it essential to find a Christian therapist? Obviously, if you can, find a person who is fully qualified and shares the same faith. That will facilitate communication, since you already are committed to the same faith and understand the same language. However, effectiveness is not limited to professionals who accept the Christian faith. There are many who do not impose their own value system on their patients, nor do they try to alter your thinking in any way. If you have to choose between an unqualified Christian helper and a qualified secular helper, you will probably receive the greatest benefit from the most qualified person. Merely being a believer does not qualify a person to be effective as a sexual helper.

SEXUAL THERAPY AND HOW IT WORKS

All sexual therapy, wherever it is practiced and by whomever it is practiced, is quite similar. The first task is to make a thorough assessment of your sexual dilemma. The counselor will attempt to understand your history, recommend any medical tests or examinations that seem necessary, and get a detailed and precise picture of your current sexual activity. Once the assessment has been made and all agree on the problem, goals will be defined together so that everyone is working in the same direction. As a rule, specific communication and experience assignments will be given. Limitations regarding sexual intercourse will be spelled out. The couple will be instructed to back up in the sexual relationship to a stage where both are comfortable; then the retraining begins. This is what sexual therapy is about: retraining the couple to function in a way that brings satisfaction to both partners. The emphasis will often have to be redirected away from the goal of achieving orgasm and toward the enjoyment of pleasure.

As the various experiences are undertaken, barriers may develop that block further progress. Sometimes these have to be dealt with either as a couple or individually before the sexual therapy can continue. Thus it becomes obvious that there is no one narrow routine that everyone must pursue. Following the general principles of sexual therapy, every treatment planned for each couple will have its own variations and special emphases. At all times, the couple will be encouraged to share their feelings with each other as well as with their helpers in an attempt to avoid any further sexual miscommunication. Your therapist will always want to know your opinions, your feelings, and your reactions. To hold back can only hurt your progress.

Be encouraged. Much change can take place in a relatively short period of time. Many have gained sexual fulfillment and happiness after years of frustration. You can, too!

36 QUESTIONS AND ANSWERS

Wherever we travel, whatever kind of group we speak to, people's questions are basically the same. For this section, we have selected the most commonly asked questions. People are searching for answers. Some need to relieve pain, while others wish to provide greater enhancement.

ABOUT THE MAN

Question: How can a man be taught to begin with words—not just fondling?

Answer: This is probably the one thing that more women ask about men than any other single item. Men seem to find their most natural expression in action, as they have been trained to do from childhood. Women, on the other hand, have learned to express themselves verbally. This disparity continues in lovemaking. Both spouses need to take responsibility. The woman obviously has to communicate to the man that she enjoys reminiscing about the day, talking about the common love they share, and whispering endearments. Unless the man knows this, he is likely to do what seems most natural for him, that is, to go directly after what he wants.

Having heard his wife express her desire for verbal communication, the man can struggle to take responsibility for his action. This becomes more complicated if he feels his wife is making an unreasonable request rather than seeing this as normal desire on her part. It is also important to attend to the location of the fondling. Most women enjoy receiving nongenital and nonbreast caressing as they are warming to the sexual experience. It is mainly direct sexual stimulation that is irritating and jarring at the beginning of the love experience for the woman.

Question: Most of the time I have an ejaculation without a full erection. Is there something wrong with me?

Answer: This pattern of sexual response seems to be a learned response (assuming the man is in good health). It was usually learned during self-stimulation activity: The boy or young man pushed himself to have an ejaculation even if anxiety prevented him from experiencing a full erection. Once learned, it was carried on into the marriage and is now causing some doubt for the man and perhaps providing less vigorous stimulation for the woman. We recommend experimenting with some of the exercises suggested in the chapter on erectile dysfunction. Be particularly attentive to stimulation before entry, even to the point of orgasm, but stimulate vigorously only when there is a full erection. Even as this pattern has been learned, it can also be unlearned.

Question: Can a man have an orgasm without ejaculation?

Answer: Some men report this as a common experience. It usually happens when a man has ejaculated in a first orgasm and then is aroused and brought to a climax shortly thereafter. A small percentage of men report the ability to be multiorgasmic even as women are.

Question: I am often unable to ejaculate after entry, needing to bring myself to orgasm outside my wife's body. Can this be changed?

Answer: This is known as ejaculatory dysfunction. It usually has to do with some early experiences with demanding women, particularly a demanding mother, or with homosexual preoccupation or fantasy. If this is your situation, professional advice can often help you understand the problem and provide a way out. The chapter "Problems with Release" in our book *Restoring the Pleasure* will guide you through the steps of learning to ejaculate inside the vagina.

ABOUT THE WOMAN

Question: How can I improve my concentration during sex?

Answer: Difficulties with concentration usually go hand in hand with passivity. As you become active in the pursuit of your pleasure, it is not likely that you will have difficulty concentrating. Focus on the good sensations in your body; go after more. Focus on the joy and delight of your husband's body and become active in heightening his joy. If there are some persistent things that are on your mind, it may be best to clear those out by having a brief conversational time before sex so that you can leave the concerns of your day aside and be totally involved in your loving.

Question: My husband loves to have me wear something sexy when home and also to strip for him. I don't feel I'm that sexy (being a little overweight bothers me, too), plus, I feel kind of cheap. But we love each other and I want our sex life fulfilled—though it's often great now. What are your thoughts on this?

Answer: As we have said many times throughout the book, anything that enhances the experience of both of you without bringing physical, psychological, or spiritual harm or demand can be enjoyed with abandonment. If something is getting in your way, work together to understand what it is. Apparently your weight doesn't hinder him from seeing you as sexy. Obviously your husband loves you. Share your hesitant feelings with him in an attempt to understand what the barrier really is. Keep in mind that teasing is a natural part of love play. As we read the Song of Songs, we keep having the feeling that the lovers were there and then they were gone; that they were with each other and then searching for one another. This may be one of those places where you push yourself past the barriers. Your husband needs to let you learn to move at your own pace so you aren't violated in the process. What is important is that you not feel like an object in the process. If each of you is reaching out with concern for the other, no one will be hurt.

Question: Regarding submissiveness in the wife, should she submit even though she is mistreated and unhappy with the sexual relationship, or does the Bible teach that she can withhold herself when her husband does not treat her or respond to her as he should? Paul said, "submitting yourselves one to another" and also "defraud not one another." What should she do? Is it her duty to respond?

Answer: As suggested in the question, all the passages that deal with submission of husband and wife include an encouragement to mutual submission, not just submission of wife to husband. I need to give myself totally whether I am the man or the woman, even as Christ gave himself for the church. There can be no greater submission than his gift of himself to us. Yet to submit oneself to unloving sexual activity is not a loving act or an act of mutuality. Communication is the starting point. Sex out of duty does not satisfy in the long-term. Ultimately, you have to be doing it for your own desire and gratification.

FANTASY

Question: I recently read an article in a Christian magazine about the difference between lust and fantasy. The author's ideas were much more liberal than I had ever heard before. Can you tell me biblically the difference between lust and fantasy?

Answer: We can make some inferences from the Scriptures, but the Bible does not talk directly about fantasy. Proverbs 23:7 says, "For as he thinks within himself, so he is" (NASB). The distinction often made between fantasy and lust is that in lust there is an intense desire with the hope or possibility of action, whereas fantasy is a picture, image, or story within a person without any intention to act.

Fantasies are often so unrealistic that they would be impossible to carry out. Lust usually has to do with real people in real places and carries with it the intent to act.

Question: I have always thought it was wrong to fantasize in one's mind about sex per se while making love. In other words, a person should think only of what is going on to get turned on. Thinking of the sex act between people in general should be avoided. Am I right?

Answer: There are many differences of opinion on this issue. Some people's thoughts while making love only enhance the experience. For others they get in the way. As we mentioned earlier, fantasies take on so many different forms that it is difficult to make a specific statement that applies to all people in all situations. For some, the only way they know to get aroused and move to orgasm is to engage in some fantasy. Since this brings pleasure to both, it is difficult to say that they should or even could avoid that activity. We encourage spouses to fantasize about each other in unique and exciting situations.

VARIETY

Question: If premarital play, not necessarily intercourse, has occurred before we became Christians and before marriage to our mate, how can we best forget those experiences and avoid comparing them to our present sex life?

Answer: Comparing usually causes difficulties only when the spouse does not measure up to the past situation. We need to be careful how we make that evaluation, however, since premarriage and preintercourse experiences can never really be compared with what happens after marriage and after we begin full lovemaking. Sometimes it is most beneficial to be able to share all these concerns with someone. A competent counselor or pastor may be just such a sounding board. This sharing is not designed to relive the past experiences but rather to get them out in the open. Sharing may free you to move on to a fully satisfying experience with your husband or wife. Keep in mind, too, that God has forgiven you. Only *you* are holding on to the past, keeping yourself from complete joy.

Question: What if you aren't in the mood? Should you go along to please your mate?

Answer: At various times, we all will not feel like it but will decide to go ahead and be involved sexually because our spouse desires sex with us. There is the possibility that we may become responsive even if we are not initially in the mood. If we never find ourselves in the mood, there is a serious barrier with which we must deal. Begin by talking with each other about this, and then seek competent help. If lack of interest is only an occasional state, it need not cause concern, since it is not likely to have significant impact on you or your spouse. There are many times when we may not be in the mood. If we are open to letting the mood change without pressure or demand, often responsiveness will come. Occasionally we might even go ahead in spite of our mood.

Question: What is the relationship between sexual fulfillment and length of marriage?

Answer: We have known couples who have been married six months who are experiencing unbelievable fulfillment. We have also known couples who have been married thirty years who have never had a fulfilling sexual experience together. And just the opposite can be true for some couples. Surprisingly, complete fulfillment keeps expanding and becoming even more fulfilling. This is one of the ways that good marriages seem to be reinforced. The Lord keeps giving more and more to enjoy as we give ourselves totally to each other.

Question: Please (not to sound smug), but how do I make something better that is already good? Both of us are satisfied and both reach orgasm. What more can be done? (This is a sincere question.)

Answer: What a delightful question! As with any other aspect of life, we can always keep growing. In the sexual area, we can keep learning to give more and experience more. We are not speaking here of greater frequency but rather greater depth of emotion and greater intensity. Expand your experiences to new places, new experimentations, new creativity, new books, or new seminars. Look for ways to outgive and outlove one another.

Question: A speaker recently said, "A woman can have six to eleven or more orgasms while the man has one." Could this be true?

Answer: The woman has an infinite capacity for orgasms, but the drive for this should not be the husband's, nor should it grow out of some demand she is putting on herself. Rather, it should come from within herself. Many women are fully satisfied with one orgasm and need nothing more. Others always prefer two or three. Some women prefer repeated orgasmic release during a given experience, but this does not say that they are freer women or better lovers. Any time we establish an outside criterion to evaluate how we are doing, we are not listening to how God made us and responding in terms of ourselves. Once we establish an outside criterion, we detract from what is natural for us.

36 FINAL WORDS

So many concepts have been presented in this book that it may seem impossible to remember them all and even more difficult to put them into practice. All that has been said rises naturally out of who and what we are. There are no radical ideas, no concepts that go against what we were designed to be. Perhaps this would be the best way to sum up the message of this book: The sexual experience is that ecstatic expression of our total being—physical, emotional, intellectual, and spiritual. When all these dimensions come together with freedom and are shared with the one to whom we are committed, usually sexual fulfillment will follow.

There are a number of *attitudes* that we can bring to our lovemaking experience and to all of our loving experiences that will positively shape us in relation to one another. We need to see the sexual response as natural and God-given. It is not a result of our perverse natures but rather a part of what we were created to express. Sexual love is a symbol of God's relationship with man. This includes the physical release dimension but is much more than that. Though it is a natural process within us, many barriers have arisen to keep nature from taking its course. Many couples have received the instruction as they prepare for marriage, "Just take your clothes off and let it happen naturally." This is fine for two animals but is not very helpful when planning to bring two complex human lives together. Because of all the input that gets in the way between birth and the time of marriage, there is no way that nature can take its course. We need education.

Even though we need education and training, we cannot think of our sexual lovemaking as merely requiring a batch of techniques or the learning of some new skills. While skills and techniques are essential ingredients to the fulfilled relationship, we need much more than just knowing the right things to do. Every part of our being is vitally involved.

How we have been trained and how we feel will affect our freedom in that loving relationship. We must be able to allow ourselves the right to receive pleasure. God has already given us that right; if we do not experience it, it is because of our own insecurity. When we deeply believe that pleasure is a possibility we will be open to variation and experimentation. We will not be limited by rules about right and wrong, but will rather be guided by our own internal desires and urges. This is one of those dimensions of life that the Bible has left open to our own desire and discretion. We have to be guided from within ourselves.

Recognizing this, we are forced to accept what the apostle Paul teaches regarding our sexual equality. We are not expected to do something for our partner that he or she is not responsible to do for us. Sex is not something we do *to* someone, neither is it something we do *for* someone. Rather, sex is a *with* experience. This is a tough balance to find. It is easy to come to the marital bed with strong expectations for one's self as well as for one's spouse, rather than letting the feelings flow freely out of one's body. When we can let those feelings flow, we accept the individual differences between two people and the differences between men and women. These will not be troublesome to us but will rather be used as an additional form of enhancement, delight, and variety. We will not think of our spouse in terms of stereotypes or clichés that usually begin, "Well, men always . . ." or "Women always . . ." We will let the other be a person who is taking responsibility for himself or herself as he or she gives to us.

Our attitudes obviously make a difference, and so do our *feelings*. If we lack the self-worth necessary to be able to receive, we will limit our own pleasure and our spouse's joy. For many, receiving is more difficult than giving. They only feel self-worth as they give. It is important to reverse that pattern. It involves the acceptance of our own sexuality, with its maleness and femaleness, as having worth in and of itself, not just in relationship to our spouse. Many past experiences of guilt, shame, and discomfort can get in the way of acceptance.

The level of commitment that we feel for our spouse is central. We must be committed to our spouse and must feel his or her commitment in return. Without the feeling of love, sexual response becomes less likely. Many barriers can get in the way of experiencing love and commitment in both directions. Whether these be anger, lack of respect, external tension, or performance anxiety, a couple can move past those barriers as they learn to express and share the love and commitment that they feel.

Even when the feelings of love and commitment are solid, they will make a difference in lovemaking only as we put them into practice. Once we start *acting* on our feelings, the joy that is a potential becomes a reality. That action can take many forms. It may evidence itself by special preparation that is made, by the spontaneity and flexibility that is shown, or by new ways of sharing ourselves in the actual sexual experience. As we accept our right to pleasure, we tend to be ready to lose control. This grows out of an inner security and follows the internal bodily rhythms. Having grown in our acceptance of ourselves and our spouse, we will also feel less need to follow the same hurried routine time after time. As we become more secure, speed will decrease, gentleness will increase, keeping score will disappear, and we will be participants rather than spectators.

The key to all this is *communication*. Sexual decisions must be made in an atmosphere of freedom and openness. There has to be the freedom to express what we want, what we need, what feels good, and what feels bad. Nonverbal communication will also be crucial, whether it is the receiver guiding the hands of the giver, a private signal system, or nonverbal communication that is felt without any prearranged meaning. In this communication, as we accept responsibility for ourselves and for any problems as a couple, we will avoid the pitfalls of blaming ourselves or our spouse and hence also avoid the put-downs and teases that may hinder rather than help. In working out problems, negotiation based on each person's having an equal vote will also often be a necessary dimension to the communication. In this negotiation it is important to keep realizing that the only rights or wrongs between you have to do with what each of you finds pleasant or unpleasant.

As you share yourselves openly you will be received with understanding and warmth, knowing that you are not being judged. You can continue to blossom from that seed of sexual freedom within you to the full sexual beauty that is there ready to be expressed.

> Set me as a seal upon thine heart,
> as a seal upon thine arm:
> for love is strong as death;
> jealousy is cruel as the grave:
> the coals thereof are coals of fire,
> which hath a most vehement flame.
> Many waters cannot quench love,
> neither can the floods drown it:
> if man would give all the substance
> of his house for love,
> it would be utterly contemned.
> —Song of Songs 8:6, 7 (KJV)

SEXUAL ENHANCEMENT EXERCISES

ILLUSTRATIONS

NOTES

Chapter 8: Our Bodies' Sexual Response

1. Adapted from Masters and Johnson, *Human Sexual Response* (Boston: Little, Brown & Co., 1966).
2. A. K. Ladas, B. Whipple, and J. D. Perry, *The G Spot* (New York: Holt, Rinehart, and Winston, 1983).
3. Ibid.
4. This and the following six graphs are adapted from Masters and Johnson, *Human Sexual Response.*

Chapter 15: Stimulating

1. Paul Popenoe, *Sex Happiness or Tragedy?* (Los Angeles: Samuel Newman Productions, 1954), pp. 40–41.

Chapter 20: Why Sexual Problems?

1. Helen Singer Kaplan, *The New Sex Therapy* (New York: Brunner/Mazel, 1974), p. 165.

Chapter 21: Differing Sexual Needs

1. John Gray, *Men Are from Mars, Women Are from Venus,* (New York: HarperCollins, 1992).

Chapter 23: You Want to Do What?
1. James C. Dobson, *Solid Answers* (Wheaton, IL: Tyndale, 1997).

Chapter 29: Less Arousal or No Release: Some Women's Frustrations
1. Diana Schwarzbein and Nancy Deville, *The Schwarzbein Principle: The Truth About Losing Weight, Being Healthy and Feeling Younger* (Deerfield Beach, FL: Health Communications, 1999).
2. Barry Sears, *The Zone* (New York: HarperCollins, 1995).

Chapter 30: Pain Reduces Pleasure
1. Fred M. Howard, C. Paul Perry, James E. Carter, Ahmed M. El-Minawi, and Rong-Zeng Li, eds., *Pelvic Pain: Diagnosis and Management* (New York: Lippincott Williams & Wilkins, 2000).

Chapter 31: Pornography and the Internet
1. Patrick Carnes, *Out of the Shadows: Understanding Sexual Addiction* (Minneapolis: Compcare Publications, 1992).
2. Patrick Carnes and Joseph Moriarty, *Sexual Anorexia: Overcoming Sexual Self-Hatred* (Center City, MN: Hazelden, 1997); Patrick Carnes, David Delmonico, Elizabeth Griffin, and Joseph Moriarity, *In the Shadows of the Net: Breaking Free of Compulsive Online Sexual Behavior* (Center City, MN: Hazelden, 1989).
3. Mark R. Laaser, *Faithful and True* (Grand Rapids, MI: Zondervan, 1996).
4. Stephen Arterburn, et al., *Every Man's Battle: Winning the War on Sexual Temptation One Victory at a Time* (Colorado Springs: Waterbrook Press, 2000).

REFERENCES

Allender, Dan B. *The Wounded Heart.* Colorado Springs: NavPress, 1990.

Arterburn, Stephen, et al. *Every Man's Battle: Winning the War on Sexual Temptation One Victory at a Time.* Colorado Springs: Waterbrook Press, 2000.

Barbach, L. G. *For Yourself: The Fulfillment of Female Sexuality.* New York: Anchor Books, 2000.

———. *The Pause: Positive Approaches to Menopause.* New York: Penguin, 1993.

Berman, Jennifer, and Laura Berman. *For Women Only: A Revolutionary Guide to Overcoming Sexual Dysfunction and Reclaiming Your Sex Life.* New York: Henry Holt and Co., 2001.

Billings, John J. *The Ovulation Method: Natural Family Planning.* Collegeville, MN: Liturgical Press, 1992.

Brauer, Alan P., and Donna Brauer. *ESO (Extended Sexual Orgasm).* New York: Warner Books, 2001.

Cane, William. *The Art of Kissing.* New York: St. Martin's Press, 1995.

Carnes, Patrick. *Contrary to Love: Helping the Sexual Addict.* Minneapolis: Compcare Publications, 1989.

————. *Out of the Shadows: Understanding Sexual Addiction.* Minneapolis: Compcare Publications, 1992.

Carnes, Patrick, David Delmonico, Elizabeth Griffin, and Joseph Moriarity. *In the Shadows of the Net: Breaking Free of Compulsive Online Sexual Behavior.* Center City, MN: Hazelden Information, 1989.

Carnes, Patrick, and Joseph Moriarity. *Sexual Anorexia: Overcoming Sexual Self-Hatred.* Center City, MN: Hazelden Information, 1997.

Dickey, Richard, P. *Oral Contraception User Guide.* Durant, OK: Infomatic Guides, Inc., 2002 (1-800-225-0694).

Dillow, Linda, and Lorraine Pintus. *Intimate Issues: Conversations Woman to Woman: 21 Questions Christian Women Ask About Sex.* Colorado Springs: Waterbrook Press, 1999.

Dobson, James C. *Solid Answers.* Wheaton, IL: Tyndale House, 1997.

Forward, Susan, and Craig Buck. *Betrayal of Innocence: Incest and Its Devastation.* New York: Penguin Books, 1988.

Foster, Richard. *Money, Sex, and Power.* San Francisco: Harper and Row, 1989.

Frank, Jan. *A Door of Hope.* Nashville: Thomas Nelson, 1995.

Gottmann, John. *Why Marriages Succeed and Fail.* New York: Simon and Schuster, 1995.

Graber, Benjamin, and Georgia Kline-Graber. *Woman's Orgasm: A Guide to Sexual Satisfaction.* Indianapolis: Bobs Merrill Co., 1986.

Gray, John. *Men Are from Mars, Women Are from Venus.* New York: HarperCollins, 1992.

Grenz, Stanley. *Sexual Ethics: An Evangelical Perspective.* Louisville, KY: Westminster John Knox, 1997.

Hart, Archibald D. *The Sexual Man.* Waco, TX: Word Publishing, 1995.

Hart, Archibald D., Catherine H. Weber, and Debra Taylor. *Secrets of Eve: Understanding the Mystery of Female Sexuality.* Waco, TX: Word Publishing, 1998.

Hendrix, Harville. *Getting the Love You Want: A Guide for Couples.* New York: Owl Books, 2001.

Heinman, Julia, and Joseph LoPiccolo. *Becoming Orgasmic.* New York: Prentice Hall, 1990.

Howard, Fred M., C. Paul Perry, James E. Carter, Ahmed M. El-Minawi, Rong-Zeng Li, eds. *Pelvic Pain: Diagnosis and Management.* New York: Lippincott Williams & Wilkins, 2000.

Jones, Stanton L., and Brenna B. Jones. *How and When to Tell Your Kids About Sex: A Lifelong Approach to Shaping Your Child's Sexual Character.* Colorado Springs: NavPress, 1993.

Kaplan, Helen Singer. *Disorders of Sexual Desire.* New York: Simon Schuster, 1983.

————. *The Illustrated Manual of Sex Therapy.* New York: Brunner/Mazel, 1974.

————. *The New Sex Therapy.* New York: Brunner/Mazel, 1974.

————. *PE: How to Overcome Premature Ejaculation.* New York: Brunner/Mazel, 1989.

Laaser, Mark. *Faithful and True.* Grand Rapids, MI: Zondervan, 1996.

Ladas, A. K., B. Whipple, and J. D. Perry. *The G Spot.* New York: Holt, Rinehart and Winston, 1983.

Masters, W. H., and V. E. Johnson. *Human Sexual Inadequacy.* Boston: Little, Brown and Company, 1970.

————. *Human Sexual Response.* Boston: Little, Brown and Company, 1966.

Mayo, Mary Ann, and Joseph L. Mayo. *Menopause Manager: A Safe Path for Natural Change.* Grand Rapids, MI: Fleming H. Revell, 1998.

McCarthy, Barry, and Emily McCarthy. *Female Sexual Awareness: Achieving Sexual Fulfillment.* New York: Carroll and Graf, 1998.

McIlhaney, Joe S., Jr. *Sexuality and Sexually Transmitted Diseases.* Grand Rapids, MI: Baker Books, 1990.

————. *1250 Health-Care Questions Women Ask.* Grand Rapids, MI: Baker Books, 1992.

Penner, Clifford, and Joyce Penner. *Counseling for Sexual Disorders.* Waco, TX: Word Books, 1994.

————. *52 Ways to Have Fun, Fantastic Sex.* Nashville: Thomas Nelson, 1994.

————. *Getting Your Sex Life Off to a Great Start.* Waco, TX: Word Books, 1994.

————. *Men and Sex.* Nashville: Thomas Nelson, 1997.

————. *Restoring the Pleasure.* Waco, TX: Word Books, 1993.

————. *Sex Facts for the Family.* Waco, TX: Word Books, 1992.

————. *What Every Wife Wants Her Husband to Know About Sex.* Nashville: Thomas Nelson, 1998.

Penner, Joyce. *What to Pray When You Are Expecting.* Ann Arbor, MI: Servant Publications, 2000.

Popenoe, Paul. *Sex Happiness or Tragedy.* Los Angeles: Samuel Newman Productions, 1954.

Rako, Susan. *The Hormone of Desire: The Truth About Testosterone, Sexuality, and Menopause.* New York: Three Rivers Press, 1999.

Schaumburg, Harry W. *False Intimacy: Understanding the Struggle of Sexual Addiction.* Colorado Springs: NavPress, 1997.

Schwarzbein, Diana, and Nancy Deville. *The Schwarzbein Principle: The Truth About Losing Weight, Being Healthy and Feeling Younger.* Deerfield Beach, FL: Health Communications, 1999.

Sears, Barry. *The Zone.* New York: HarperCollins, 1995.

Shedd, Charlie, and Martha Shedd. *Celebration of the Bedroom.* Waco, TX: Word Books, 1979.

Shippen, Eugene, and William Frye. *The Testosterone Syndrome.* New York: M. Evans & Co., 1998.

Short, Ray E. *Sex, Love, or Infatuation: How Can I Really Know?* Minneapolis: Augsburg Publishing House, 1990.

Smedes, Lewis B. *The Art of Forgiving: When You Need to Forgive and Don't Know How.* New York: Ballantine, 1997.

————. *Forgive and Forget: Healing the Hurts We Don't Deserve.* San Francisco: Harper and Row, 1996.

————. *Sex for Christians: The Limits and Liberties of Sexual Living.* Grand Rapids, MI: Eerdmans, 1996.

Warren, Neil C. *Learning to Live with the Love of Your Life and Loving It.* Wheaton, IL: Tyndale House, 1995.

————. *Make Anger Your Ally.* Wheaton, IL: Tyndale House, 1999.

Williams, Warwick. *Rekindling Desire: Bring Your Sexual Relationship Back to Life.* Oakland, CA: New Harbinger Publications, 1988.

Zilbergeld, Bernie. *The New Male Sexuality.* New York: Bantam Books, 1999.

INDEX

129755